AF678763

Handbook of Global Fixed Income Calculations

The Frank J. Fabozzi Series

Frank J. Fabozzi, PhD, is an adjunct Professor of Finance at Yale University's School of Management. A CFA and CPA, he is also the editor of the *Journal of Portfolio Management*, which is read by thousands of institutional investors. He is editor or author of over 100 books on finance for the professional and academic markets. He is a Fellow of the International Center for Finance at Yale University and serves on the board of directors of the BlackRock complex of funds and the Guardian Life family of funds.

Comprised of nearly 100 titles, The Frank J. Fabozzi Series is a key resource for finance professionals and academics, strategists and students, investors in college courses, executive and company training programs, and prep courses for the CFA. The series is overseen by its eponymous editor, whose expert instruction and presentation of new ideas have been at the forefront of financial publishing for over twenty years.

Also in The Frank J. Fabozzi Series:

Focus on Value by James L. Grant and James A. Abate
Real Options & Option-Embedded Securities by William T. Moore

Handbook of Global Fixed Income Calculations

Dragomir Krgin

John Wiley & Sons, Inc.

Copyright © 2002 by Dragomir Krgin. All rights reserved.

Published by John Wiley & Sons, Inc.
Published simultaneously in Canada.

No part of this publication may be reproduced, stored in a retrieval system, or transmitted in any form or by any means, electronic, mechanical, photocopying, recording, scanning, or otherwise, except as permitted under Sections 107 or 108 of the 1976 United States Copyright Act, without either the prior written permission of the Publisher or authorization through payment of the appropriate per-copy fee to the Copyright Clearance Center, 222 Rosewood Drive, Danvers, MA 01923, (978) 750–8400, fax (978) 750–4744. Requests to the Publisher for permission should be addressed to the Permissions Department, John Wiley & Sons, Inc., 605 Third Avenue, New York, NY 10158–0012, (212) 850–6011, fax (212) 850–6008, E-Mail: PERMREQ @ WILEY.COM.

This publication is designed to provide accurate and authoritative information in regard to the subject matter covered. It is sold with the understanding that the publisher is not engaged in rendering professional services. If professional advice or other expert assistance is required, the services of a competent professional person should be sought.

ISBN 0471218359

Printed in the United States of America.

10 9 8 7 6 5 4 3 2 1

To my wife Bojana and sons Branimir and Borivoj

Contents

General Price/Yield Formula: Periodic Payment Fixed Income Securities....... 1

DEFINITIONS: SOME DATES AND COUPON PERIODS 2
Date and Coupon Period Illustrations 3
GENERAL P/Y FORMULA: SETTLEMENT DATE NOT IN LAST COUPON PERIOD....... 6
Cum-Dividend Trading 6
Ex-Dividend Trading 6
ANALYZING THE FORMULA 13
YIELD CALCULATION BY ITERATIONS WHEN PRICE IS GIVEN 15
GENERAL P/Y FORMULA WHEN SETTLEMENT DATE IS IN LAST COUPON PERIOD 16
Simple Interest: Cum-Dividend Trading 16
Simple Interest: Ex-Dividend Trading 16
Compound Interest: Cum-Dividend Trading 17
Compound Interest: Ex-Dividend Trading 17
FULL PRICE 20
DAY COUNT METHODS 21
Rules for the 30/360 and 30/365 Day Count Methods 22
Rules for the 30E/360 Day Count Method 22
Rules for the ACT/365 (366 in Leap Year) Day Count Method 23
Day Count Methods: Clarification 23
EXAMPLE OF AN ACCRUED-INTEREST FACTOR CALCULATION 25
APPLICABLE MARKETS AND CONVENTIONS 27
DATE ASSUMPTIONS AND CONVENTIONS 27
TEST EXAMPLES 33
Example 1 33
Example 2 34
Example 3 35
Example 4 36
Example 5 37

Accrued-Interest Calculations 39

GENERAL FORMULA FOR ACCRUED INTEREST 39
Cum-Dividend Trading 39
Ex-Dividend Trading 40

AUSTRALIAN GOVERNMENT BONDS 41
Conventions 41
CANADIAN GOVERNMENT BONDS 42
Conventions 42
CZECH GOVERNMENT BONDS 45
Conventions 45
DANISH GOVERNMENT BONDS 46
Conventions 46
EMU COUNTRIES BONDS 47
Conventions 47
EURO BONDS 51
Conventions 51
HUNGARIAN GOVERNMENT BONDS 52
Conventions 52
JAPANESE GOVERNMENT BONDS 52
Conventions 52
NEW ZEALAND GOVERNMENT BONDS 55
Conventions 55
NORWEGIAN GOVERNMENT BONDS 57
Conventions 57
POLISH GOVERNMENT BONDS 58
Conventions 58
SOUTH AFRICAN GOVERNMENT BONDS 60
Conventions 60
SWEDISH GOVERNMENT BONDS 61
Conventions 61
SWISS GOVERNMENT BONDS 62
Conventions 62
UNITED KINGDOM 63
Gilts 63
Index-Linked Gilts 66
U.S. GOVERNMENT BONDS 68
Conventions 68
U.S. CORPORATE BONDS 70
Conventions 70

Other Calculations 72

CURRENT YIELD 72
SETTLEMENT DATE NOT IN LAST COUPON PERIOD 72
First Derivative of Price with Respect to Yield 72
Second Derivative of Price with Respect to Yield 73
Duration 75
Modified Duration 75
Convexity 75

Price Value of 0.01 (Basis Point Value) 75
Price Value of ΔY Change in Yield 76
Yield Value of 0.01 76
Yield Value of 1/32 76
Taylor Series of Price as a Function of Yield 76
SETTLEMENT DATE IS IN THE LAST COUPON PERIOD 77
Simple Interest 77
Compound Interest 78
EXAMPLE 79
Accrued Interest 80
Price 81
Full Price 81
Current Yield 81
First Derivative of Price with Respect to Yield 81
Second Derivative of Price with Respect to Yield 82
Duration 82
Modified Duration 83
Convexity 83
Price Value of 0.01 83
Yield Value of 0.01 83
Yield Value of 1/32 83

SAMPLE CALCULATIONS: PERIODIC PAYMENT FIXED INCOME SECURITIES 84

TIME LINE 85
FACTORS 85
Accrued-Interest Factor 85
First Coupon Factor 85
Discount Factor 85
Last Coupon Factor 86
Last Discount Factor 86
ACCRUED INTEREST 86
PRICE 86
FULL PRICE 86
FIRST DERIVATIVE OF PRICE WITH RESPECT TO YIELD (RISK FACTOR) 87
Using the General Price/Yield Formula 87
By Approximation 87
By Summation 88
DURATION 89
MODIFIED DURATION 89
PRICE VALUE OF 0.01 (BASIS POINT VALUE) 89
SECOND DERIVATIVE OF PRICE WITH RESPECT TO YIELD 89
Using the General Price/Yield Formula 89
By Approximation 90
By Summation 91

CONVEXITY 92
PERCENTAGE CHANGE IN FULL PRICE PER ΔY 92
Predicted by Modified Duration and Convexity 92
Actual 92
PERCENTAGE CHANGE IN FULL PRICE NOT EXPLAINED BY MODIFIED DURATION AND CONVEXITY—RESIDUAL 93
YIELD VALUE OF 0.01 93

DETERMINING COUPON DATES FOR PERIODIC PAYMENT FIXED INCOME SECURITIES 94

ALL COUPON PERIODS ARE NORMAL 94
End-Of-Month (EOM) Rule in Effect 94
End-Of-Month Rule Not in Effect 95
SHORT-OR-LONG FIRST COUPON PERIOD 95
End-Of-Month Rule in Effect 95
End-Of-Month Rule Not in Effect 96
SHORT-OR-LONG LAST COUPON PERIOD 96
End-Of-Month Rule in Effect 96
End-Of-Month Rule Not in Effect 96
BOTH FIRST AND LAST COUPON DATES ARE GIVEN 97
End-Of-Month Rule in Effect 97
End-Of-Month Rule Not in Effect 97

CASH FLOW CALCULATIONS 98

CASH FLOW CALCULATIONS 98
Settlement Date Not in Last Coupon Period 98
Settlement Date in Last Coupon Period 98
TIME IN YEARS TO EACH CASH FLOW 99
Settlement Date Not in Last Coupon Period 99
Settlement Date in Last Coupon Period 99

FORWARD PRICING ANALYSIS 103

INTRODUCTION 103
FORWARD PRICE FORMULAS 104
Proceeds Method 104
CD Method 109
Scientific Method 110
Continuous Compounding Method 111
OTHER CALCULATIONS 111
Drop 111
Invoice Payment at the Settlement Date 111
Invoice Payment at the Termination Date 111
Net Profit/Loss 111
Forward Yield 112
CALCULATION OF BREAKEVEN REPO RATE GIVEN FORWARD PRICE 112

FORWARD PRICE FOR TREASURY BILLS ... 113
Example 1 ... 113
Example 2 ... 116
Example 3 ... 119
Example 4 ... 120
Example 5 ... 122
Example 6 ... 123
Example 7 ... 124
Example 8 ... 126
Example 9 ... 127
Example 10 ... 128

CONVERSION FACTOR ... 130

DEFINITIONS ... 130
CONVENTIONS ... 131
Canadian 10-Year Government Bond Futures Contract (on MSE—Montreal Stock Exchange) ... 131
Canadian 5-Year Government Bond Futures Contract (on MSE) ... 131
Euro 2-Year, 5-Year, and 10-Year Bond Futures Contract (on MATIF—Marché a Terme International de France, Paris) ... 131
E-Bond 30-Year Bond Futures Contract (on MATIF) ... 131
German 2-Year (SCHATZ), 5-Year (BOBL), 10-Year (BUND), and 30-Year (BUXL) Government Bond Futures Contract (on EUX—Eurex Frankfurt). 132
German 10-Year Government Bond Futures Contract (BUND) (on LIFFE —London International Financial Futures and Options Exchange) ... 132
Italian 10-Year Government Bond Futures Contract (on MIF—Mercato Italiano Futures, Milan) ... 132
Japanese 5-Year, 10-year, and 20-Year Government Bond Futures Contract (on TSE—Tokyo Stock Exchange) and 10-Year (on LIFFE) ... 132
Spanish 10-Year Futures Contract (on MEFF RENTA FIJA, Barcelona) ... 133
Swiss 10-Year Government Bond Futures Contract (on Eurex—Zurich) ... 133
U.K. Long GILT (10-Year) Futures Contract (on LIFFE) ... 134
U.S. Treasury Bond (20-Year) and 10-Year Treasury Note Futures Contract (on CBOT—Chicago Board of Trade) ... 134
U.S. 2-Year and 5-Year Treasury Note Futures Contract (on CBOT) ... 134
U.S. Index-Linked Note Futures Contract ... 134
EXAMPLES ... 135
1. Canadian 10-Year Government Bond ... 135
2. Euro 10-Year Notional Bond (French Government Bond on MATIF) ... 135
3. Euro 10-Year Notional Bond (German Government Bond on MATIF) ... 136
4. Italian 10-Year Government Bond ... 137
5. Japanese 10-Year Government Bond ... 138
6. Japanese 5-Year Government Bond ... 139

7. Spanish 10-Year Government Bond ... 139
8. Spanish 10-Year Government Bond ... 140
9. Spanish 10-Year Government Bond ... 140
10. Swiss Government Bond ... 141
11. Swiss Government Bond ... 142
12. U.K. Long GILT ... 142
13. U.S. 2-Year Treasury Note ... 143
14. U.S. 10-Year Treasury Note ... 144
15. U.S. Treasury Bond ... 145

FUTURES ANALYTICS ... 146

FUTURES CALCULATIONS ... 146
Futures Calculations for n ≥ 2 ... 146
Futures Calculations for n = 1 ... 148
Futures Calculations for n = 0 ... 148
CALCULATION OF IMPLIED REPO RATE BY ITERATIONS ... 149
COST OF FINANCING ... 151
COUPON INCOME ... 151
GROSS BASIS ... 151
GROSS BASIS IN 32NDS ... 152
COST OF CARRY ... 152
NET BASIS ... 152
NET BASIS IN 32NDS ... 152
EXAMPLE 1 ... 152
Implied Repo Rate ... 154
Cost of Financing ... 154
Coupon Income ... 154
Gross Basis ... 154
Gross Basis in 32nds ... 154
Cost of Carry ... 154
Net Basis ... 155
Net Basis in 32nds ... 155
EXAMPLE 2 ... 155
EXAMPLE 3 ... 156

U.S. SECURITIES ... 158

TREASURY NOTES AND BONDS ... 158
Conventions ... 158
TREASURY BILLS ... 161
Discount in Dollars ... 161
Price ... 162
Discount Rate ... 162
Yields ... 162
STRIPS (SEPARATELY TRADED REGISTERED INTEREST AND PRINCIPAL SECURITIES) ... 174

Example 1 174
Example 2 174
CORPORATE SECURITIES 175
Bonds and Notes 175
TREASURY INVESTMENT GROWTH RECEIPTS (TIGRS) 237

FOREIGN GOVERNMENT BONDS 239

EMU (EUROPEAN MONETARY UNION) COUNTRIES 239
Conventions 239
AUSTRALIA 250
Conventions 250
CANADA 257
Conventions 257
CZECH REPUBLIC 268
Conventions 268
DENMARK 271
Conventions 271
GREECE 275
Conventions 275
HUNGARY 277
Conventions 277
Settlement Date Is More Than One Year from Maturity Date 278
Settlement Date Is in the Last Coupon Period 281
Settlement Date Is in the Next-To-Last Coupon Period When Frequency of Payments per Year Is Semiannual 282
IRELAND 292
Conventions 292
ITALY 303
Conventions 303
JAPAN 314
Conventions 314
NEW ZEALAND 327
Conventions 327
NORWAY 329
Conventions 329
POLAND 335
Conventions 335
PORTUGAL 338
Conventions 338
SOUTH AFRICA 340
Conventions 340
SPAIN 347
Conventions 347
SWEDEN 352
Conventions 352

SWITZERLAND 354
Conventions 354
UNITED KINGDOM GILTS 357
Conventions 357
INDEX-LINKED GILTS 363
Conventions 363
Calculation of Cash Flows 365

Index........ 375

Acknowledgments

In preparing this book, I received help from a number of people, and I would like to thank all of them for their generosity. I would like especially to express my appreciation to Naidu Guttapalle, Patricia Potts, Shilpa Switalski, Alison Switalski, and Barbara Hallnan, all from Merrill Lynch. Special thanks go to Frank J. Fabozzi, who encouraged me to publish this book and gave me very helpful comments. He also helped me to clarify some definitions.

Foreword

Global investors face the difficult task of pricing sovereign bonds and derivative instruments throughout the world. Not only is the global investor confronted with the different structural characteristics of bonds and derivatives in different markets, but there are conventions that must be taken into consideration in pricing and yield calculation—for example, accrued interest calculations, determining coupon dates for periodic payments, and cash flow calculations. While global investors can turn to a good number of excellent books on bond and derivative analytics in covering the U.S. market, when it comes to pricing sovereign specific instruments, there has not been a comprehensive source available in the literature that provides all the possible scenarios and the corresponding conventions for all major bond markets. Understanding these conventions has been very difficult even for experts in the field.

Handbook of Global Fixed Income Calculations by Dragomir Krgin fills this void, providing the most comprehensive and detailed coverage of the calculations of price, accrued interest, yield measures, price sensitivity measures, forward price, and futures analytics for most of the world's bond markets. It reflects the most recent changes in EMU (European Monetary Union) countries.

In writing this book, Mr. Krgin has combined his two decades of industry experience with practical implementation of a very successful and widely used fixed income analytics library for Merrill Lynch. A key feature of this book is the simple approach presented to evaluate any sovereign security using the same general formulas. All variations in sovereign conventions and their effects on pricing are clearly illustrated with ample examples.

This book should be on the desk of traders, quantitative analysts, sales people, and fixed income analytics library developers. It is sure to become the standard reference book for global bond investors.

Frank J. Fabozzi

Chapter 1

General Price/Yield Formula: Periodic Payment Fixed Income Securities

A bond's full price is the sum of the present values of its future cash flows at the settlement date. In practice, however, other pricing conventions must be correctly specified for bond prices to be calculated accurately. These conventions (such as day count methods, ex-dividend trading, frequency of payments per year, etc.) vary from country to country, and for different markets within a country. Two dealers in the same market may not always agree on the conventions to be used.

In our support of the fixed income trading activities of Merrill Lynch, we have spent years researching these pricing conventions, and have put them into practice, creating analytical products that rely on accurate calculations of price and yield, as well as other measures. As a result, we have developed generalized formulas that have proven their accuracy and reliability in day-to-day usage.

The purpose of this book is to provide these detailed, yet straightforward, conventions and formulas for calculating prices, yields, and other measures on periodic payment fixed income instruments (hereafter called *bonds*).

Definitions: Some Dates and Coupon Periods

Trade Date (Transaction Date, Bargain Date): This is the date on which a transaction is initiated.

Settlement Date: This is the date on which a trade is cleared by delivery of securities against funds.

Issue Date: This is the first (earliest) date on which settlement can occur.

Dated Date (Interest Accrue Date): This is the date from which the interest starts to accrue when the security is issued. It can be on, before or after issue date. The dated date must be less than two normal coupon periods before the first coupon date. For calculation purposes, the dated date is important, not the issue date.

Coupon Dates: They are the dates when the issuer pays the interest.

First Coupon Date: This is the date when the first interest payment, after the issue date, is made.

Last Coupon Date: This is the last coupon date prior to maturity date.

Last-Paid Coupon Date (previous coupon date): This is the coupon date *on,* or *just before,* the settlement date.

Next Coupon Date: This is the coupon date *just after* the settlement date. It is the same as first coupon date, when settlement date is in the first coupon period.

The Normal (Regular) Coupon Period: This is the period from any coupon date (except the last coupon date) until the following coupon date. We assume that all normal coupon periods have the same length.

The First Coupon Period: This is the period from the dated date until the first coupon date.

The Last Coupon Period: This is the period from the last coupon date (inclusive) until maturity date. The first and last coupon periods may be shorter, longer, or the same length as the normal coupon period, and are called **short**, **long**, or **normal periods**, accordingly.

The Normal Issue Date (for bonds with a short or long first coupon period): This is the date one normal coupon period before the first coupon date. For a bond with a short first coupon period, the normal issue date is before the dated date. For a bond with a long first coupon period, the normal issue date is after the dated date.

The Pseudo Issue Date (for bonds with long first coupon period only): This is the date two normal coupon periods before the first coupon date. The pseudo issue date is always *before* the dated date.

The Normal Maturity Date (for bonds with short or long last coupon periods): This is the date one normal coupon period *after* the last coupon date. For a bond with a short last coupon period, the normal maturity date is after the maturity date. For a bond with a long last coupon period, the normal maturity date is before the maturity date.

The Pseudo Maturity Date (for bonds with long last coupon period only): This is the date two normal coupon periods after the last coupon date. The pseudo maturity date is *always* after the maturity date.

The Current Coupon Period: This is the period in which the settlement date occurs. When the settlement date coincides with the coupon date, the current coupon period begins with that coincidental date. The current coupon period is the same as the first coupon period, when settlement date is in the first coupon period.

Date and Coupon Period Illustrations

Let us look at several visual illustrations of these definitions. The first three examples show bonds with normal, short, and long first coupon period. The second set of three examples shows bonds with normal, short, and long last coupon period.

Normal First Coupon Period

A bond with a dated date of March 15, 1999, paying interest on March 15 and September 15 of each year and having its first coupon date on September 15, 1999, would have a normal first coupon period.

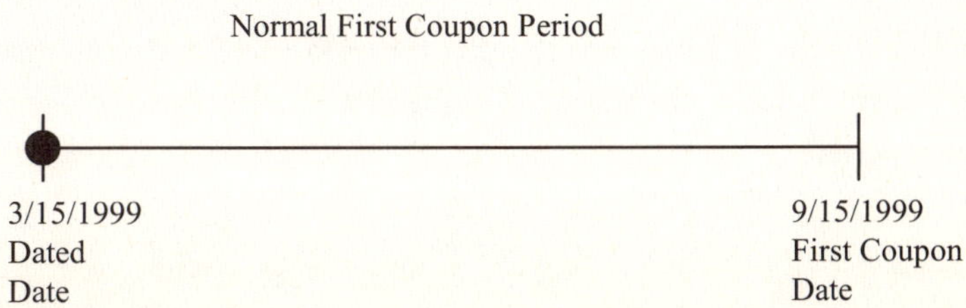

Short First Coupon Period

A bond with a dated date of June 1, 1999, paying interest on the March 15 and September 15 of each year and having its first coupon date on September 15, 1999, would have a short first coupon period. Its normal issue date would be March 15, 1999.

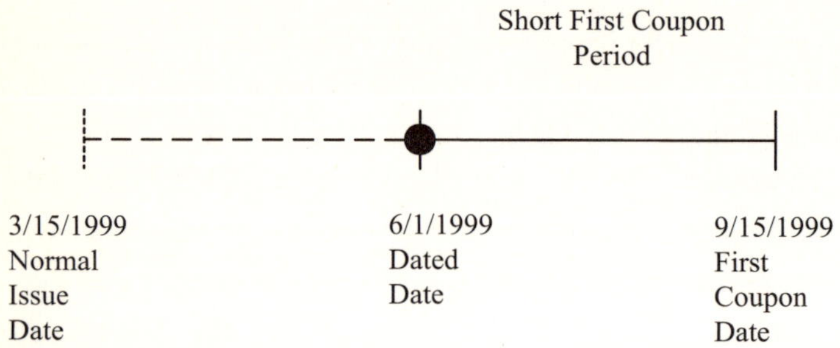

Long First Coupon Period

A bond with a dated date of December 1, 1999, paying interest on March 15 and September 15 of each year and having its first coupon date on September 15, 2000, would have a long first coupon period. Its normal issue date would be March 15, 2000, and its pseudo issue date would be September 15, 1999.

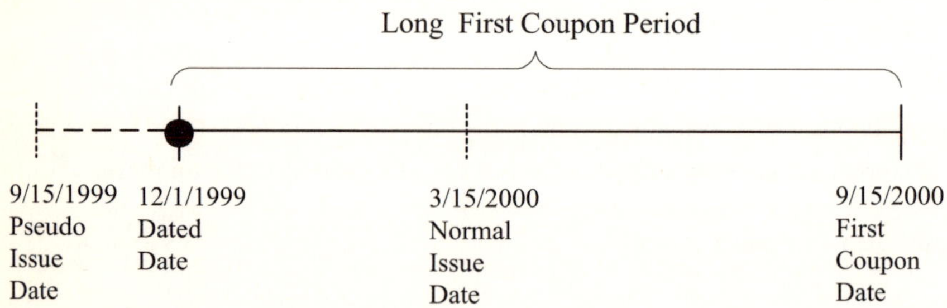

Normal Last Coupon Period

A bond maturing on March 15, 2000, paying interest on March 15 and September 15 of each year and having its last coupon date on September 15, 1999, would have a normal last coupon period.

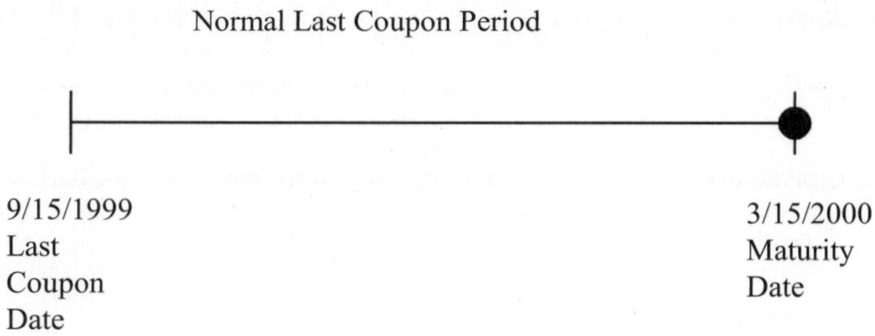

Short Last Coupon Period

A bond maturing on January 1, 2000, paying interest on March 15 and September 15 of each year and having its last coupon date on September 15, 1999, would have a short last coupon period. Its normal maturity date would be March 15, 2000.

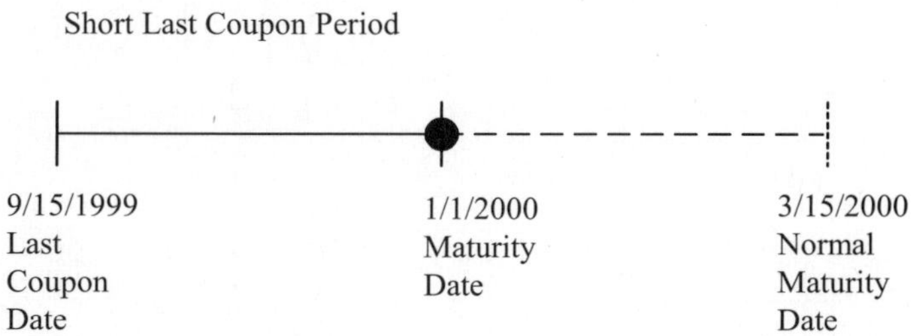

Long Last Coupon Period

A bond maturing on July 1, 2000, paying interest on March 15 and September 15 of each year and having its last coupon date on September 15, 1999, would have a long last coupon period. Its normal maturity date would be March 15, 2000, and its pseudo maturity date would be September 15, 2000.

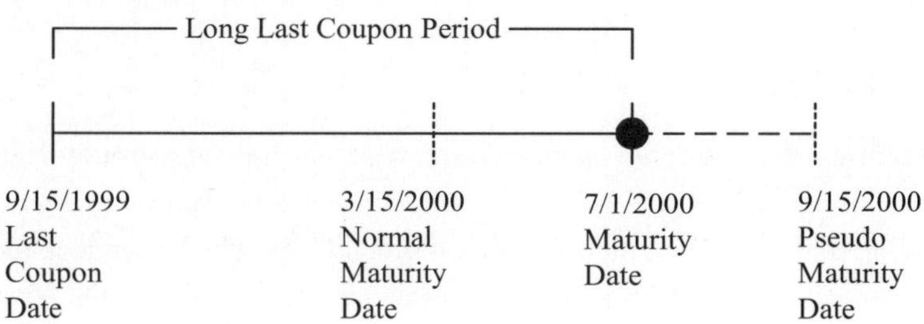

General P/Y Formula: Settlement Date Not in Last Coupon Period

Below we assume that all coupon periods are normal, except the first and last, which might be short or long. We also assume that all coupon payments (cash flows), except first and at-maturity, are the same and equal to the coupon rate divided by the number of coupon payments per year.

Cum-Dividend Trading

$$P = \left(1+\frac{Y}{F}\right)^{-DF} \cdot \left\{ \frac{C(1-TX)}{F} \cdot FCF + \frac{C(1-TX)}{Y}\left[1-\frac{1}{\left(1+\frac{Y}{F}\right)^{n}}\right] \right.$$

$$+\left[RV - TXG(RV1-P0) + \frac{C(1-TX)}{F} \cdot LCF\right]$$

$$\left. \cdot \left(1+\frac{Y}{F}\right)^{-n-LDF} \right\} - \frac{C(1-TX)}{F} \cdot AIF \qquad (1)$$

If the given yield is zero, use the following formula:

$$P = \frac{C(1-TX)}{F}(FCF + n + LCF - AIF) + RV - TXG(RV1-P0)$$

Ex-Dividend Trading

In some countries, there is *ex-dividend trading*, which occurs when settlement date is on or after ex-dividend date and before the next coupon date. Before every coupon date (including maturity date), there is an ex-dividend date which is independent on settlement date. The ex-dividend date is a date close to the coupon date. How close depends on the convention for a particular country and security. The accrued interest factor is the fraction of the current coupon period between the settlement date and the next coupon date. The accrued interest factor, in this case, is expressed as a negative number, that is, AIF = –DF. Accrued interest is paid by the seller to the buyer, and the full next coupon payment will be received by the seller, which means that FCF = 0.

So, the price/yield formula for ex-dividend trading is the same as for cum-dividend trading, where FCF = 0 and AIF = –DF.

Note that, for some countries (as of this writing, South Africa when the Settlement Date is not in the Last Coupon Period, and Australia when the Settlement Date is in the Last Coupon Period), the accrued-interest factor has a different day count method than the discount factor. In this case, both factors should be calculated with the proper day count method.

The variables of the formula are:

P is the bond **P**rice (per 1 currency unit of face value), excluding accrued interest.

F is the number of coupon payments (**F**requency of coupon payments) per year.

Y is the nominal annual **Y**ield to maturity, compounded **F** times per year, expressed as a decimal.

C is the nominal annual **C**oupon rate, expressed as a decimal.

n is two less than the **n**umber of coupon payments remaining.

RV is the **R**edemption **V**alue per 1 currency unit of face value of the bond.

RV1 is the redemption value per 1 currency unit of face value of the bond of which the amount to be taxed is calculated. It is usually equal to RV but can be something else, such as accreted price for municipal bonds.

TX is the **TaX** rate for interest income, expressed as a decimal.

TXG is the **TaX** rate for capital **G**ains, expressed as a decimal.

P0 is the base **P**rice for taxes (fiscal price), expressed as a decimal.

The formula assumes the compound discounting of cash flows. This is the rule for almost all securities in the world.

There are five different factors shown in the formula:

AIF **A**ccrued **I**nterest **F**actor—used to calculate accrued interest.

DF **D**iscount **F**actor—used as an exponent to discount the cash flow from next coupon date back to settlement date.

FCF **F**irst **C**oupon **F**actor (current coupon factor)—used to calculate next coupon payment.

LCF **L**ast **C**oupon **F**actor—used to calculate the coupon payment on maturity date.

LDF **L**ast **D**iscount **F**actor—used as an exponent to discount cash flow at maturity date back to last coupon date.

Three of these factors (AIF, FCF, and DF) depend on the nature of the first coupon period (or current coupon period if settlement date is not in first coupon period) and the settlement date's relationship to it (not for FCF). The factors require calculation of the number of days between two dates.

The general rules for such calculations follow:

R1 The order in which the components of these factors are listed below is the order in which they must be calculated. If you change the order, you may obtain erroneous values.

R2 The components must be calculated with the appropriate day count method explained in "Day count methods" in this chapter (see "Applicable Markets and Conventions").

R3 Any part of any coupon period must be divided by the length of the normal coupon period to which it belongs.

We show the calculations of AIF, DF, and FCF for all cases where settlement date is not in the last coupon period. We then provide the calculation of the LCF and LDF.

- If the settlement date occurs in a normal first coupon period, then:

DDF is the number of days from the **D**ated **D**ate to the **F**irst coupon date.

DDS is the number of days from the **D**ated **D**ate to the **S**ettlement date.

SF is the number of days from the **S**ettlement date to the **F**irst coupon date.

Note that **SF** is calculated as **DDF**   **DDS** only when the day count method is 30/360 or 30E/360.

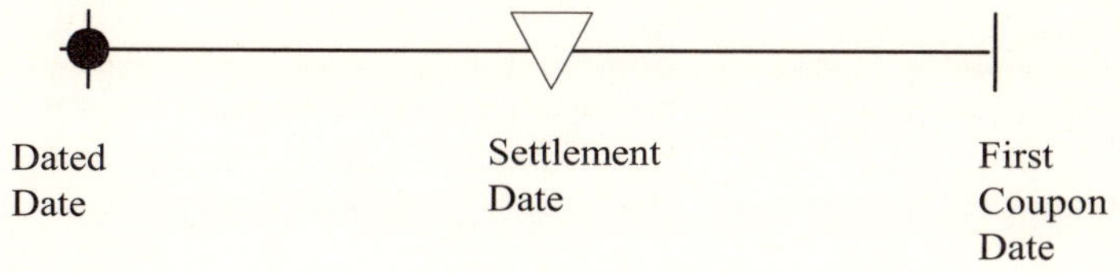

$$\text{AIF} = \frac{\text{DDS}}{\text{DDF}} \qquad \text{FCF} = 1 \qquad \text{DF} = \frac{\text{SF}}{\text{DDF}}$$

- If the settlement date occurs in a short first coupon period, then:

NIF is the number of days from the **N**ormal **I**ssue date to the **F**irst coupon date.

DDF is the number of days from the **D**ated **D**ate to the **F**irst coupon date.

DDS is the number of days from the **D**ated **D**ate to the **S**ettlement date.

SF is the number of days from the **S**ettlement date to the **F**irst coupon date.

Note that **SF** is calculated as **DDF**   **DDS** only when the day count method is 30/360 or 30E/360.

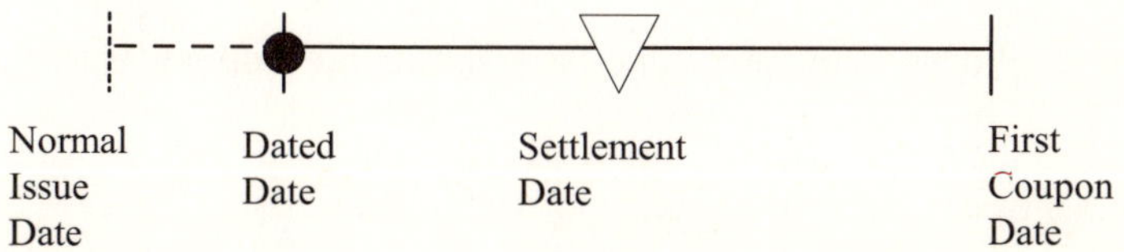

$$\text{AIF} = \frac{\text{DDS}}{\text{NIF}} \qquad \text{FCF} = \frac{\text{DDF}}{\text{NIF}} \qquad \text{DF} = \frac{\text{SF}}{\text{NIF}}$$

- If the settlement date occurs in a long first coupon period and is on or before the normal issue date, then:

PINI is the number of days from the **P**seudo **I**ssue date to **N**ormal **I**ssue date.

DDNI is the number of days from the **D**ated **D**ate to **N**ormal **I**ssue date.

DDS is the number of days from **D**ated **D**ate to the **S**ettlement date.

SNI is the number of days from **S**ettlement date to the **N**ormal **I**ssue date.

Note that **SNI** is calculated as **DDNI** **DDS** only when the day count method is 30/360 or 30E/360.

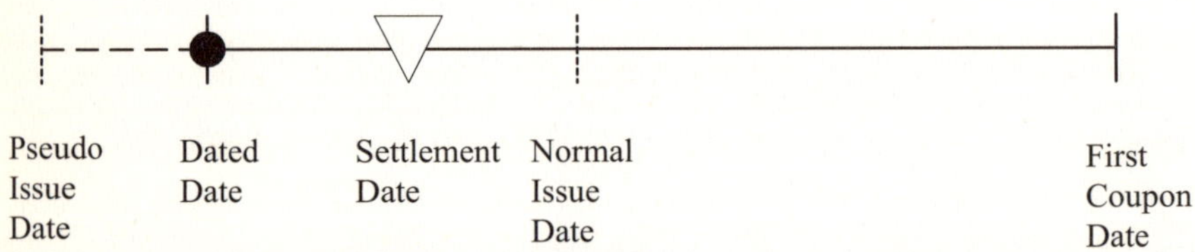

$$\text{AIF} = \frac{\text{DDS}}{\text{PINI}} \qquad \text{FCF} = \frac{\text{DDNI}}{\text{PINI}} + 1 \qquad \text{DF} = \frac{\text{SNI}}{\text{PINI}} + 1$$

- If the settlement date occurs in a long first coupon period and is after the normal issue date, then:

PINI is the number of days from the **P**seudo **I**ssue date to the **N**ormal **I**ssue date.

DDNI is the number of days from **D**ated **D**ate to **N**ormal **I**ssue date.

NIF is the number of days from **N**ormal **I**ssue date to **F**irst coupon date.

NIS is the number of days from **N**ormal **I**ssue date to **S**ettlement date.

SF is the number of days from **S**ettlement date to **F**irst coupon date.

Note that **SF** is calculated as **NIF** **NIS** only when the day count method is 30/360 or 30E/360.

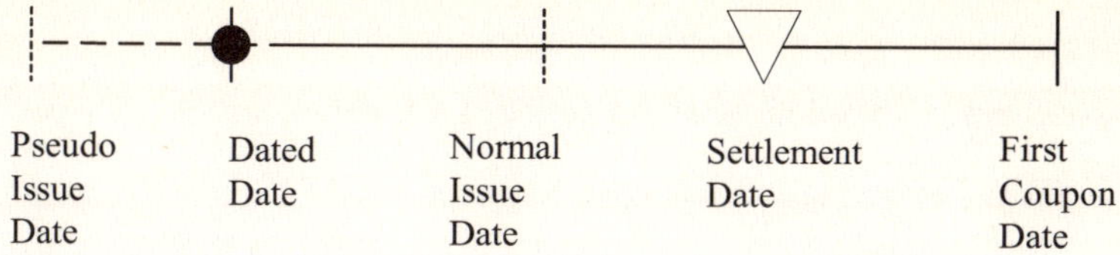

$$AIF = \frac{DDNI}{PINI} + \frac{NIS}{NIF} \qquad FCF = \frac{DDNI}{PINI} + 1 \qquad DF = \frac{SF}{NIF}$$

- If the settlement date is not in the bond's first coupon period, then:

LPN is the number of days from **L**ast **P**aid coupon date to the **N**ext coupon date.

LPS is the number of days from **L**ast **P**aid coupon date to **S**ettlement date.

SN is the number of days from **S**ettlement date to the **N**ext coupon date.

Note that **SN** is calculated as **LPN** **LPS** only when the day count method is 30/360 or 30E/360.

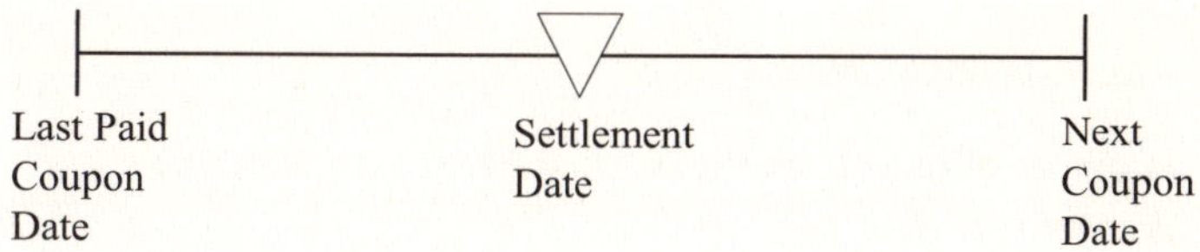

$$AIF = \frac{LPS}{LPN} \qquad FCF = 1 \qquad DF = \frac{SN}{LPN}$$

- If settlement date coincides with a coupon date, then:

$$AIF = 0 \qquad FCF = 1 \qquad DF = 1$$

In this case, the coincidental date is not counted in determining n in the price/yield formula.

For all the cases illustrated earlier, we calculated LCF as follows:

- If the bond has a normal last coupon period, **LCF = 1**.
- If the bond has a short last coupon period, then:

LNM is the number of days from the **L**ast coupon date to the **N**ormal **M**aturity date.

LM is the number of days from the **L**ast coupon date to the **M**aturity date.

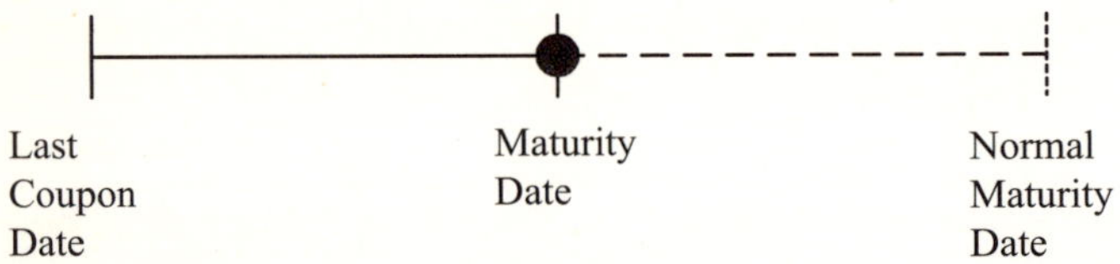

$$\text{LCF} = \frac{\text{LM}}{\text{LNM}}$$

- If the bond has a long last coupon period, then:

NMPM is the number of days from the **N**ormal **M**aturity date to the **P**seudo **M**aturity date.

NMM is the number of days from the **N**ormal **M**aturity date to **M**aturity date.

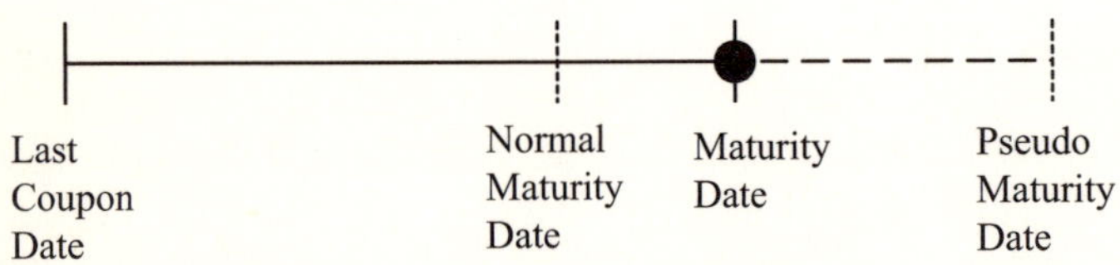

$$\text{LCF} = 1 + \frac{\text{NMM}}{\text{NMPM}}$$

LDF **L**ast **D**iscount **F**actor has the same definition as **LCF**, but it may have a different day count method.

Analyzing the Formula

Let's look at the price/yield formula again.

$$P = \left(1+\frac{Y}{F}\right)^{-DF}\left\{\frac{C(1-TX)}{F}\cdot FCF + \frac{C(1-TX)}{Y}\left[1-\frac{1}{\left(1+\frac{Y}{F}\right)^{n}}\right]\right.$$

$$\left. + \left[RV - TXG(RV1-P0) + \frac{C(1-TX)}{F}\cdot LCF\right]\left(1+\frac{Y}{F}\right)^{-n-LDF}\right\} - \frac{C(1-TX)}{F}\cdot AIF$$

Now let's look at each of the components of the formula:

$$\frac{C(1-TX)}{F}\cdot FCF$$

This component represents the amount of the next coupon payment.

$$\frac{C(1-TX)}{Y}\left[1-\frac{1}{\left(1+\frac{Y}{F}\right)^{n}}\right]$$

This component represents the sum of the present values at the next coupon date of all of the bond's future coupon payments except the next coupon payment and the final payment (payment at maturity date).

$$\left[RV - TXG(RV1-P0) + \frac{C(1-TX)}{F}\cdot LCF\right]\cdot\left(1+\frac{Y}{F}\right)^{-n-LDF}$$

This component represents the sum of the present values at the next coupon date of the bond's final coupon payment and face value.

$$\left(1+\frac{Y}{F}\right)^{-DF}$$

This component represents the discount applied to the sum of the three terms above from the next coupon date back to the settlement date.

$$\frac{C(1-TX)}{F}\cdot AIF$$

This component represents the accrued interest.

The derivation of the second term in braces in the price/yield formula would be

$$\sum_{t=1}^{n}\frac{\frac{C(1-TX)}{F}}{\left(1+\frac{Y}{F}\right)^{t}}=\frac{\frac{C(1-TX)}{F}}{1+\frac{Y}{F}}+\frac{\frac{C(1-TX)}{F}}{\left(1+\frac{Y}{F}\right)^{2}}+\ldots+\frac{\frac{C(1-TX)}{F}}{\left(1+\frac{Y}{F}\right)^{n}}$$

This is the geometric progression with quotient, **q**:

$$q=\frac{1}{1+\frac{Y}{F}}$$

$$=\left(\frac{\frac{C(1-TX)}{F}}{1+\frac{Y}{F}}\cdot\frac{1-\frac{1}{\left(1+\frac{Y}{F}\right)^{n}}}{1-\frac{1}{1+\frac{Y}{F}}}\right)=\frac{\frac{C(1-TX)}{F}}{1+\frac{Y}{F}}\cdot\frac{1-\frac{1}{\left(1+\frac{Y}{F}\right)^{n}}}{\frac{1+\frac{Y}{F}-1}{1+\frac{Y}{F}}}$$

$$=\frac{C(1-TX)}{Y}\left[1-\frac{1}{\left(1+\frac{Y}{F}\right)^{n}}\right]$$

Formula (1) can be used to calculate the price/yield to call date (put date or any redemption date) by applying the following procedures:

- Substitute the call date (put date or any redemption date) for maturity date when determining the values of **n**, **DF**, **LCF**, and **LDF**.
- Substitute call price (put price or any redemption date value) per 1 currency unit of face value for **RV**.

If these substitutions cause the settlement date to fall in the last coupon period, use Formula (2) or (3) (later in this chapter) to calculate the price or yield.

Yield Calculation by Iterations When Price Is Given

For calculations involving Formula (1), where settlement date is not in the last coupon period and we know the price, we calculate the yield by going through a series of iterations. We will use the Newton-Raphson (Tangent) method:

Formula (1) can be written as follows: $P = f(Y)$.

1. First guess for the yield is:

$$Y_1 = \frac{C \cdot N + RV - P}{N - (RV - P)\dfrac{2N+1}{4}}$$

C	is the **C**oupon rate, expressed as a decimal.
N	is the **N**umber of years from Settlement Date to redemption date with the corresponding Day Count method.
RV	is the **R**edemption **V**alue per 1 currency unit of face value.
P	is the **Price** per 1 currency unit of face value.

2. $P_1 = f(Y_1)$

3. We now compare the given price, *P,* with the calculated price, P_1:

$\lvert P - P_1 \rvert \le 10^{-k}$	Stop iteration. Y_1 is the solution. We decide the level of accuracy by setting k.
$\lvert P - P_1 \rvert > 10^{-k}$	Continue with step 4.

4. $$\left(\frac{dP}{dY}\right)_{Y=Y_1} = f'(Y_1)$$

$\frac{dP}{dY}$ is the first derivative of price with respect to yield, as explained in Chapter 3.

5. The correction for Y_1 is:

$$\Delta Y_1 = \frac{P - P_1}{f'(Y_1)}$$

6. The new guess for yield is: $Y_2 = Y_1 + \Delta Y_1$

7. Continue with step 2, giving Y_1 the value of Y_2 and calculating a new P_1.

General P/Y Formula When Settlement Date Is in Last Coupon Period

Simple Interest: Cum-Dividend Trading

$$P = \frac{RV - TXG \cdot (RV1 - P0) + \dfrac{C(1-TX)}{F} \cdot LCF}{1 + \dfrac{Y}{F} \cdot DF} - \frac{C(1-TX)}{F} \cdot AIF \quad (2)$$

To calculate yield, use the following formula:

$$Y = \left(\frac{RV - TXG \cdot (RV1 - P0) + \dfrac{C(1-TX)}{F} \cdot LCF}{P + \dfrac{C(1-TX)}{F} \cdot AIF} - 1 \right) \cdot \frac{F}{DF}$$

Simple Interest: Ex-Dividend Trading:

Formulas are the same as for cum-dividend trading, where LCF = 0 and AIF = –DF.

Note that for some countries (as of this writing, Australia only), the accrued-interest factor has a different day count method than the discount factor. In this case, both factors should be calculated with the proper day count method.

Compound Interest: Cum-Dividend Trading

$$P = \frac{RV - TXG\left(RV1 - P0\right) + \dfrac{C\left(1-TX\right)}{F} \cdot LCF}{\left(1+\dfrac{Y}{F}\right)^{DF}} - \frac{C\left(1-TX\right)}{F} \cdot AIF \qquad (3)$$

$$Y = \left\{\left[\frac{RV - TXG\left(RV1 - P0\right) + \dfrac{C\left(1-TX\right)}{F} LCF}{P + \dfrac{C\left(1-TX\right)}{F} \cdot AIF}\right]^{\frac{1}{DF}} - 1\right\} \cdot F$$

Compound Interest: Ex-Dividend Trading

The formulas are the same as for cum-dividend trading, where LCF = 0 and AIF = –DF.

Note that for some countries, the accrued-interest factor may have a different day count method than the discount factor. In this case, both factors should be calculated with the proper day count method.

All variables (except **AIF**, **LCF**, and **DF**) have been explained earlier.

We now show the calculations of **AIF**, **LCF**, and **DF**.

- If the bond has a normal last coupon period, then:

LM is the number of days from the **L**ast coupon date to the **M**aturity date.

LS is the number of days from the **L**ast coupon date to the **S**ettlement date.

SM is the number of days from the **S**ettlement date to the **M**aturity date.

Note that **SM** is calculated as **LM** **LS** only when the day count method is 30/360 or 30E/360.

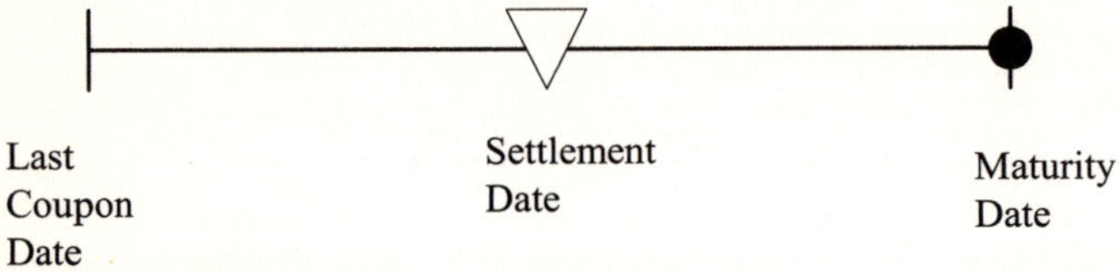

$$AIF = \frac{LS}{LM} \qquad LCF = 1 \qquad DF = \frac{SM}{LM}$$

- If the bond has a short last coupon period, then:

LNM is the number of days from the **L**ast Coupon date to the **N**ormal **M**aturity date.

LM is the number of days from the **L**ast Coupon date to the **M**aturity date.

LS is the number of days from the **L**ast Coupon date to the **S**ettlement date.

SM is the number of days from the **S**ettlement date to the **M**aturity date.

Note that **SM** is calculated as **LM** **LS** only when the day count method is 30/360 or 30E/360.

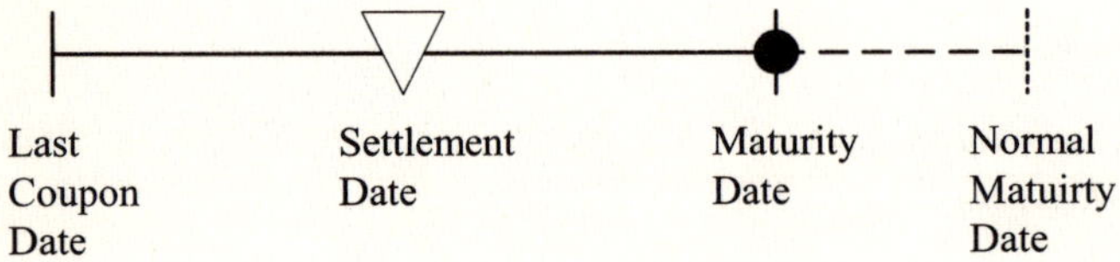

$$AIF = \frac{LS}{LNM} \qquad LCF = \frac{LM}{LNM} \qquad DF = \frac{SM}{LNM}$$

- If a bond has a long last coupon period and the settlement date is on or before the normal maturity date, then:

NMPM is the number of days from the **N**ormal **M**aturity date to the **P**seudo **M**aturity date.

LNM is the number of days from the **L**ast coupon date to the **N**ormal **M**aturity date.

LS is the number of days from the **L**ast coupon date to the **S**ettlement date.

SNM is the number of days from the **S**ettlement date to the **N**ormal **M**aturity date.

Note that **SNM** is calculated as **LNM**   **LS** only when the day count method is 30/360 or 30E/360.

NMM is the number of days from the **N**ormal **M**aturity date to the **M**aturity date.

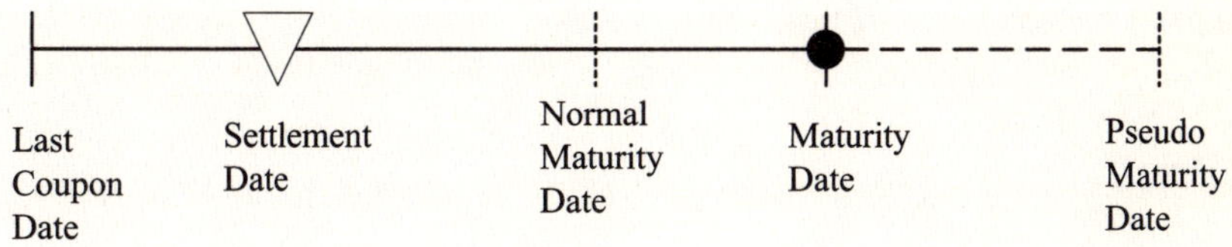

$$AIF = \frac{LS}{LNM} \qquad LCF = 1 + \frac{NMM}{NMPM} \qquad DF = \frac{SNM}{LNM} + \frac{NMM}{NMPM}$$

- If the bond has a long last coupon period and the settlement date is after the normal maturity date, then:

NMPM is the number of days from the **N**ormal **M**aturity date to the **P**seudo **M**aturity date.

NMM is the number of days from the **N**ormal **M**aturity date to the **M**aturity date.

NMS is the number of days from the **N**ormal **M**aturity date to the **S**ettlement date.

SM is the number of days from the **S**ettlement date to the **M**aturity date.

Note that **SM** is calculated as **NMM** **NMS** only when the day count method is 30/360 or 30E/360.

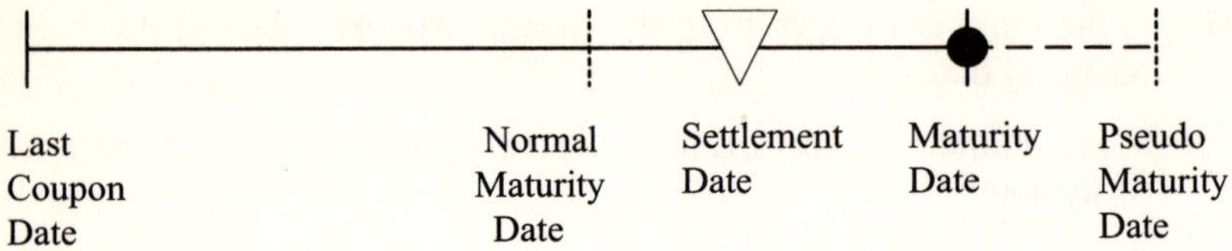

$$\text{AIF} = 1 + \frac{\text{NMS}}{\text{NMPM}} \qquad \text{LCF} = 1 + \frac{\text{NMM}}{\text{NMPM}} \qquad \text{DF} = \frac{\text{SM}}{\text{NMPM}}$$

Remember to follow the rule given earlier stating that you must calculate the components of the factors in the order given in the formulas above.

To calculate the price/yield, other calculations (see Chapter 3), or cash flows (see Chapter 6) to the call date (the put date or any redemption date), substitute the call date (the put date or any redemption date) for the maturity date in the calculations of DF and LCF and replace RV with the call price (the put price or any redemption date value) per 1 currency unit of face value.

Full Price

$$P_{FULL} = P + AI$$

P_{FULL} is the **Full** (dirty) **Price** per 1 currency unit of face value.

AI is the **A**ccrued **I**nterest per one currency unit of face value (see Chapter 2).

Day Count Methods

The day count basis indicates the method by which the days in a month and the days in a year are to be counted. The day count basis is usually expressed as follows:

Number of days in month/Number of days in year

There are eight day count methods in current use:

1. Actual/Actual (in Period)
2. Actual/365
3. Actual (NL)/365 (NL – No Leap). This is the same as Actual/365, but February 29 is not counted.
4. Actual/365 (366 in a leap year)
5. Actual/360
6. 30/360 [SIA-Standard Industry Association (published in *Standard Securities Calculations Methods*, Volume 1, 1996)]
7. 30/365
8. 30E/360 (ISMA-30/360-International Securities Market Association) where **E** stands for European

When calculating the actual number of days between two dates, only one of the dates should be included.

If the number of days in a year is 360, 365, or 366, then the denominator in all factors (AIF, FCF, DF, LCF, and LDF) is 360/F, 365/F, or 366/F, respectively.

Rules for the 30/360 and 30/365 Day Count Methods

The number of days calculation between the dates $M_1/D_1/Y_1$ and $M_2/D_2/Y_2$ on 30/360 and 30/365 day count bases (where $M_1/D_1/Y_1$ is the earlier date) is as follows.

Corrections that must be performed in the exact order as shown below:

1. If D2 is the last day of February (28 in a non–leap year; 29 in a leap year) and D1 is the last day of February, change D2 to 30 (only if the End-of-Month rule is in effect: see Chapter 5).

2. If D_1 is the last day of February, change D_1 to 30 (only if the End-of-Month rule is in effect: see Chapter 5).

3. If D_2 is 31 and D_1 is 30 or 31, change D_2 to 30.

4. If D_1 is 31, change D_1 to 30.

Number of days = $(Y_2 - Y_1)360 + (M_2 - M_1)30 + D_2 - D_1$

There is a lot of confusion with the 30/360 day count method, so I strongly recommend the following rule:
If D_1 or D_2 is the end of the month, change it to 30, and then apply the above formula.
This is consistent with the definition of 30/360, which means 30 days in each month and 360 days in a year. Corporate issuers with which we had trouble calculate this way.

Rules for the 30E/360 Day Count Method

The number of days between the dates $M_1/D_1/Y_1$ and $M_2/D_2/Y_2$ on a 30E/360 day count basis is as follows.

Corrections that must be performed are shown below:

1. If $D_1 = 31$, change D_1 to $D_1 = 30$.

2. If $D_2 = 31$, change D_2 to $D_2 = 30$.

Number of days $= (Y_2 - Y_1)360 + (M_2 - M_1)30 + D_2 - D_1$

Rules for the ACT/365 (366 in Leap Year) Day Count Method

In calculating AIF, FCF, and LCF with the ACT/365 (366 in leap year) day count method, the portion in a non–leap year should be divided by 365/F and the portion in a leap year should be divided by 366/F.

Example

Maturity Date:	11/15/2007
Settlement Date:	1/12/2000
Frequency of Coupon Payments per year:	2

Find the Accrued-Interest Factor.

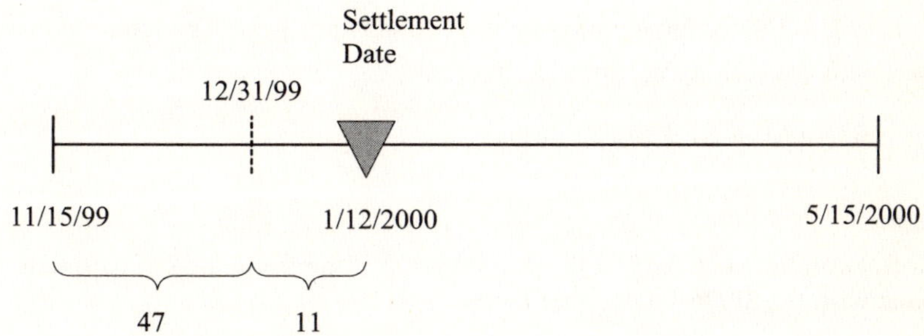

$$AIF = \frac{47}{182.5} + \frac{11}{183}$$

Day Count Methods: Clarification

Day count methods need some clarification. For that purpose we will use the Actual/360 and 30/360 day count methods.

Actual/360 Day Count Method

The denominators in all factors (AIF, DF, FCF, LCF, LDF) will, in this case, be 360/F, where F is the frequency of coupon payments per year.

The numerator will be the actual number of days between two dates, even if there is more than one year between them. One year means the period between the same dates [or 2/28 of one year and 2/29 of the next year (if it is a leap year) or vice versa] of two consecutive years.

Note that, if there is more than one year in the numerator, this does not mean that one year should be replaced by 360 days and then continue adding days to 360.

Example

Find the fraction between 3/15/2002 and 5/3/2003 if the frequency of payments per year is one with the **Actual/360** day count method.

Numerator: 3/15/2002 to 5/3/2003 = 414 days (actual number of days), not 3/15/2002 to 5/3/2003 = 3/15/2002 to 3/15/2003 + 3/15/2003 to 5/3/2003 → 360 + 49 = 409
Denominator: 360/1 = 360
The fraction is 414/360.

30/360 Day Count Method

The denominators in all factors (AIF, DF, FCF, LCF, LDF) will in this case be 360/F, where F is the frequency of coupon payments per year. The numerator will be calculated with the following formula after applying corrections, if any:

$$(Y_2 - Y_1)360 + (M_2 - M_1)30 + D_2 - D_1$$

Example:

Find the fraction between 3/15/2002 and 5/3/2003 if the frequency of payments per year is one with the **30/360** day count method.

Numerator: 3/15/2002 to 5/3/2003 = (2003 – 2002)360 + (5 – 3)30 + 3 – 15 = 408

Denominator: 360/1 = 360
The fraction is 408/360.

Example of an Accrued-Interest Factor Calculation

Assume the following: (1) coupon payments are semiannual, (2) maturity date 1/15/2005, and (3) settlement date 5/31/2000. Using the day count methods described earlier, determine the accrued-interest factor (the fraction of the period between the last paid coupon date and the settlement date).

1. Actual/Actual (in period)

   1/15/2000 to 5/31/2000 = 137

   1/15/2000 to 7/15/2000 = 182

   $$AIF = \frac{137}{182}$$

2. Actual/365

   1/15/2000 to 5/31/2000 = 137

   1/15/2000 to 7/15/2000 → 365/2 = 182.5

   $$AIF = \frac{137}{182.5}$$

3. Actual (NL)/365

   1/15/2000 to 5/31/2000 = 136 (February 29th is not counted)

   1/15/2000 to 7/15/2000 → 365/2 = 182.5

   $$AIF = \frac{136}{182.5}$$

4. Actual/365 (366 in leap year)

   1/15/2000 to 5/31/2000 = 137

   1/15/2000 to 7/15/2000 → 366/2 = 183

   $$AIF = \frac{137}{183}$$

5. Actual/360

   1/15/2000 to 5/31/2000 = 137

   1/15/2000 to 7/15/2000 → 360/2 = 180

   $$AIF = \frac{137}{180}$$

6. 30/360

   1/15/2000 to 5/31/2000 = (2000 – 2000)360 + (5–1)30 + 31 – 15 = 136

   1/15/2000 to 7/15/2000 → 360/2 = 180

   $$AIF = \frac{136}{180}$$

7. 30/365

   1/15/2000 to 5/31/2000 → (2000 – 2000)360 + (5 – 1)30 +31 – 15 = 136

   1/15/2000 to 7/15/2000 → 365/2 = 182.5

   $$AIF = \frac{136}{182.5}$$

8. 30E/360

   1/15/2000 to 5/31/2000 → 1/15/2000 to 5/30/2000 =
   (2000 – 2000)360 + (5–1) 30 + 30 – 15 = 135

   1/15/2000 to 7/15/2000 → 360/2 = 180

   $$AIF = \frac{135}{180}$$

Applicable Markets and Conventions

The default conventions by market and type (i.e., governments, agencies, corporates, and municipals) are summarized in Exhibit 1.1.

Date Assumptions and Conventions

The following is a description of the assumptions and conventions in determining the dates that are not provided as input.

1. The term **Maturity-Anniversary** (Mat-anniv) refers to any date that is a set of normal coupon periods away from maturity. For a bond with normal first and last coupon periods, all coupon payment dates are on Mat-anniv dates. For example, if the maturity date is 5/15/2006 and the frequency of payments per year (F) is 2, then Mat-anniv dates are 5/15 and 11/15. [Note that it is necessary to take into account the End-of-Month (EOM) rule (see Chapter 5).]

2. If the dated date and the first coupon date are given, then the dated date must be less than two normal coupon periods before the first coupon date.

3. First coupon date (FCPNDATE) and the last coupon date (LCPNDATE) *must be* on the anniversary of each other, or equal to each other. For example:

    a) FCPNDATE: 3/5

       F: 2 (semi-annual)

       The **last coupon date** might be 3/5 or 9/5.

    b) FCPNDATE: 5/31

       F: 4 (quarterly)

       The **last coupon date** might be 5/31 or 8/31 or 11/30 or 2/28 (2/29 in a leap year).

4. The **first coupon date** should be provided only if the first coupon period is short or long and if settlement date is in the first coupon period. (See the assumptions listed below if the **first coupon date** is not given.)

5. The **last coupon date** should be provided only if the last coupon period is short or long. See the assumptions listed below if the **last coupon date** is not given.

Several fields in the Assumptions column in Exhibit 1.2 refer to the assumed FCPNDATE. These fields are marked with an asterisk (*). The assumed FCPNDATE falls either on a maturity anniversary date, or on a last coupon date's anniversary date, or on the last coupon date itself. The assumed FCPNDATE is then the closest date to the dated date (DDATE), making the first coupon period long.

Examples

1. Semi-annual coupon payments:

Maturity Date:	5/20/2007
Dated Date:	12/1/2001
Last Coupon Date:	2/15/2007
Assumed FCPNDATE:	8/15/2002

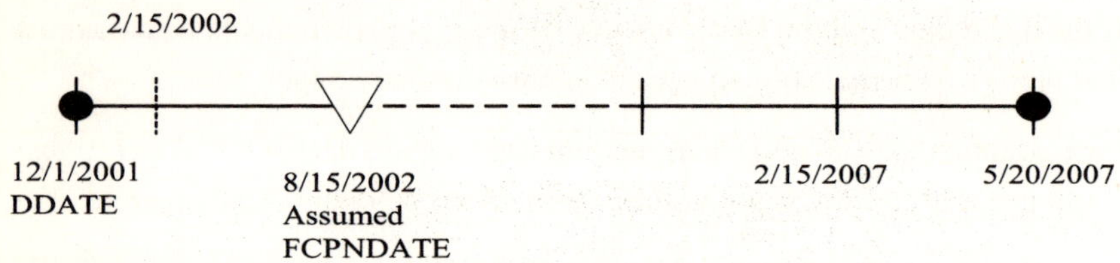

2. Semi-annual coupon payments

Maturity date:	3/21/2005
Dated date:	12/10/2002

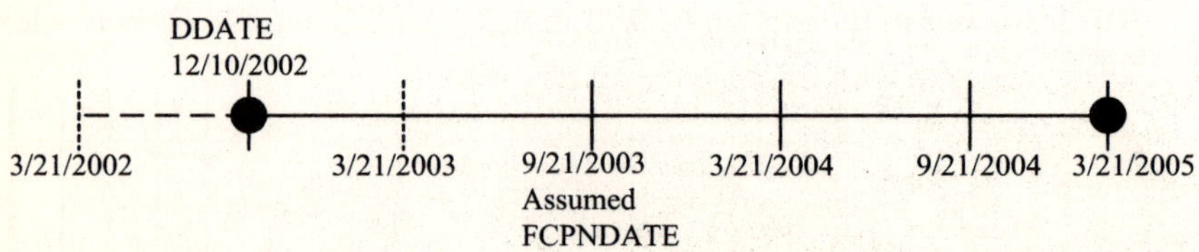

Assumed FCPNDATE:	9/21/2003

Exhibit 1.1: Applicable Markets and Conventions

		Day Count Methods									
Market	Coupon Payment Frequency	Accrued Interest (AI) to Be Paid	AI (Price/Yield)	FCF	DF	LCF	LDF	DF in Last Coupon Period	DF For Normal Coupon Periods	Ex-Div. Trading	End-of-Month Rule
Australian Gov't	Semiannual	Act/Act	Act/Act	Act/Act	Act/Act	Act/Act	Act/Act	Act/365	1	Y	Y
Canadian Gov't	Semiannual	Act/365	Act/Act	Act/Act	Act/Act	Act/Act	Act/Act	Act/365	1	N	Y
Czech Gov't	Annual	30E/360	30E/360	30E/360	30E/360	30E/360	30E/360	30E/360	1	Y	Y
Danish Gov't	Annual	Act/Act	Act/Act	Act/Act	Act/Act	Act/Act	Act/Act	Act/Act	1	Y	Y
EMU Countries	Annual	Act/Act	Act/Act	Act/Act	Act/Act	Act/Act	Act/Act	Act/Act	1	N	Y
Eurobond	Annual	30E/360	30E/360	30E/360	30E/360	30E/360	30E/360	30E/360	1	N	Y
Finnish Gov't	Annual	30E/360	30E/360	30E/360	30E/360	30E/360	30E/360	30E/360	1	N	Y
Greek Gov't	Annual	30E/360	30E/360	30E/360	30E/360	30E/360	30E/360	30E/360	1	N	Y
Irish Gov't	Annual	30E/360	30E/360	30E/360	30E/360	30E/360	30E/360	30E/360	1	Y	Y
Italian Gov't	Semiannual	30E/360	30E/360	30E/360	Act/365	30E/360	Act/365	30E/360	1	N	Y
New Zealand Gov't	Semiannual	Act/Act	Act/Act	Act/Act	Act/Act	Act/Act	Act/Act	Act/Act	1	Y	Y
Norwegian Gov't	Semiannual	Act/365	Act/365	Act/365	Act/365	Act/365	Act/365	Act/365	1	Y	N
Polish Gov't	Annual	Act/Act	Act/Act	Act/Act	Act/Act	Act/Act	Act/Act	Act/Act	1	N	Y
South African Gov't	Semiannual	Act/365	Act/365	Act/Act	Act/Act	Act/Act	Act/Act	Act/365	1	Y	Y
Swedish Gov't	Annual	30E/360	30E/360	30E/360	30E/360	30E/360	30E/360	30E/360	1	Y	Y
Swiss Gov't	Annual	30E/360	30E/360	30E/360	30E/360	30E/360	30E/360	30E/360	1	N	Y
U.S. Gov't	Semiannual	Act/Act	Act/Act	Act/Act	Act/Act	Act/Act	Act/Act	Act/Act	1	N	Y

Exhibit 1.1 (continued)

		Day Count Methods									
Market	**Coupon Payment Frequency**	**Accrued Interest (AI) to be Paid**	**AI (Price/ Yield)**	**FCF**	**DF**	**LCF**	**LDF**	**DF in Last Coupon Period**	**DF For Normal Coupon Periods**	**Ex-Div. Trading**	**End-of-Month Rule**
U.S. Corporate	Semiannual	30/360	30/360	30/360	30/360	30/360	30/360	30/360	1	N	Y
U.S. Gov't Agency	Semiannual	30/360	30/360	30/360	30/360	30/360	30/360	30/360	1	N	Y
U.S. Municipal	Semiannual	30/360	30/360	30/360	30/360	30/360	30/360	30/360	1	N	Y

Exhibit 1.2: Date Assumptions and Conventions

DDATE	FCPNDATE	LCPNDATE	ASSUMPTIONS
No Date Is Given			
not given	not given	not given	normal coupon period in which settlement date occurs; normal last coupon period
One Date Is Given			
not given	not given	on Mat-anniv	normal coupon period in which settlement date occurs
not given	not given	not on Mat-anniv	normal coupon period in which settlement date occurs
not given	on Mat-anniv	not given	normal coupon period in which settlement date occurs; normal last coupon period
not given	not on Mat-anniv	not given	normal coupon period in which settlement date occurs; short last coupon period
on Mat-anniv	not given	not given	normal first coupon period; normal last coupon period
not on Mat-anniv	not given	not given	*ERROR if settlement date is before assumed FCPNDATE (user must provide FCPNDATE); otherwise, normal coupon period in which settlement date occurs; normal last coupon period
Two Dates Are Given			
not given	on Mat-anniv	on Mat-anniv	normal period in which settlement date occurs
not given	on Mat-anniv	not on Mat-anniv	ERROR (FCPNDATE and LCPNDATE MUST be on the anniversary of each other)
not given	not on Mat-anniv	on Mat-anniv	ERROR (FCPNDATE and LCPNDATE MUST be on the anniversary of each other)

Exhibit 1.2 (continued)

not given	not on Mat-anniv but on LCPNDATE anniversary	not on Mat-anniv	normal coupon period in which settlement date occurs
not given	not on Mat-anniv and not on LCPNDATE anniversary	not on Mat-anniv	ERROR (FCPNDATE and LCPNDATE MUST be on the anniversary of each other)
on Mat-anniv	not given	on Mat-anniv	normal first coupon period
on Mat-anniv	not given	not on Mat-anniv	*ERROR if settlement date is before assumed FCPNDATE (user must provide FCPNDATE); otherwise, normal coupon period in which settlement date occurs
not on Mat-anniv	not given	on Mat-anniv	*ERROR if settlement date is before assumed FCPNDATE (user must provide FCPNDATE); otherwise, normal coupon period in which settlement date occurs
not on Mat-anniv but on LCPNDATE anniversary	not given	not on Mat-anniv	normal first coupon period
not on Mat-anniv and not on LCPNDATE anniversary	not given	not on Mat-anniv	*ERROR if settlement date is before assumed FCPNDATE (user must provide FCPNDATE); otherwise, normal coupon period in which settlement date occurs
any date	on Mat-anniv	not given	normal last coupon period; ERROR if the dated date is two or more normal coupon periods before the first coupon date and settlement date is in the first coupon period
any date	not on Mat-anniv	not given	short last coupon period; ERROR if the dated date is two or more normal coupon periods before the first coupon date and settlement date is in the first coupon period
Three Dates Are Given			
any date	on Mat-anniv	not on Mat-anniv	ERROR (FCPNDATE and LCPNDATE MUST be on the anniversary of each other)
any date	not on Mat-anniv	on Mat-anniv	ERROR (FCPNDATE and LCPNDATE MUST be on the anniversary of each other)

Test Examples

This section provides examples of accrued-interest and price/yield calculations. In all the examples we assume RV = 1, TX = 0, and TXG = 0.

Example 1

This example illustrates a United States government bond with normal last coupon period. The settlement date is neither in the first nor in the last coupon period.

Maturity Date:	6/1/2013
Settlement Date:	8/24/2002
Nominal Annual Coupon Rate:	8%
Nominal Annual Yield to Maturity:	8.5%
Frequency of Payments per Year:	2
Day Count Method:	Actual/Actual (in period)

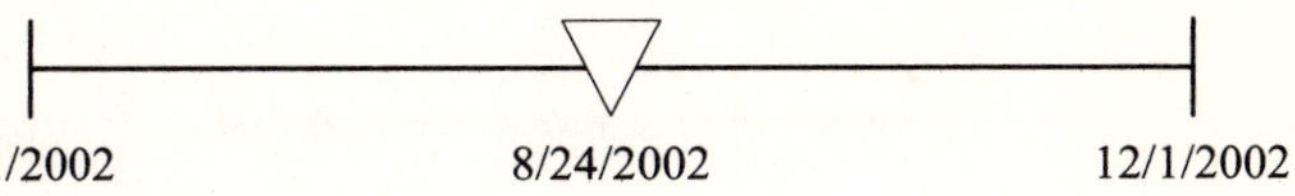

LPN:	6/1/2002 to 12/1/2002	=	183 days
LPS:	6/1/2002 to 8/24/2002	=	84 days
SN:	8/24/2002 to 12/1/2002	=	99 days

AIF:	LPS/LPN	=	84/183
FCF:		=	1
DF:	SN/LPN	=	99/183
n:		=	20
LCF:		=	1
LDF:		=	1

AI:	=	0.0183606557
P:	=	0.9649678765

Example 2

This example illustrates a United States government note that has a long first coupon period and a normal last coupon period. The settlement date is in the first coupon period before the normal issue date.

Maturity Date:	5/15/2006
Settlement Date:	4/16/2001
Dated Date:	3/10/2001
First Coupon Date:	11/15/2001
Nominal Annual Coupon Rate:	8%
Nominal Annual Yield to Maturity:	9%
Frequency of Payments per Year:	2
Day Count Method:	Actual/Actual (in period)
Normal Issue Date:	5/15/2001
Pseudo Issue Date:	11/15/2000

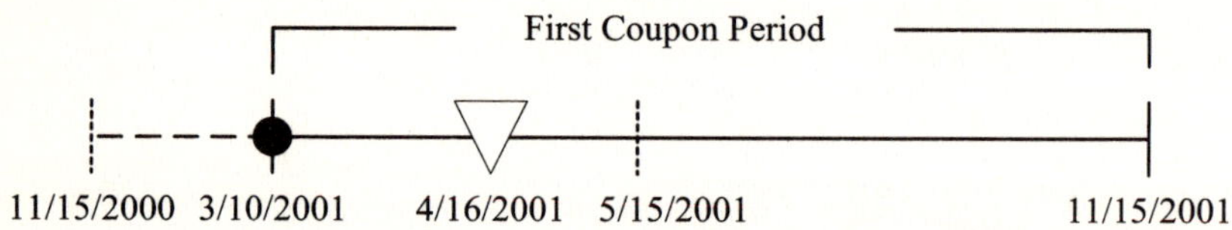

PINI:	11/15/2000 to 5/15/2001	=	181 days
DDNI:	3/10/2001 to 5/15/2001	=	66 days
DDS:	3/10/2001 to 4/16/2001	=	37 days
SNI:	4/16/2001 to 5/15/2001	=	29 days

AIF:	DDS/PINI	=	37/181
FCF:	(DDNI/PINI) +1	=	(66/181) + 1
DF:	(SNI/PINI) + 1	=	(29/181) +1
n:		=	8
LCF:		=	1
LDF:		=	1

AI:	=	0.00817679558
P:	=	0.95936948973

Example 3

This example is a United States corporate bond that has a long first coupon period and a normal last coupon period. Settlement date is in the first coupon period, after the normal issue date.

Maturity Date:	10/31/2003
Settlement Date:	7/10/1999
Dated Date:	2/16/1999
First Coupon Date:	10/31/1999
Nominal Annual Coupon Rate:	9%
Nominal Annual Yield to Maturity:	11%
Frequency of Payments per Year:	2
Day Count Method:	30/360
Normal Issue Date:	4/30/1999
Pseudo Issue Date:	10/31/1998

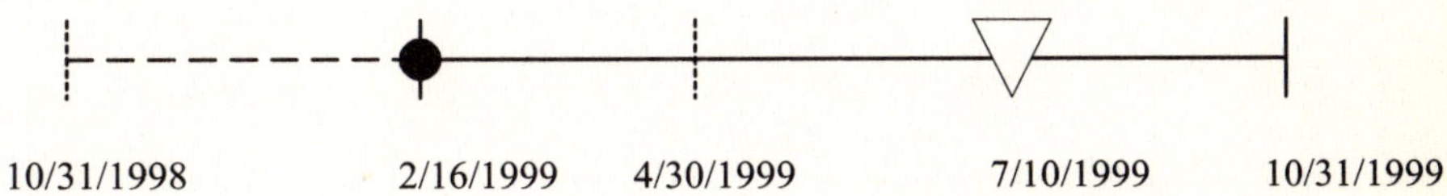

PINI:	10/31/1998 to 4/30/1999	=	180 days
DDNI:	2/16/1999 to 4/30/1999	=	74 days
NIF:	4/30/1999 to 10/31/1999	=	180 days
NIS:	4/30/1999 to 7/10/1999	=	70 days
SF:	NIF – NIS	=	110 days
AIF:	(DDNI/PINI) + (NIS/NIF)	=	144/180
FCF:	(DDNI/PINI) +1	=	254/180
DF:	SF/NIF	=	110/180

n:	=	7
LCF:	=	1
LDF:	=	1
AI:	=	0.036
P:	=	0.9319595020

Example 4

This example illustrates a U.S. corporate bond with a short first and short last coupon period. Settlement date is in the first coupon period.

Maturity Date:	1/20/2008
Settlement Date:	2/12/2001
Dated Date:	1/5/2001
First Coupon Date:	5/15/2001
Last Coupon Date:	11/15/2007
Nominal Annual Coupon Rate:	9%
Nominal Annual Yield to Maturity:	11%
Frequency of Payments per Year:	2
Day Count Method:	30/360
Normal Issue Date:	11/15/2000
Normal Maturity Date:	5/15/2008

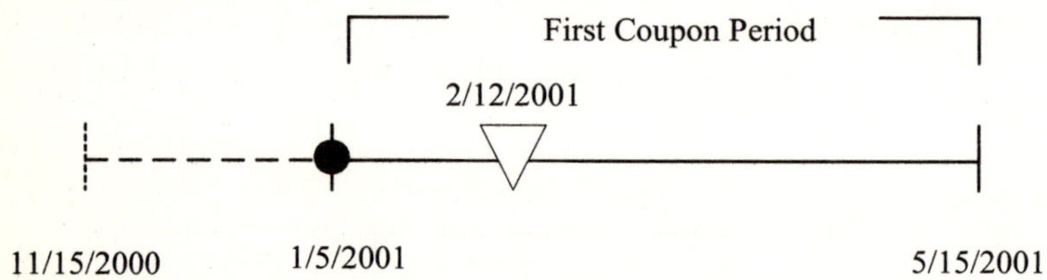

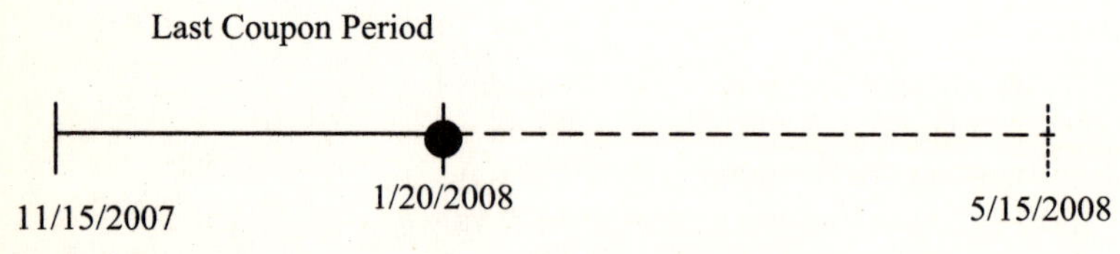

NIF:	11/15/2000 to 5/15/2001	=	180 days
DDF:	1/5/2001 to 5/15/2001	=	130 days

DDS:	1/5/2001 to 2/12/2001	=	37 days
SF:	DDF – DDS	=	93 days
LNM:	11/15/2007 to 5/15/2008	=	180 days
LM:	11/15/2007 to 1/20/2008	=	65 days
AIF:	DDS/NIF	=	37/180
FCF:	DDF/NIF	=	130/180
DF:	SF/NIF	=	93/180
n:		=	13
LCF:	LM/LNM	=	65/180
LDF:	LM/LNM	=	65/180
AI:		=	0.00925
P:		=	0.9048398137

Example 5

This example illustrates a United States government note with a short last coupon period. The settlement date is in the last coupon period.

Maturity Date:	10/15/2002
Settlement Date:	7/20/2002
Last Coupon Date:	6/1/2002
Nominal Annual Coupon Rate:	10%
Nominal Annual Yield to Maturity:	11%
Frequency of Payments per Year:	2
Day Count Method:	Actual/Actual (in period)
Normal Maturity Date:	12/1/2002

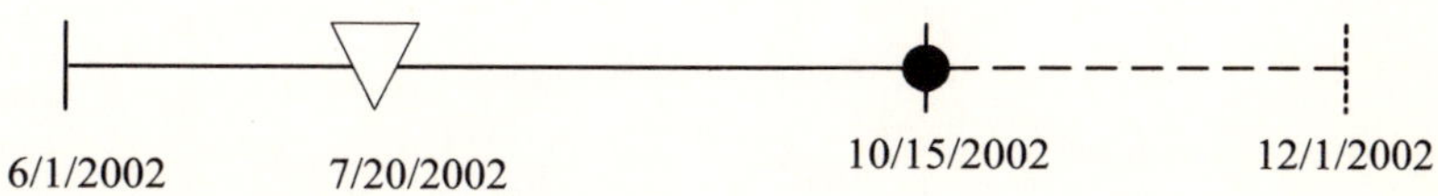

LNM:	6/1/2002 to 12/1/2002	=	183 days
LM:	6/1/2002 to 10/15/2002	=	136 days
LS:	6/1/2002 to 7/20/2002	=	49 days
SM:	7/20/2002 to 10/15/2002	=	87 days

AIF:	LS/LNM	=	49/183
LCF:	LM/LNM	=	136/183
DF:	SM/LNM	=	87/183
AI:		=	0.0133879781
P:		=	0.9973423784

Chapter 2

Accrued-Interest Calculations

General Formula for Accrued Interest

Cum-Dividend Trading

Accrued interest is a portion of the next coupon payment between the last-paid coupon date (or dated date if the settlement date is in the first coupon period) and the settlement date. The buyer will pay this portion to the seller and the buyer will get the full next coupon payment.

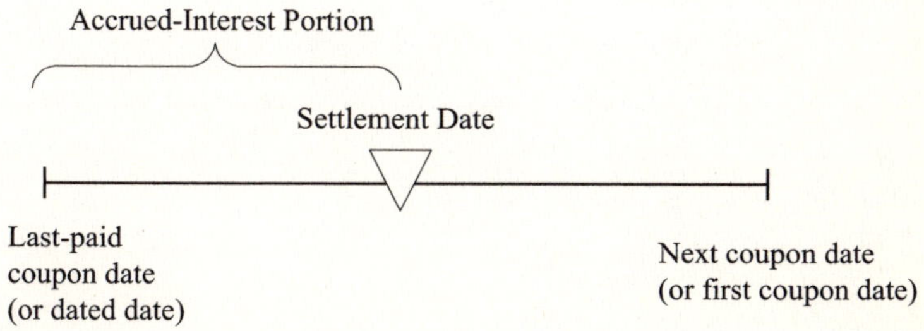

The formula is:

$$AI = \frac{C}{F} \cdot (1 - TX) \cdot AIF$$

AI	is the **A**ccrued **I**nterest per one currency unit (for example \$1) of face value.
C	is the Nominal annual **C**oupon Rate, expressed as a decimal.
F	is the **F**requency of coupon payments per year.

TX is the **T**a**X** rate for interest income, expressed as a decimal.

AIF is the **A**ccrued **I**nterest **F**actor, explained with the general price/yield formula (Chapter 1).

Ex-Dividend Trading

In some countries there is ex-dividend trading, which occurs when the settlement date is on, or after, the ex-dividend date. The ex-dividend date is a date close to the coupon date. How close depends on the convention for the particular country and security. The **A**ccrued **I**nterest **F**actor is the fraction of the current coupon period between the settlement date and the next coupon date (or first coupon date). The accrued interest factor in this case is equal to **D**iscount **F**actor and is expressed as a negative number, i.e., **AIF = DF**. Accrued Interest is paid by the seller to the buyer, and the full next coupon payment will be received by the seller. Note that for some countries (Australia and South Africa only, as of this writing), the accrued-interest factor may have a different day count method than the discount factor. In this case, both factors should be calculated with the proper day count method.

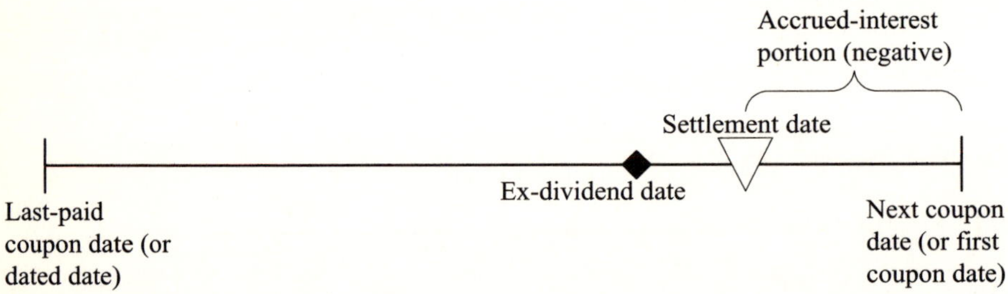

The formula is:

$$AI = -\frac{C}{F} \cdot (1 - TX) \cdot DF$$

DF is the **D**iscount **F**actor, as explained in the general price/yield formula.

In calculation of the **A**ccrued **I**nterest **F**actor and **D**iscount **F**actor, we need to use the day count method that corresponds to the particular country and security. The day count methods are explained in the general price/yield formula. In all examples that follow, we will assume TX = 0, except for Italian government bonds.

Australian Government Bonds

Conventions

- The day count method is Actual/Actual (in a period).
- Ex-dividend date is the seventh calendar day before the coupon date.
- Coupon payment frequency is semiannual.
- Accrued interest is rounded to five decimal places per one Australian dollar of face value.

Example 1

Maturity Date:	8/15/2006
Settlement Date:	9/17/2001
Nominal Annual Coupon Rate:	7%

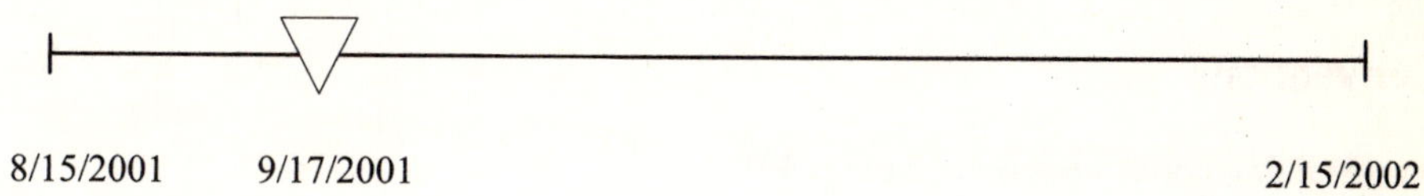

Ex-dividend date: 2/8/2002

This is cum-dividend trading.

$$AIF = \frac{8/15/2001 \text{ to } 9/17/2001}{8/15/2001 \text{ to } 2/15/2002} = \frac{33}{184}$$

$$AI = \frac{0.07}{2} \cdot \frac{33}{184} = 0.006277173913 \approx 0.00628$$

Example 2

Maturity Date:	9/15/2012
Settlement Date:	9/8/2001
Nominal Annual Coupon Rate:	9%

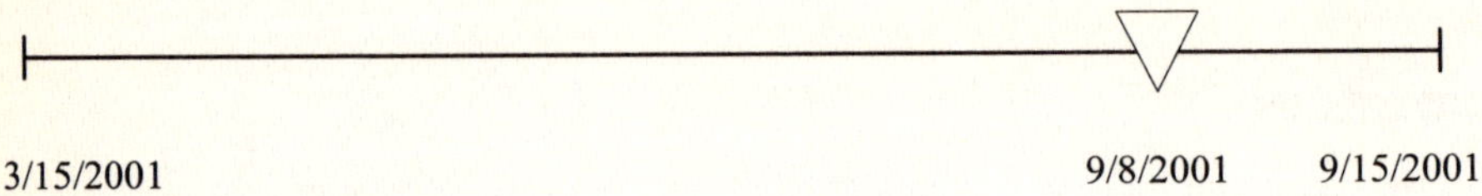

Ex-dividend date: 9/8/2001

This is ex-dividend trading.

$$\text{AIF} = -\frac{9/8/2001 \text{ to } 9/15/2001}{3/15/2001 \text{ to } 9/15/2001} = -\frac{7}{184}$$

$$\text{AI} = \frac{0.09}{2}\left(\frac{-7}{184}\right) = -0.001711956522 \approx -0.00171$$

Canadian Government Bonds

Conventions

- The day count method is Actual/365.
- No ex-dividend trading
- Coupon payment frequency is semiannual.
- A special case exists if the number of accrued interest days is 183, then accrued interest should be calculated with this formula:

$$\text{AI} = \frac{\text{C}}{2} \cdot (1 - \text{TX}) \cdot \left(1 - \frac{1}{182.5}\right)$$

Note that, if the actual number of accrued interest days is 182, then the accrued interest factor is 182/182.5. If the actual number of accrued-interest days is 183, then the accrued-interest factor is:

$$1 - \frac{1}{182.5} = \frac{182.5 - 1}{182.5} = \frac{181.5}{182.5}$$

This means that when the actual number of accrued interest days is 182, accrued interest is higher than accrued interest when the actual number of accrued-interest days is 183.

Example 1

Maturity Date:	7/1/2005
Settlement Date:	9/21/2001
Nominal Annual Coupon Rate:	7.5%

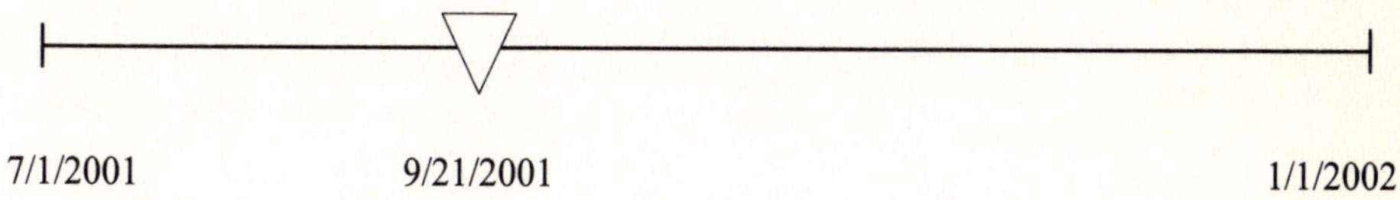

$$\text{AIF} = \frac{7/1/2001 \text{ to } 9/21/2001}{7/1/2001 \text{ to } 1/1/2002} = \frac{82}{182.5}$$

$$\text{AI} = \frac{0.075}{2} \cdot \frac{82}{182.5} = 0.016849315068$$

Example 2

Maturity Date:	9/1/2008
Settlement Date:	8/31/2001
Nominal Annual Coupon Rate:	11.5%

Because the actual number of accrued-interest days between 3/1/2001 and 8/31/2001 is 183, we will use the special case formula:

$$\text{AI} = \frac{0.115}{2} \cdot \left(1 - \frac{1}{182.5}\right) = 0.05718493$$

Example 3

The settlement date is in the short first coupon period:

Maturity Date:	9/1/2006
Settlement Date:	7/5/2001
Dated Date:	5/1/2001
First Coupon Date:	9/1/2001
Nominal Annual Coupon Rate:	6.5%

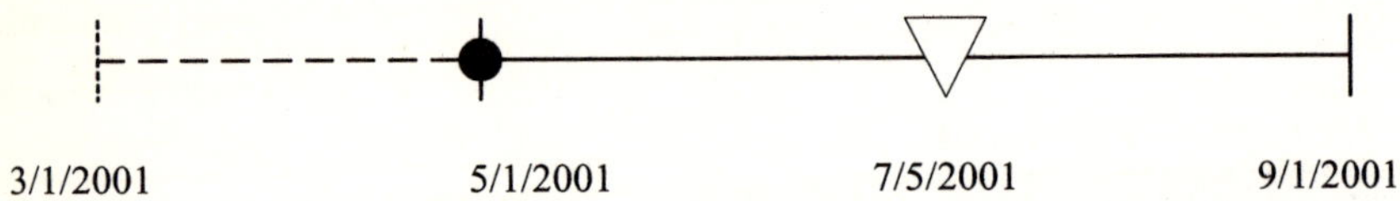

$$AIF = \frac{5/1/2001 \text{ to } 7/5/2001}{3/1/2001 \text{ to } 9/1/2001} = \frac{65}{182.5}$$

$$AI = \frac{0.065}{2} \cdot \frac{65}{182.5} = 0.01157534$$

Example 4

The settlement date is in the last coupon period:

Maturity Date:	12/6/2001
Settlement Date:	9/17/2001
Nominal Annual Coupon Rate:	7%

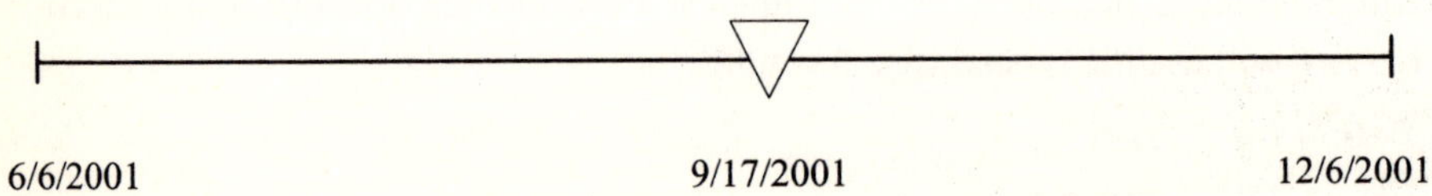

$$AIF = \frac{6/6/2001 \text{ to } 9/17/2001}{6/6/2001 \text{ to } 12/6/2001} = \frac{103}{182.5}$$

$$AI = \frac{0.07}{2} \cdot \frac{103}{182.5} = 0.019753424658$$

Czech Government Bonds

Conventions

- The day count method is 30E/360.
- The ex-dividend date is the 30th calendar day before the coupon date.
- The coupon payment frequency is annual.

Example 1

Maturity Date:	8/15/2006
Settlement Date:	7/16/2002
Coupon Rate:	12.2%

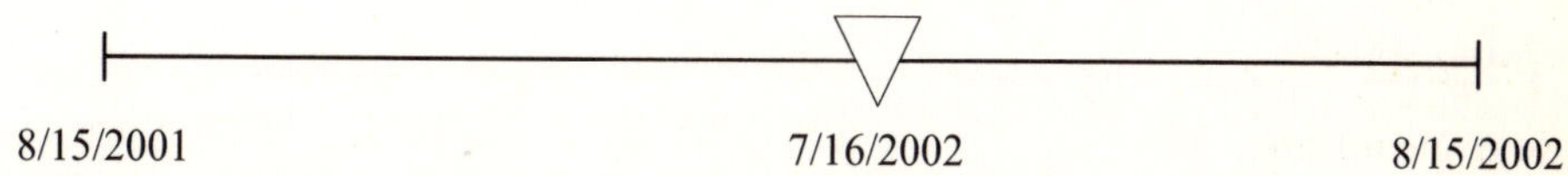

Ex-dividend date: 7/16/2002

This is ex-dividend trading.

$$AIF = -\frac{7/16/2002 \text{ to } 8/15/2002}{8/15/2001 \text{ to } 8/15/2002} = -\frac{29}{360}$$

$$AI = 0.122\left(-\frac{29}{360}\right) = -0.009827778$$

Danish Government Bonds

Conventions

- The day count method is actual / actual (in period).
- The ex-dividend date is one month before the coupon date. "One month before the coupon date" means the same day one month earlier or the ends of two consecutive months.
- The coupon payment frequency is annual.

Example 1

Bond:	Bullet
Maturity Date:	11/15/2009
Settlement Date:	2/6/2002
Coupon Rate:	6%

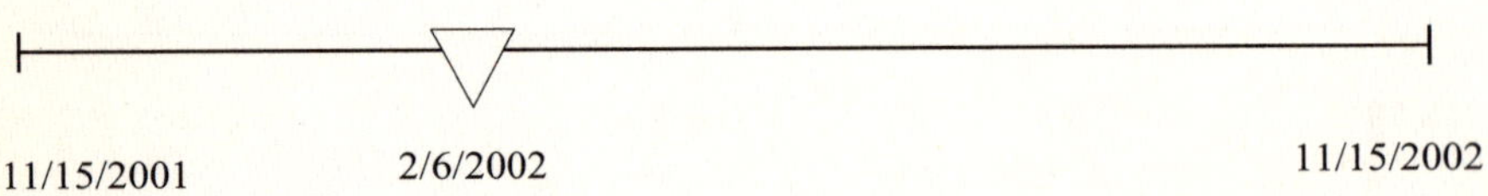

Ex-dividend date: 10/15/2002

This is cum-dividend trading.

$$AIF = \frac{11/15/2001 \text{ to } 2/6/2002}{11/15/2001 \text{ to } 11/15/2002} = \frac{83}{365}$$

$$AI = 0.06 \cdot \frac{83}{365} = 0.01364384$$

Example 2

Bond:	Bullet
Maturity Date:	12/15/2004
Settlement Date:	11/15/2001
Coupon Rate:	7%

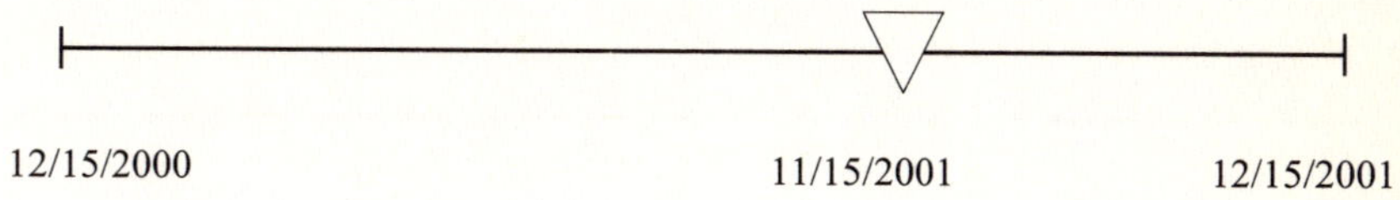

Ex-dividend date: 11/15/2001

This is ex-dividend trading.

$$AIF = -\frac{11/15/2001 \text{ to } 12/15/2001}{12/15/2000 \text{ to } 12/15/2001} = -\frac{30}{365}$$

$$AI = 0.07 \cdot \left(\frac{-30}{365}\right) = -0.005753425$$

EMU Countries Bonds

This section deals with EMU countries' bonds issued on or after 1/1/1999 or reconventioned bonds that existed.

Conventions

- The day count method is Actual/Actual (in period), except Ireland for reconventioned bonds, where it can be Actual/365 or 30E/360, and Greece, where it is 30E/360 for bonds issued before 1/1/2001.
- No ex-dividend trading

- Coupon payment frequency is annual, except Italy, Ireland, and Portugal, where it can be semiannual.

Example 1: German Government Bond

Maturity Date:	7/4/2008
Settlement Date:	3/20/2001
Coupon Rate:	4.75%

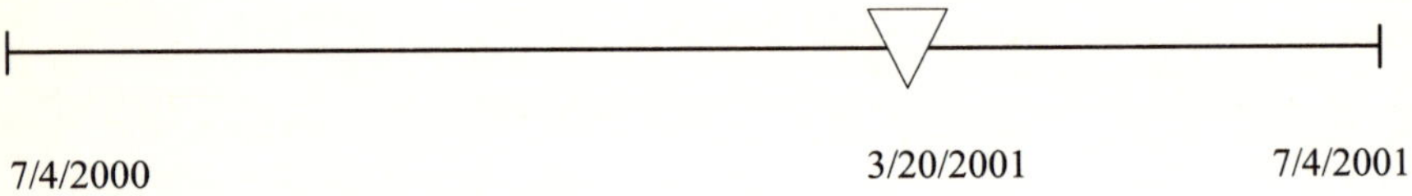

$$\text{AIF} = \frac{7/4/2000 \text{ to } 3/20/2001}{7/4/2000 \text{ to } 7/4/2001} = \frac{259}{365}$$

$$\text{AI} = 0.0475 \cdot \frac{259}{365} = 0.033705479$$

Example 2: Portuguese Government Bond

Maturity Date:	9/23/2013
Settlement Date:	12/14/2000
Coupon Rate:	5.45%

Coupon Payment Frequency per Year is annual.

Accrued interest for Portuguese government bonds is calculated in three steps:

1. Calculate accrued interest per one day and per one escudo of face value.
2. Round amount from step 1 to eleven decimal places.
3. Multiply amount from step 2 by the number of accrued-interest days.

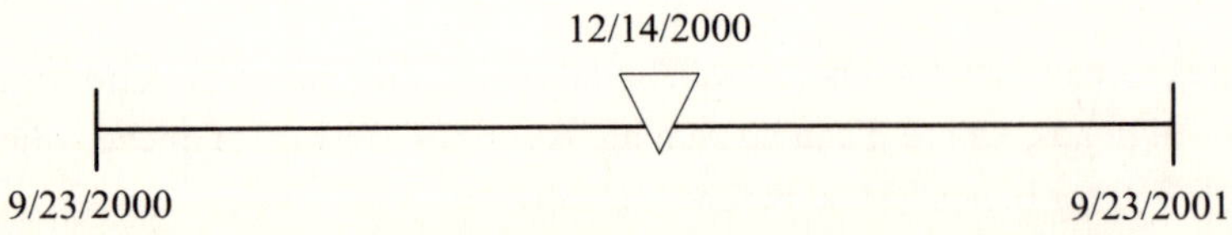

Number of accrued-interest days = 9/23/2000 to 12/14/2000 = 82

AI_1 (Accrued interest per one day and per one escudo of face value)

$$= \frac{0.0545}{365} = 0.0001493150685 \approx 0.00014931507$$

$$AI = 0.00014931507 \cdot 82 = 0.01224383574$$

Example 3: Italian Government Bond

Maturity Date:	5/1/2009
Settlement Date:	1/10/2001
Nominal Annual Coupon Rate:	4.5%

Coupon Payment Frequency per Year is semiannual.

Accrued interest of Italian government bonds is rounded to seven decimal places per one lira of face value.

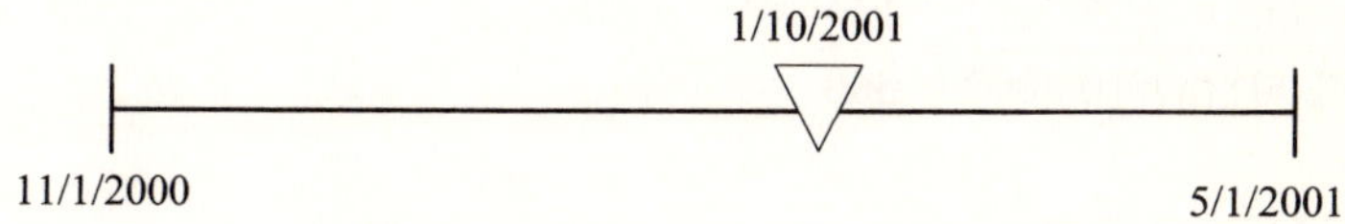

$$AIF = \frac{11/1/2000 \text{ to } 1/10/2001}{11/1/2000 \text{ to } 5/1/2001} = \frac{70}{181}$$

$$AI = \frac{0.045}{2} \cdot \frac{70}{181} = 0.008701657 \approx 0.0087017$$

Example 4: Irish Government Bond

Maturity Date:	10/1/2010
Settlement Date:	2/9/2001
Nominal Annual Coupon Rate:	8.5%
Day Count Method:	ACT/365

Coupon Payment Frequency per Year is semiannual.

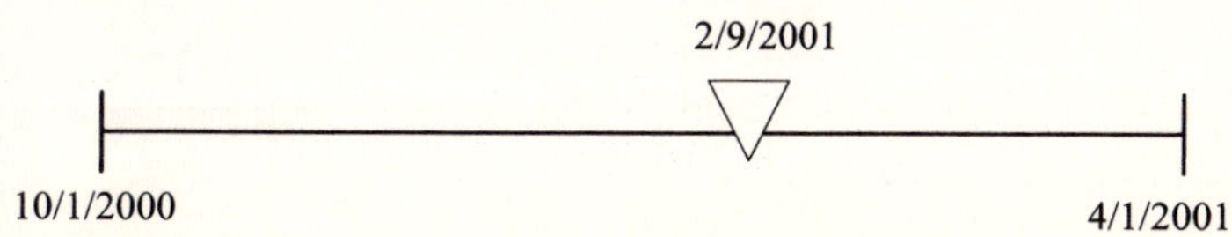

$$AIF = \frac{10/1/2000 \text{ to } 2/9/2001}{10/1/2000 \text{ to } 4/1/2001} = \frac{131}{182.5}$$

$$AI = \frac{0.085}{2} \cdot \frac{131}{182.5} = 0.030506849$$

Example 5: Greek Government Bond

Maturity Date:	1/10/2007
Settlement Date:	5/23/2001
Coupon Rate:	6%
Day Count Method:	30E/360

$$AIF = \frac{1/10/2001 \text{ to } 5/23/2001}{1/10/2001 \text{ to } 1/10/2002} = \frac{133}{360}$$

$$AI = 0.06 \cdot \frac{133}{360} = 0.02216667$$

Example 6: Spanish Government Bond

Maturity date	1/31/2010
Settlement date:	6/6/2001
Coupon Rate:	4%

$$AIF = \frac{1/31/2001 \text{ to } 6/6/2001}{1/31/2001 \text{ to } 1/31/2002} = \frac{126}{365}$$

$$AI = 0.04 \cdot \frac{126}{365} = 0.013808219$$

Euro Bonds

Conventions

- The day count method is 30E/360.
- No ex-dividend trading
- Coupon payment frequency is annual.

Example 1

Settlement date in short first coupon period:

Maturity Date:	4/15/2006
Settlement Date:	7/23/2001
Dated Date:	6/1/2001
First Coupon Date:	4/15/2002
Coupon Rate:	6%

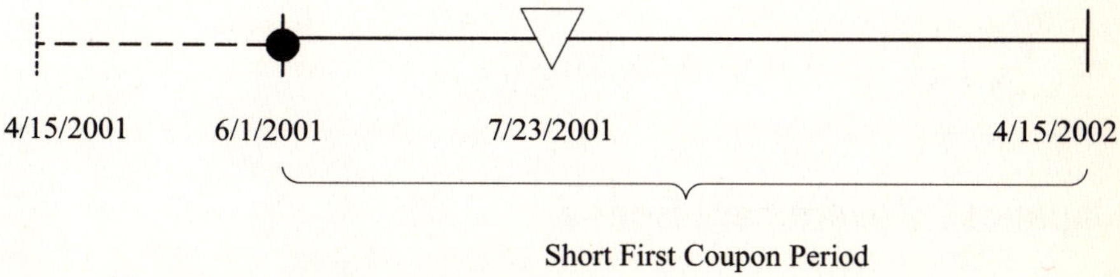

$$AIF = \frac{6/1/2001 \text{ to } 7/23/2001}{4/15/2001 \text{ to } 4/15/2002} = \frac{52}{360}$$

$$AI = 0.06 \cdot \frac{52}{360} = 0.00866667$$

Hungarian Government Bonds

Conventions

- The day count method is Actual (NL)/365.
- No ex-dividend trading
- Coupon payment frequency is semiannual.
- Accrued interest is rounded to six decimal places per one forint of face value.

Example 1

Maturity Date:	2/12/2009
Settlement Date:	6/21/2000
Nominal Annual Coupon Rate:	9.5%

$$AIF = \frac{2/12/2000 \text{ to } 6/21/2000}{2/12/2000 \text{ to } 8/12/2000} = \frac{129}{182.5}$$

February 29th is not counted.

$$AI = \frac{0.095}{2} \cdot \frac{129}{182.5} = 0.033575342 \approx 0.033575$$

Japanese Government Bonds

Conventions

- The day count method is Actual/365.
- No ex-dividend trading
- Coupon payment frequency is semiannual.

If the settlement date is in the first coupon period, then both the dated date and settlement date should be included in the number of accrued-interest days.

Note that, if the settlement date is on the dated date, the number of accrued-interest days is zero (the above rule does not apply). If the settlement date is one day after the dated date, the number of accrued-interest days is 2 (the above rule applies).

For bonds issued on or after 3/1/2001, only one date should be included.

A special case exists if the number of accrued-interest days is 183 or 184 (if settlement date is in the first coupon period), when accrued interest is equal to the full semiannual coupon payment, that is, C/2. This means that the buyer will lose one day of interest on the C/2 amount of money.

Accrued interest is truncated to nine decimal places per one yen of face value.

Example 1

Settlement date in short first coupon period:

Maturity Date:	1/20/2003
Settlement Date:	7/12/2001
Dated Date:	1/25/2001
First Coupon Date:	7/20/2001
Nominal Annual Coupon Rate:	3.2%

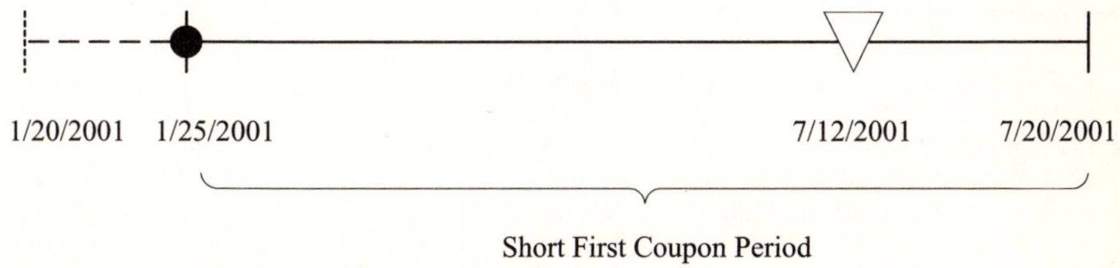

$$\text{AIF} = \frac{1/25/2001 \text{ to } 7/12/2001}{1/20/2001 \text{ to } 7/20/2001} = \frac{169}{182.5}$$

$$\text{AI} = \frac{0.032}{2} \cdot \frac{169}{182.5} = 0.014816438$$

Example 2

Maturity Date:	3/20/2002
Settlement Date:	9/19/2001
Nominal Annual Coupon Rate:	1.2%

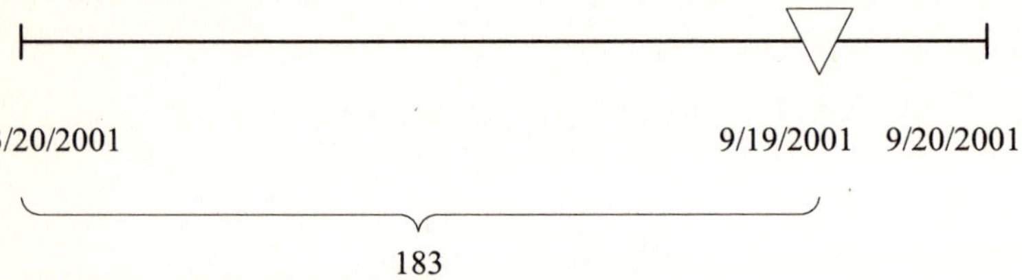

The number of accrued-interest days is 183.

$$AI = \frac{0.012}{2} = 0.006 \text{ (full coupon payment)}$$

Example 3

The settlement date is in the long first coupon period, before the normal issue date:

Maturity Date:	12/22/2008
Settlement Date:	6/19/99
Dated Date:	10/20/98
First Coupon Date:	6/20/99
Nominal Annual Coupon Rate:	0.9%
Tax Rate for Interest Income:	20%

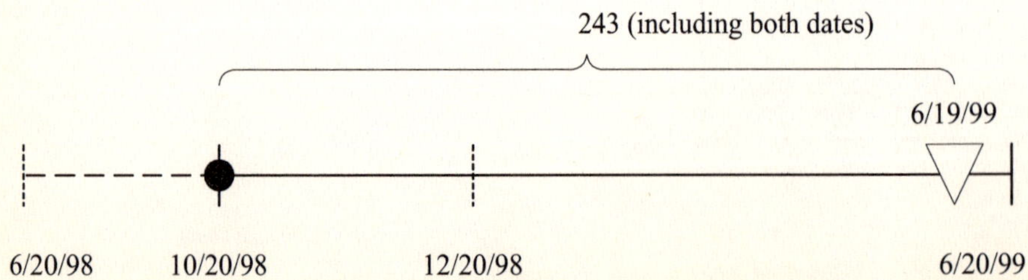

$$\text{AIF} = \frac{243}{182.5}$$

Before tax:

$$\text{AI} = \frac{0.009}{2} \cdot \frac{243}{182.5} = 0.005991780$$

After tax:

$$\text{AI} = \frac{0.009(1-0.20)}{2} \cdot \frac{243}{182.5} = 0.004793424$$

New Zealand Government Bonds

Conventions

- The day count method is Actual/Actual (in period).
- The ex-dividend date is the ninth calendar day before the coupon date.
- The coupon payment frequency is semiannual.

Example 1

Maturity Date: 11/15/2006

Settlement Date: 4/12/2001

Nominal Annual Coupon Rate: 8%

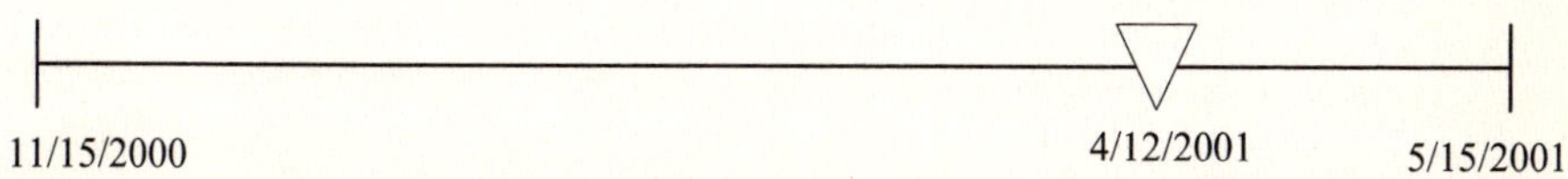

Ex-dividend date: 5/6/2001

This is cum-dividend trading.

$$\text{AIF} = \frac{11/15/2000 \text{ to } 4/12/2001}{11/15/2000 \text{ to } 5/15/2001} = \frac{148}{181}$$

$$\text{AI} = \frac{0.08}{2} \cdot \frac{148}{181} = 0.032707182$$

Example 2

Maturity Date:	7/15/2009
Settlement Date:	1/11/2001
Nominal Annual Coupon Rate:	7%

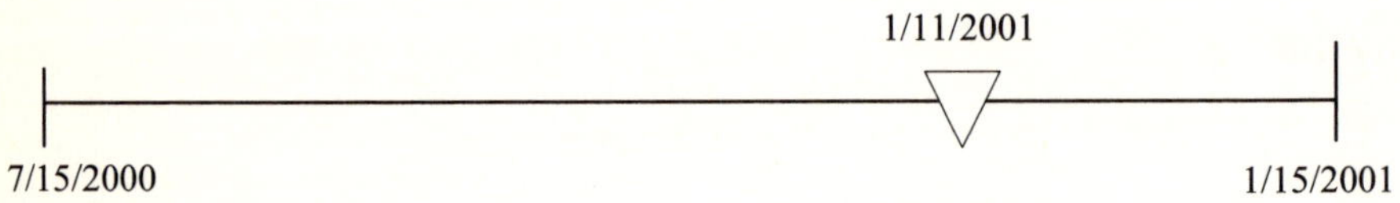

Ex-dividend date: 1/6/2001

This is ex-dividend trading.

$$\text{AIF} = -\frac{1/11/2001 \text{ to } 1/15/2001}{7/15/2000 \text{ to } 1/15/2001} = -\frac{4}{184}$$

$$\text{AI} = \frac{0.07}{2} \cdot \left(-\frac{4}{184}\right) = -0.00076087$$

Norwegian Government Bonds

Conventions

- The day count method is Actual/365.
- The ex-dividend date is the 14th calendar day before the coupon date.
- The coupon payment frequency is semiannual.
- The End-of-Month rule is not in effect.

Example 1

Maturity Date:	3/30/2005
Settlement Date:	5/4/2001
Nominal Annual Coupon Rate:	13%

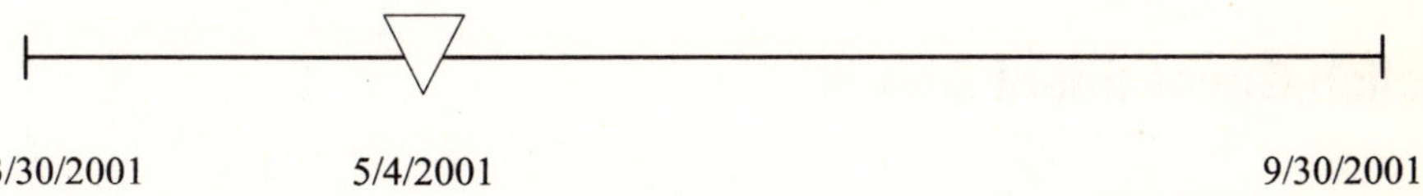

Ex-dividend date: 9/16/2001

This is cum-dividend trading.

$$AIF = \frac{3/30/2001 \text{ to } 5/4/2001}{3/30/2001 \text{ to } 9/30/2001} = \frac{35}{182.5}$$

$$AI = \frac{0.13}{2} \cdot \frac{35}{182.5} = 0.012465753$$

Example 2

Maturity Date:	1/15/2003
Settlement Date:	7/9/2001
Nominal Annual Coupon Rate:	13.1%

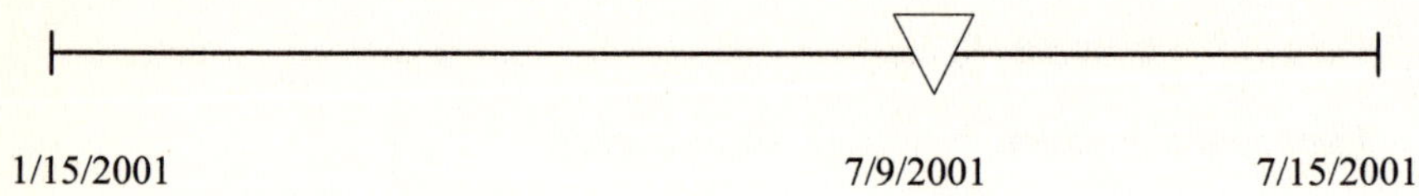

Ex-dividend date: 7/1/2001

This is ex-dividend trading.

$$\text{AIF} = -\frac{7/9/2001 \text{ to } 7/15/2001}{1/15/2001 \text{ to } 7/15/2001} = -\frac{6}{182.5}$$

$$\text{AI} = \frac{0.131}{2} \cdot \left(-\frac{6}{182.5}\right) = -0.002153424$$

Polish Government Bonds

Conventions

- The day count method is Actual/Actual (in period).
- The ex-dividend date is the tenth business day before the coupon date.
- The coupon payment frequency is annual.

Accrued interest is rounded to five decimal places per one Zloty of face value.

Example 1

Maturity Date:	6/12/2002
Settlement Date:	12/11/2001
Coupon Rate:	12%

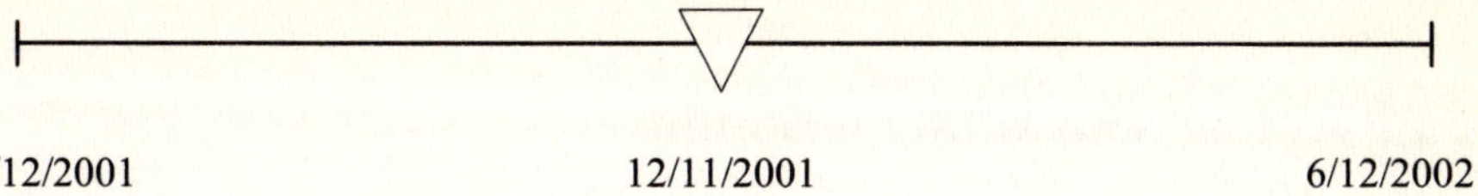

Ex-dividend date: 5/28/2002

This is cum-dividend trading.

$$\text{AIF} = \frac{6/12/2001 \text{ to } 12/11/2001}{6/12/2001 \text{ to } 6/12/2002} = \frac{182}{365}$$

$$\text{AI} = 0.12 \cdot \frac{182}{365} = 0.059835616 \approx 0.05984$$

Example 2

Maturity Date:	11/24/2009
Settlement Date:	11/15/2001
Coupon Rate:	6%

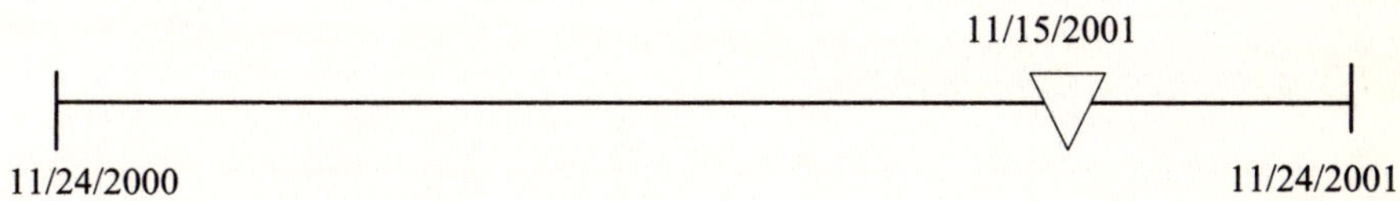

Ex-dividend date: 11/12/2001

This is ex-dividend trading.

$$\text{AIF} = -\frac{11/15/2001 \text{ to } 11/24/2001}{11/24/2000 \text{ to } 11/24/2001} = -\frac{9}{365}$$

$$\text{AI} = 0.06\left(-\frac{9}{365}\right) = -0.001479452 \approx -0.00148$$

South African Government Bonds

Conventions

- The day count method is Act/365.
- The ex-dividend date is one month before the coupon date. One month before the coupon date means the same day one month earlier, or the ends of two consecutive months.
- The coupon payment frequency is semiannual.

Accrued interest is rounded to seven decimal places per one rand of face value.

Example 1

Maturity Date:	4/15/2004
Settlement Date:	5/22/2001
Nominal Annual Coupon Rate:	9%

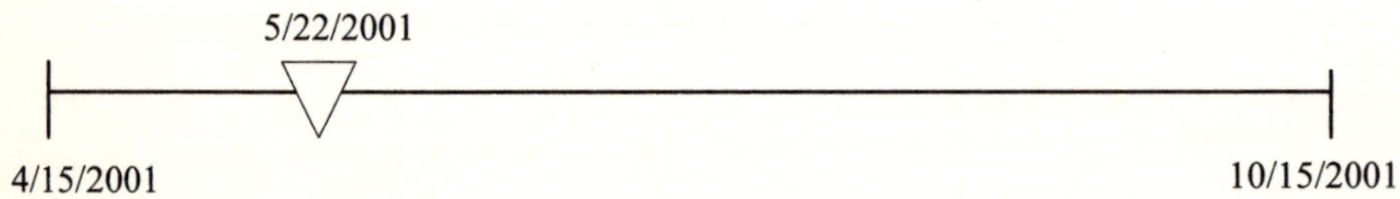

Ex-dividend date: 9/15/2001

This is cum-dividend trading.

$$AIF = \frac{4/15/2001 \text{ to } 5/22/2001}{4/15/2001 \text{ to} 10/15/2001} = \frac{37}{182.5}$$

$$AI = \frac{0.09}{2} \cdot \frac{37}{182.5} = 0.009123288 \approx 0.0091233$$

Example 2

Maturity Date:	9/30/2007
Settlement Date:	3/2/2001
Nominal Annual Coupon Rate:	13.45%

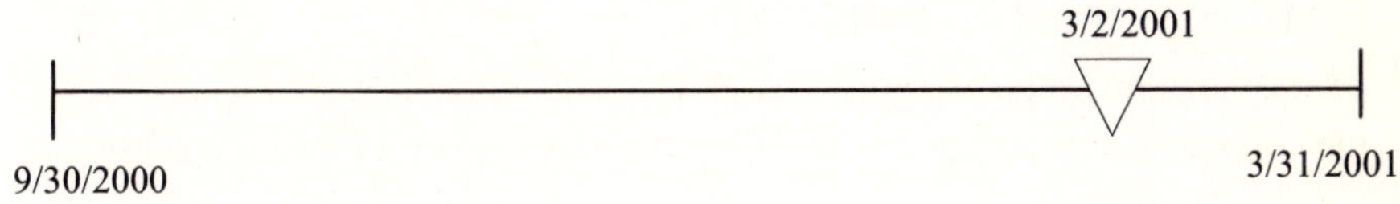

Ex-dividend date: 2/28/2001

This is ex-dividend trading.

$$\text{AIF} = -\frac{3/2/2001 \text{ to } 3/31/2001}{9/30/2000 \text{ to } 3/31/2001} = -\frac{29}{182.5}$$

$$\text{AI} = \frac{0.1345}{2} \cdot \left(-\frac{29}{182.5}\right) = -0.010686301 \approx -0.0106863$$

Swedish Government Bonds

Conventions

- The day count method is 30E/360.
- The ex-dividend date is the fourth business day before the coupon date.
- The coupon payment frequency is annual.

Example 1

Maturity Date:	10/25/2006
Settlement Date:	7/9/2001
Coupon Rate:	6.5%

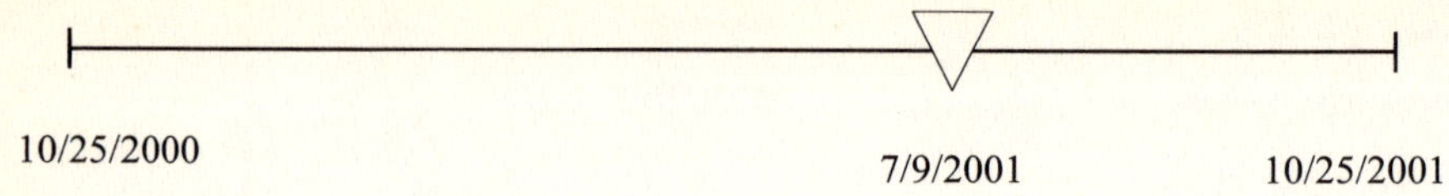

Ex-dividend date: 10/19/2001

This is cum-dividend trading.

$$AIF = \frac{10/25/2000 \text{ to } 7/9/2001}{10/25/2000 \text{ to } 10/25/2001} = \frac{254}{360}$$

$$AI = 0.065 \cdot \frac{254}{360} = 0.04586111$$

Swiss Government Bonds

Conventions

- The day count method is 30E/360.
- No ex-dividend trading
- The coupon payment frequency is annual.

Example 1

Maturity Date:	6/10/2007
Settlement Date:	3/31/2001
Coupon Rate:	4.5%

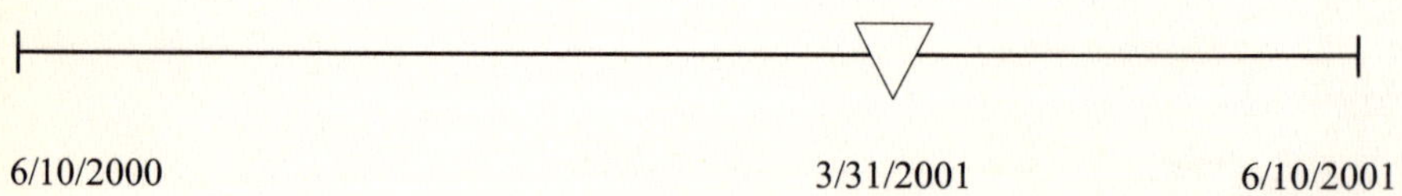

$$AIF = \frac{6/10/2000 \text{ to } 3/31/2001}{6/10/2000 \text{ to } 6/10/2001} \rightarrow \frac{6/10/2000 \text{ to } 3/30/2001}{6/10/2000 \text{ to } 6/10/2001} = \frac{290}{360}$$

$$AI = 0.045 \cdot \frac{290}{360} = 0.03625$$

United Kingdom

Gilts

Conventions

- The day count method is Actual/Actual (In period).
- The ex-dividend date is the 6th business day before the coupon date. The exception is for 3.5% war loans, where the ex-dividend date is the 9th business day before the coupon date.
- The coupon payment frequency is semiannual.
- The End-of-Month rule is not in effect.

A special case exists when stock is in partly paid form (see Chapter 11) and the settlement date is in the first coupon period, before the ex-dividend date:

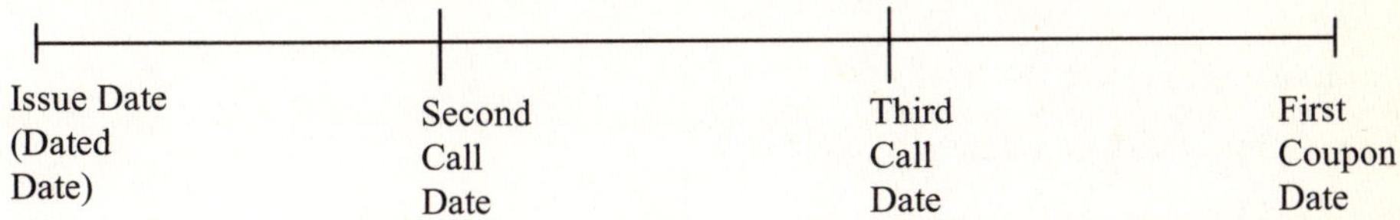

$$AIF = \frac{1}{d} \sum_{i=1}^{m} \left[A_i (d_{cs})_i \right]$$

d is the actual number of **d**ays in the normal first coupon period. If the first coupon period is long, then two normal coupon periods before the first coupon date should be taken into account.

m is the number of partial calls before the settlement date (including issue date).

$\mathbf{A_i}$ is the *i*th partial **a**mount, expressed as a decimal.

$\mathbf{(d_{cs})_i}$ is the actual number of **d**ays between the *i*th partial payment (**c**all) date (including issue date) and **s**ettlement date.

Example 1

Maturity Date:	12/7/2005
Settlement Date:	7/30/2001
Nominal Annual Coupon Rate:	8.5%

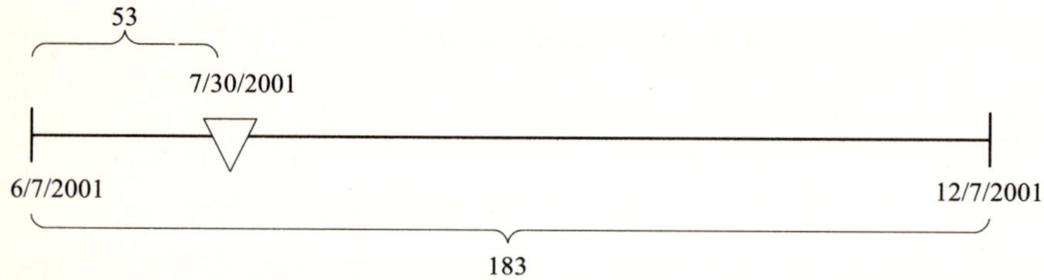

Ex-dividend date: 11/29/2001

This is cum-dividend trading.

$$AIF = \frac{53}{183}$$

$$AI = \frac{0.085}{2} \cdot \frac{53}{183} = 0.012308743$$

Example 2

Maturity Date:	8/25/2017
Settlement Date:	8/20/2001
Nominal Annual Coupon Rate:	8.75%

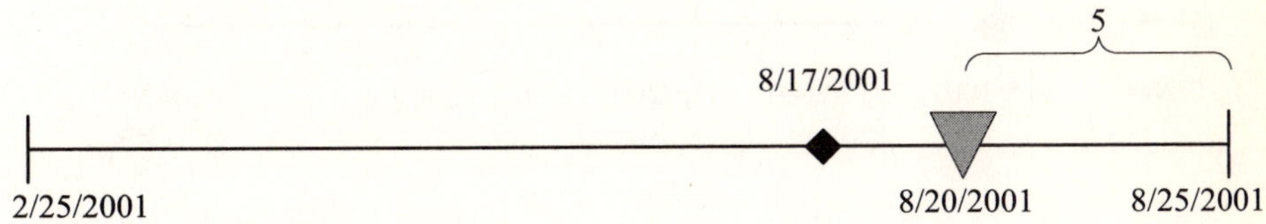

Ex-dividend date: 8/17/2001

This is ex-dividend trading.

$$\text{AIF} = -\frac{5}{181}$$

$$\text{AI} = \frac{0.0875}{2} \cdot \left(-\frac{5}{181}\right) = -0.001208564$$

Example 3

Partly paid stock with short first coupon period.

The settlement date is in the short first coupon period:

Maturity Date:	10/10/2015
Settlement Date:	6/20/2001
Dated Date:	4/15/2001
Issue Date:	4/15/2001
First Coupon Date:	10/10/2001
Amount at Issue:	0.34
Second Call Date:	5/15/2001
Amount at Second Call Date:	0.23
Third Call Date:	6/15/2001

Amount at Third Call Date: 0.43

Nominal Annual Coupon Rate: 10%

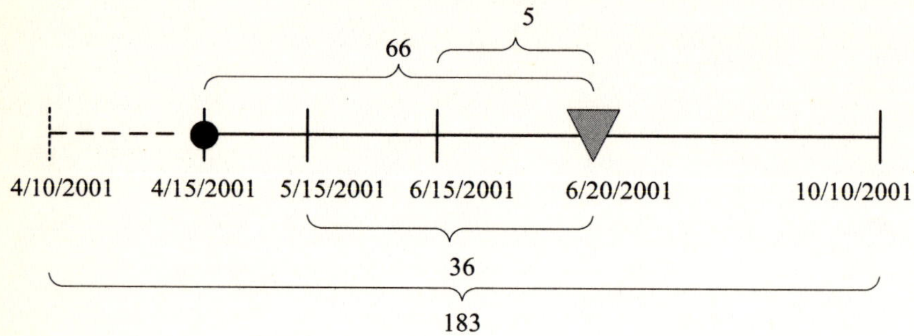

$m = 3$

$A_1 = 0.34 \qquad d_{cs1} = 66$

$A_2 = 0.23 \qquad d_{cs2} = 36$

$A_3 = 0.43 \qquad d_{cs3} = 5$

$$AIF = \frac{1}{183}(0.34 \cdot 66 + 0.23 \cdot 36 + 0.43 \cdot 5)$$

$$AIF = 0.179617486$$

$$AI = \frac{0.10}{2} \cdot 0.179617486 = 0.008980874$$

Index-Linked Gilts

Conventions

- The day count method is Actual/Actual (In period).
- The ex-dividend date is the sixth business day before the coupon date.
- The coupon payment frequency is semiannual.
- The End-of-Month rule is not in effect.

See chapter 11 for more details.

Example 1

Maturity Date:	8/16/2013
Settlement Date:	6/18/2001
Nominal Annual Coupon Rate:	2.5%
Base RPI:	89.2015
RPI_1:	172.2 for 12/2000 (eight months before the next coupon date of 8/16/2001)

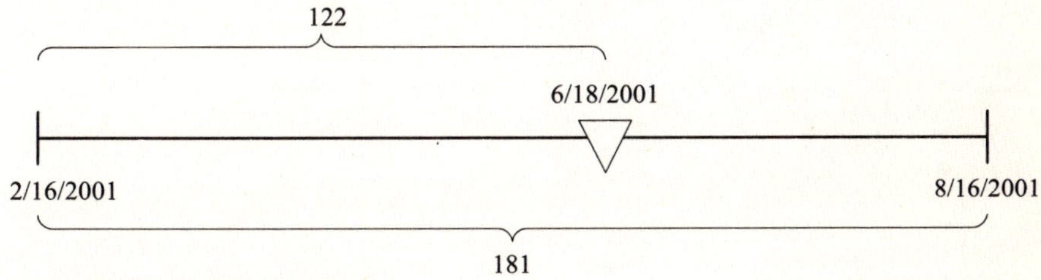

Ex-dividend date: 8/8/2001

This is cum-dividend trading.

$$CF_1 = \frac{0.025}{2} \cdot \frac{172.2}{89.2015} = 0.02413076 \approx 0.024130$$

$$AIF = \frac{122}{181}$$

$$AI = 0.024130 \cdot \frac{122}{181} = 0.01626442$$

Example 2

Maturity Date:	7/19/2006
Settlement Date:	7/13/2001
Nominal Annual Coupon Rate:	2%
Base RPI	69.4803

RPI_1	172.1 for 11/2000 (8 months before the next coupon date of 7/19/2001)

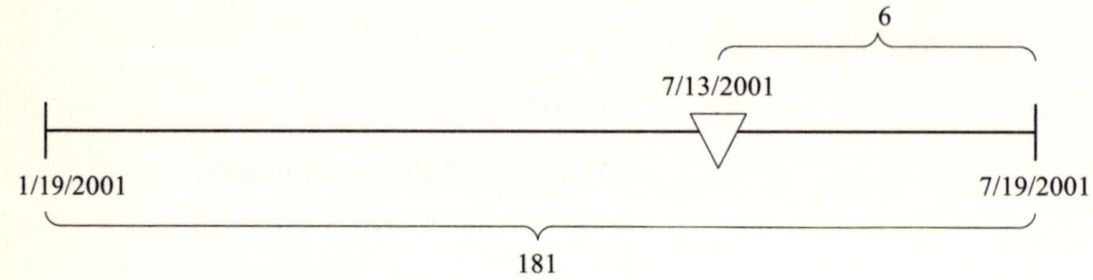

Ex-dividend date: 7/11/2001

This is ex-dividend trading.

$$CF_1 = \frac{0.02}{2} \cdot \frac{172.1}{69.4803} = 0.0247$$

$$AIF = -\frac{6}{181}$$

$$AI = 0.0247 \cdot (-\frac{6}{181}) = -0.000818785$$

Note: CF_1 is truncated to four decimal places per £1 of face value.

U.S. Government Bonds

Conventions

- The day count method is Actual/Actual (in period).
- No ex-dividend trading
- The coupon payment frequency is semiannual.

Example 1

Maturity Date:	8/15/2007
Settlement Date:	2/23/2001

Nominal Annual Coupon Rate: 6.125%

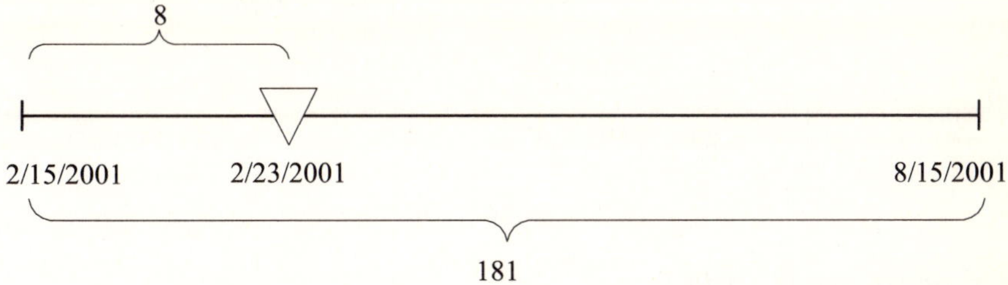

$$\text{AIF} = \frac{\text{2/15/2001 to 2/23/2001}}{\text{2/15/2001 to 8/15/2001}} = \frac{8}{181}$$

$$\text{AI} = \frac{0.06125}{2} \cdot \frac{8}{181} = 0.00135359116$$

Example 2

The settlement date is in a long first coupon period, after the normal issue date.

Maturity Date:	8/15/2007
Settlement Date:	3/5/2001
Nominal Annual Coupon Rate:	6%
Dated Date:	1/21/2001
First Coupon Date:	8/15/2001

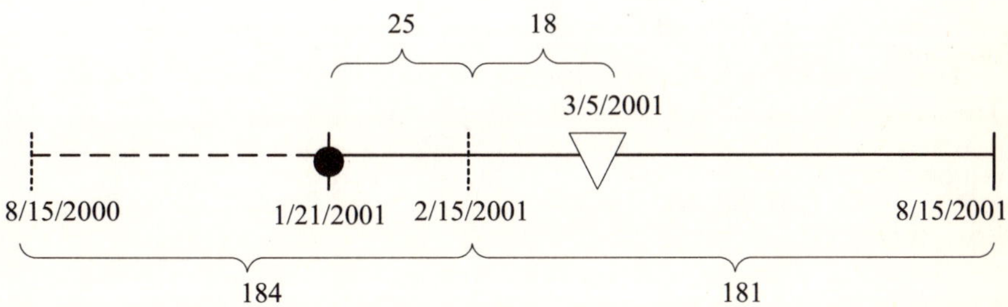

$$\text{AIF} = \frac{1/21/2001 \text{ to } 2/15/2001}{8/15/2000 \text{ to } 2/15/2001} + \frac{2/15/2001 \text{ to } 3/5/2001}{2/15/2001 \text{ to } 8/15/2001} = \frac{25}{184} + \frac{18}{181}$$

$$\text{AI} = \frac{0.06}{2}\left(\frac{25}{184} + \frac{18}{181}\right) = 0.00705951237$$

U.S. Corporate Bonds

Conventions

- The day count method is 30/360.
- No ex-dividend trading
- The coupon payment frequency is semiannual.

Example 1

Maturity Date:	1/21/2007
Settlement Date:	3/19/2001
Nominal Annual Coupon Rate:	8%

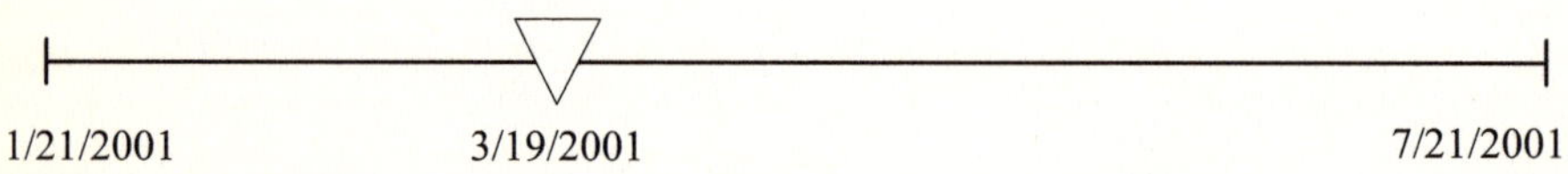

$$\text{AIF} = \frac{1/21/2001 \text{ to } 3/19/2001}{1/21/2001 \text{ to } 7/21/2001} = \frac{58}{180}$$

$$\text{AI} = \frac{0.08}{2} \cdot \frac{58}{180} = 0.012888889$$

Example 2

The settlement date is in the short last coupon period.

Maturity Date:	6/25/2001
Settlement Date:	3/19/2001
Last Coupon Date:	2/1/2001
Nominal Annual Coupon Rate:	8%

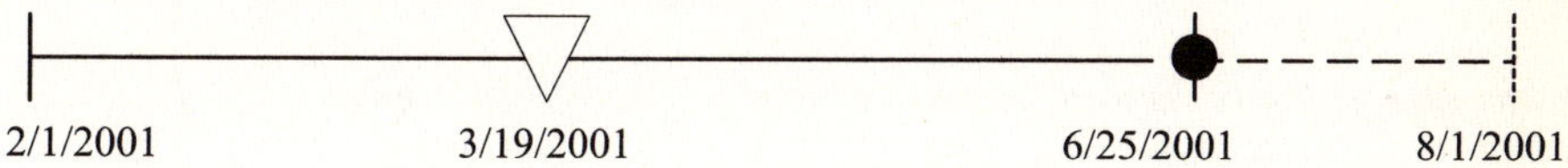

$$\text{AIF} = \frac{2/1/2001 \text{ to } 3/19/2001}{2/1/2001 \text{ to } 8/1/2001} = \frac{48}{180}$$

$$\text{AI} = \frac{0.08}{2} \cdot \frac{48}{180} = 0.010666667$$

Chapter 3

Other Calculations

In this chapter the basis for other types of calculations is presented.

Current Yield

$$Y = \frac{C}{P}$$

Y	is the Current **Y**ield, expressed as a decimal.
C	is the Nominal Annual **C**oupon Rate, expressed as a decimal.
P	is the **P**rice per one currency unit of face value.

Settlement Date Not in Last Coupon Period

The formulas presented are for both cum-dividend and ex-dividend trading.

First Derivative of Price with Respect to Yield

The first derivative of price with respect to yield approximately represents the number of basis points change in price (flat or full) per 1 bp (0.01%) change in yield. The first derivative of price with respect to yield is the slope of the tangent line of the price/yield curve.

1. Using the price/yield formula.

$$\frac{dP}{dY} = P' = -\frac{DF}{F}\cdot\left(1+\frac{Y}{F}\right)^{-1}\cdot P_{FULL} + \left(1+\frac{Y}{F}\right)^{-DF}\cdot\left\{-\frac{C(1-TX)}{Y^2}\right.$$

$$\cdot\left[1-\frac{1}{\left(1+\frac{Y}{F}\right)^{n}}\right] + \frac{C(1-TX)}{Y}\cdot\frac{n}{F}\cdot\left(1+\frac{Y}{F}\right)^{-n-1} - \frac{1}{F}\cdot(n+LDF)$$

$$\left.\cdot\left[RV - TXG(RV1-P0) + \frac{C(1-TX)}{F}\cdot LCF\right]\cdot\left(1+\frac{Y}{F}\right)^{-n-1-LDF}\right\}$$

2. By approximation.

$$\frac{dP}{dY} = P' \approx \frac{P(Y+\Delta Y) - P(Y-\Delta Y)}{2\cdot\Delta Y}, \quad \Delta Y > 0$$

ΔY as a decimal

Prices are per one currency unit of value.

3. By summation.

$$\frac{dP}{dY} = P' = -\frac{1}{F}\cdot\left\{\frac{\frac{C(1-TX)}{F}\cdot FCF\cdot DF}{\left(1+\frac{Y}{F}\right)^{DF+1}} + \sum_{t=1}^{n}\left[\frac{\frac{C(1-TX)}{F}\cdot(DF+t)}{\left(1+\frac{Y}{F}\right)^{DF+t+1}}\right]\right.$$

$$\left. + \frac{\left[RV - TXG(RV1-P0) + \frac{C(1-TX)}{F}\cdot LCF\right]\cdot(n+LDF+DF)}{\left(1+\frac{Y}{F}\right)^{n+LDF+DF+1}}\right\}$$

Second Derivative of Price with Respect to Yield

1. Using the price/yield formula.

$$\frac{d^2P}{dY^2} = P'' = -\frac{DF}{F^2}\cdot\left(1+\frac{Y}{F}\right)^{-2}\cdot P_{FULL}\cdot(DF-1) - 2\cdot\frac{DF}{F}\cdot\left(1+\frac{Y}{F}\right)^{-1}\cdot P'$$

$$+\left(1+\frac{Y}{F}\right)^{-DF}\cdot\left\{\frac{2C(1-TX)}{Y^3}\left[1-\frac{1}{\left(1+\frac{Y}{F}\right)^{n}}\right]-\frac{2C(1-TX)}{Y^2}\cdot\frac{n}{F}\cdot\left(1+\frac{Y}{F}\right)^{-n-1}\right.$$

$$-\frac{C(1-TX)}{Y}\cdot\frac{n}{F^2}\cdot(n+1)\left(1+\frac{Y}{F}\right)^{-n-2}+\frac{1}{F^2}\cdot(n+LDF)$$

$$\cdot(n+1+LDF)\cdot\left[RV-TXG(RV1-P0)+\frac{C(1-TX)}{F}\cdot LCF\right]$$

$$\left.\cdot\left(1+\frac{Y}{F}\right)^{-n-2-LDF}\right\}$$

2. By approximation.

$$\frac{d^2P}{dY^2} = P'' \approx \frac{P(Y+\Delta Y)+P(Y-\Delta Y)-2P(Y)}{(\Delta Y)^2}, \quad \Delta Y > 0$$

ΔY as a decimal

Prices are per one currency unit of face value.

3. By summation.

$$\frac{d^2P}{dY^2} = P'' = \left\{\frac{1}{F^2}\frac{\frac{C(1-TX)}{F}FCF\cdot DF(DF+1)}{\left(1+\frac{Y}{F}\right)^{DF+2}}+\sum_{t=1}^{n}\left[\frac{\frac{C(1-TX)}{F}\cdot(DF+t)(DF+t+1)}{\left(1+\frac{Y}{F}\right)^{DF+t+2}}\right]\right.$$

$$\left.+\frac{(DF+n+LDF)\cdot(DF+n+LDF+1)\cdot\left[RV-TXG(RV1-P0)+\frac{C(1-TX)}{F}\cdot LCF\right]}{\left(1+\frac{Y}{F}\right)^{DF+n+LDF+2}}\right\}$$

Duration

Duration is the weighted average time to future cash flows, where weight is the present value of the future cash flows.

$$DUR = \frac{-\frac{dP}{dY}}{P_{FULL}}\left(1+\frac{Y}{F}\right)$$

Unit of duration is **years.**

Modified Duration

Modified duration represents an approximate percentage change in full price per 100 bp (1%) change in yield.

$$MD = \frac{DUR}{1+\frac{Y}{F}}$$

Unit of modified duration is **years.**

Convexity

Convexity is the second derivative of price with respect to yield divided by the full price.

$$CONV = \frac{\frac{d^2P}{dY^2}}{P_{FULL}}$$

Unit of convexity is **years²**.

Price Value of 0.01 (Basis Point Value)

Price (dollar) value of 0.01 is the approximate change in price (flat or full) per 100 currency units of face value, per 1 bp = 0.01% = 0.0001 change in yield.

$$PV01Y = \frac{\left|\frac{dP}{dY}\right|}{100}$$

Price Value of Y Change in Yield

Price (dollar) value of ΔY (any number of basis points) is the approximate change in price (flat or full) per 100 currency units of face value, per ΔY bp = $\Delta Y/100\%$ = $\Delta Y/10000$ change in yield.

$$PV\Delta Y = P(Y + \Delta Y) - P(Y)$$

Prices per 100 currency units of face value

Yield Value of 0.01

Yield value of 0.01 is the approximate change in yield (as a percent) per 1 bp = 0.01% = 0.0001 change in price.

$$YV01P = \frac{1}{100 \cdot \left|\frac{dP}{dY}\right|}$$

$$\text{NOTE}: YV01P = \frac{1}{10000 \cdot PV01Y}$$

Yield Value of 1/32

Yield value of 1/32 is the approximate change in yield (as a percent) per 1/32 = 0.03125 change in price per 100 currency units of face value.

$$YV32P = \frac{1}{32 \cdot \left|\frac{dP}{dY}\right|}$$

Taylor Series of Price as a Function of Yield

$$\left(\frac{\Delta P}{P}\right)_{FULL} \approx \left[-MD \cdot (\Delta Y) + \frac{1}{2} \cdot CONV \cdot (\Delta Y)^2\right] \cdot 100$$

ΔY as a decimal

This represents the percentage change in full price per ΔY change in yield.

Settlement Date Is in the Last Coupon Period

Simple Interest

The formulas presented are for both cum-dividend and ex-dividend trading.

First Derivative of Price with Respect to Yield:

$$\frac{dP}{dY} = -P_{FULL} \cdot \frac{DF}{F\left(1 + \frac{Y}{F}DF\right)}$$

Second Derivative of Price with Respect to Yield:

$$\frac{d^2P}{dY^2} = P_{FULL} \cdot \frac{2 \cdot DF^2}{F^2\left(1 + \frac{Y}{F} \cdot DF\right)^2}$$

Duration

$$DUR = \frac{-\frac{dP}{dY}}{P_{FULL}}\left(1 + \frac{Y}{F}DF\right) = \frac{DF}{F}$$

Modified Duration

$$MD = \frac{DUR}{1 + \frac{Y}{F} \cdot DF}$$

Convexity

$$CONV = \frac{\frac{d^2P}{dY^2}}{P_{FULL}}$$

Price Value of 0.01 (Basis Point Value)

$$\mathrm{PV01Y} = \frac{\left|\dfrac{dP}{dY}\right|}{100}$$

Yield Value of 0.01

$$\mathrm{YV01P} = \frac{1}{100\left|\dfrac{dP}{dY}\right|}$$

Yield Value of 1/32

$$\mathrm{YV32P} = \frac{1}{32\left|\dfrac{dP}{dY}\right|}$$

Compound Interest

The formulas presented are for both cum-dividend and ex-dividend trading.

First Derivative of Price with Respect to Yield

$$\frac{dP}{dY} = -P_{FULL} \cdot \frac{DF}{F\left(1+\dfrac{Y}{F}\right)}$$

Second Derivative of Price with Respect to Yield

$$\frac{d^2P}{dY^2} = P_{FULL} \cdot \frac{DF(DF+1)}{F^2\left(1+\dfrac{Y}{F}\right)^2}$$

Duration

$$\mathrm{DUR} = \frac{-\dfrac{dP}{dY}}{P_{FULL}}\left(1+\frac{Y}{F}\right)$$

Modified Duration

$$MD = \frac{DUR}{1 + \frac{Y}{F}}$$

Convexity

$$CONV = \frac{\frac{d^2P}{dY^2}}{P_{FULL}}$$

Price Value of 0.01 (Basis Point Value)

$$PV01Y = \frac{\left|\frac{dP}{dY}\right|}{100}$$

Yield Value of 0.01

$$YV01P = \frac{1}{100\left|\frac{dP}{dY}\right|}$$

Yield Value of 1/32

$$YV32P = \frac{1}{32 \cdot \left|\frac{dP}{dY}\right|}$$

Example

U.S. government bond

The settlement date is in the short first coupon period:

Maturity Date:	4/30/2007
Settlement Date:	6/28/2002
Dated Date:	5/2/2002

First Coupon Date:	10/31/2002
Nominal Annual Coupon Rate:	6.5%
Nominal Annual Yield to Maturity:	6.9%
Day Count Method:	Actual/Actual (in period)
Frequency of Payments per Year:	2
Redemption Value:	1
Tax for Interest Income:	0%
Tax for Capital Gains:	0%

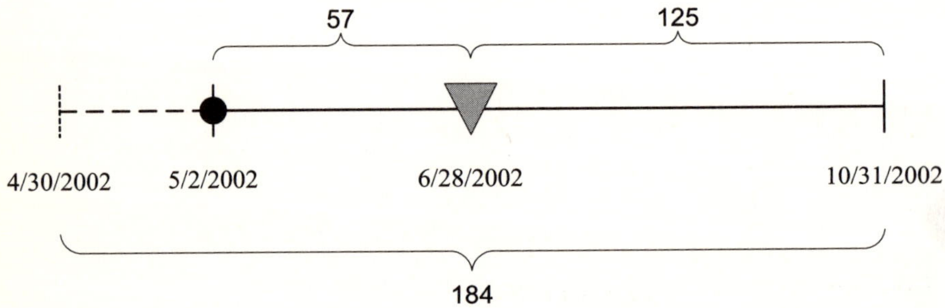

$$AIF = \frac{57}{184}, \quad FCF = \frac{182}{184}, \quad DF = \frac{125}{184}, \quad LCF = 1, \quad LDF = 1, \quad n = 8$$

Accrued Interest

$$AI = \frac{0.065}{2} \cdot \frac{57}{184} = 0.010067934783$$

Price

$$P = \left(1+\frac{0.069}{2}\right)^{-\frac{125}{184}} \left\{ \frac{0.065}{2}\cdot\frac{182}{184} + \frac{0.065}{0.069}\left[1-\frac{1}{\left(1+\frac{0.069}{2}\right)^{8}}\right] + \left(1+\frac{0.065}{2}\right)\left(1+\frac{0.069}{2}\right)^{-8-1} \right\}$$

$$-\ 0.010067934783$$

$$P = 0.983664603066$$

Full Price

$$P = 0.983664603066 + 0.010067934783 = 0.993732537849$$

Current Yield

$$Y = \frac{6.5}{0.983664603066} = 6.60794338\%$$

First Derivative of Price with Respect to Yield

Note that, in this case, we use the general price/yield formula.

$$\frac{dP}{dY} = P' = -\frac{125}{2\cdot 184}\left(1+\frac{0.069}{2}\right)^{-1}\cdot 0.99373254 + \left(1+\frac{0.069}{2}\right)^{-\frac{125}{184}}$$

$$\cdot\left\{-\frac{0.065}{0.069^{2}}\left[1-\frac{1}{\left(1+\frac{0.069}{2}\right)^{8}}\right] + \frac{0.065}{0.069}\cdot\frac{8}{2}\left(1+\frac{0.069}{2}\right)^{-8-1}\right.$$

$$\left.-\frac{1}{2}(8+1)\left(1+\frac{0.065}{2}\right)\left(1+\frac{0.069}{2}\right)^{-8-1-1}\right\}$$

$$P' = -4.01767761597$$

Second Derivative of Price with Respect to Yield

Note that, in this case, we use the general price/yield formula.

$$\frac{d^2P}{dY^2} = P'' = -\frac{125}{2^2 \cdot 184}\left(1+\frac{0.069}{2}\right)^{-2} \cdot 0.99373254 + \left(\frac{125}{184}-1\right)$$

$$-2\left(\frac{125}{2 \cdot 184}\right) \cdot \left(1+\frac{0.069}{2}\right)^{-1}(-4.0176776) + \left(1+\frac{0.069}{2}\right)^{-\frac{125}{184}}$$

$$\cdot \left\{\frac{2 \cdot 0.065}{0.069^3}\left[1-\frac{1}{\left(1+\frac{0.069}{2}\right)^8}\right] + \frac{2 \cdot 0.065}{0.069^2} \cdot \frac{8}{2}\right.$$

$$\cdot \left(1+\frac{0.069}{2}\right)^{-8-1} - \frac{0.065}{0.069} \cdot \frac{8}{2^2}(8+1)\left(1+\frac{0.069}{2}\right)^{-8-2} + \frac{1}{2^2}$$

$$\left. \cdot (8+1)(8+1+1)\left[1+\frac{0.065}{2}\right]\left(1+\frac{0.069}{2}\right)^{-8-2-1}\right\}$$

$$P'' = 19.76439500844$$

Duration

$$\text{DUR} = \frac{-(-4.0176776)}{0.99373254}\left(1+\frac{0.069}{2}\right) = 4.1825012$$

Modified Duration

$$\text{MD} = \frac{4.1825012}{1 + \frac{0.069}{2}} = 4.0430171$$

Convexity

$$\text{CONV} = \frac{19.764395}{0.99373254} = 19.889049$$

Price Value of 0.01

$$\text{PV01Y} = \frac{|-4.0176776|}{100} = 0.040176776$$

Yield Value of 0.01

$$\text{YV01P} = \frac{1}{100 \cdot |-4.0176776|} = 0.002489000103$$

Yield Value of 1/32

$$\text{YV32P} = \frac{1}{32 \cdot |-4.0176776|} = 0.00777812532$$

Chapter 4

Sample Calculations: Periodic Payment Fixed Income Securities

The example in this chapter provides detailed calculations for accrued-interest, price, duration, and other measures for a fixed income periodic payment security with short first and short last coupon period.

Maturity Date:	1/15/2008
Nominal Annual Coupon Rate:	8%
Issue Date:	6/20/2001
Dated Date:	6/20/2001
First Coupon Date:	11/15/2001
Last Coupon Date:	11/15/2007
Frequency of Payments per Year:	2
Day Count Method:	Actual/Actual (in period)
Settlement Date:	8/10/2001
Nominal Annual Yield to Maturity:	9%
Redemption Value:	1
Tax for Interest Income:	0%
Tax for Capital Gains:	0%

Time Line

The time line for the example appears below.

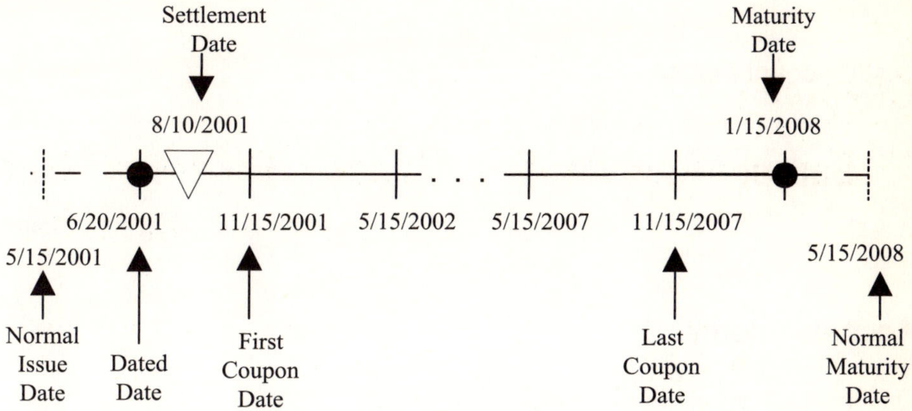

Factors

Factors for the example are presented in this section.

Accrued-Interest Factor

$$\text{AIF} = \frac{6/20/2001 \text{ to } 8/10/2001}{5/15/2001 \text{ to } 11/15/2001} = \frac{51}{184}$$

First Coupon Factor

$$\text{FCF} = \frac{6/20/2001 \text{ to } 11/15/2001}{5/15/2001 \text{ to } 11/15/2001} = \frac{148}{184}$$

Discount Factor

$$\text{DF} = \frac{8/10/2001 \text{ to } 11/15/2001}{5/15/2001 \text{ to } 11/15/2001} = \frac{97}{184}$$

Last Coupon Factor

$$\text{LCF} = \frac{11/15/2007 \text{ to } 1/15/2008}{11/15/2007 \text{ to } 5/15/2008} = \frac{61}{182}$$

Last Discount Factor

$$\text{LDF} = \frac{11/15/2007 \text{ to } 1/15/2008}{11/15/2007 \text{ to } 5/15/2008} = \frac{61}{182}$$

$$n = 12$$

Accrued Interest

$$\text{AI} = \frac{C}{F} \cdot \text{AIF} = \frac{0.08}{2} \cdot \frac{51}{184} = 0.0110869565$$

Price

$$P = \left(1 + \frac{Y}{F}\right)^{-DF} \left\{ \frac{C}{F} \cdot \text{FCF} + \frac{C}{Y}\left[1 - \frac{1}{\left(1 + \frac{Y}{F}\right)^{n}}\right] + \left(\text{RV} + \frac{C}{F} \cdot \text{LCF}\right) \cdot \left(1 + \frac{Y}{F}\right)^{-n-\text{LDF}} \right\} - \text{AI}$$

$$P = \left(1 + \frac{0.09}{2}\right)^{-\frac{97}{184}} \left\{ \frac{0.08}{2} \cdot \frac{148}{184} + \frac{0.08}{0.09}\left[1 - \frac{1}{\left(1 + \frac{0.09}{2}\right)^{12}}\right] + \left(1 + \frac{0.08}{2} \cdot \frac{61}{182}\right) \cdot \left(1 + \frac{0.09}{2}\right)^{-12-\frac{61}{182}} \right\}$$

$$- 0.0110869565 = 0.9520380596 = 95.20380596\%$$

Full Price

$$P_{\text{FULL}} = P + \text{AI} = 0.9520380596 + 0.0110869565 = 0.9631250161 = 96.31250161\%$$

First Derivative of Price with Respect to Yield (Risk Factor)

Using the General Price/Yield Formula

$$\frac{dP}{dY} = P' = -\frac{DF}{F}\cdot\left(1+\frac{Y}{F}\right)^{-1}\cdot P_{FULL} + \left(1+\frac{Y}{F}\right)^{-DF}\left\{-\frac{C}{Y^2}\left[1-\frac{1}{\left(1+\frac{Y}{F}\right)^{n}}\right]\right.$$

$$\left. + \frac{C}{Y}\cdot\frac{n}{F}\cdot\left(1+\frac{Y}{F}\right)^{-n-1} - \frac{1}{F}\cdot(n+LDF)\left(RV+\frac{C}{F}\cdot LCF\right)\left(1+\frac{Y}{F}\right)^{-n-1-LDF}\right\}$$

$$\frac{dP}{dY} = P' = \left(-\frac{97}{2\cdot 184}\right)\left(1+\frac{0.09}{2}\right)^{-1}\cdot 0.9631250161$$

$$+\left(1+\frac{0.09}{2}\right)^{-\frac{97}{184}}\left\{-\frac{0.08}{0.09^2}\left[1-\frac{1}{\left(1+\frac{0.09}{2}\right)^{12}}\right] + \frac{0.08}{0.09}\cdot\frac{12}{2}\right.$$

$$\left.\cdot\left(1+\frac{0.09}{2}\right)^{-12-1} - \frac{1}{2}\cdot\left(12+\frac{61}{182}\right)\cdot\left(1+\frac{0.08}{2}\cdot\frac{61}{182}\right)\cdot\left(1+\frac{0.09}{2}\right)^{-12-1-\frac{61}{182}}\right\}$$

$$\frac{dP}{dY} = P' = -4.6577473495$$

By Approximation

$$\frac{dP}{dY} = P' \approx \frac{P(Y+\Delta Y) - P(Y-\Delta Y)}{2\cdot\Delta Y}$$

$$\Delta Y = 1bp = 0.01\% = 0.0001$$

$$\frac{dP}{dY} = P' \approx \frac{P(0.09 + 0.0001) - P(0.09 - 0.0001)}{2 \cdot 0.0001}$$

$$\frac{dP}{dY} = P' \approx \frac{0.9515724270 - 0.9525039765}{2 \cdot 0.0001}$$

$$\frac{dP}{dY} = P' \approx -4.6577475$$

By Summation

$$\frac{dP}{dY} = P' = -\frac{1}{F}\left\{\frac{\frac{C}{F} \cdot FCF \cdot DF}{\left(1+\frac{Y}{F}\right)^{DF+1}} + \sum_{t=1}^{n}\left[\frac{\frac{C}{F} \cdot (DF + t)}{\left(1+\frac{Y}{F}\right)^{DF+t+1}}\right]\right.$$

$$\left. + \frac{\left(RV + \frac{C}{F} \cdot LCF\right) \cdot (n + LDF + DF)}{\left(1+\frac{Y}{F}\right)^{n+LDF+DF+1}}\right\}$$

$$\frac{dP}{dY} = P' = -\frac{1}{2}\left\{\frac{\frac{0.08}{2} \cdot \frac{148}{184} \cdot \frac{97}{184}}{\left(1+\frac{0.09}{2}\right)^{\frac{97}{184}+1}} + \sum_{t=1}^{12}\left[\frac{\frac{0.08}{2} \cdot \left(\frac{97}{184} + t\right)}{\left(1+\frac{0.09}{2}\right)^{\frac{97}{184}+t+1}}\right]\right.$$

$$\left. + \frac{\left(1 + \frac{0.08}{2} \cdot \frac{61}{182}\right) \cdot \left(12 + \frac{61}{182} + \frac{97}{184}\right)}{\left(1+\frac{0.09}{2}\right)^{12+\frac{61}{182}+\frac{97}{184}+1}}\right\} = -4.6577473$$

Duration

$$\mathrm{DUR} = \frac{-\dfrac{dP}{dY}}{P_{FULL}}\left(1+\frac{Y}{F}\right) = -\frac{(-4.6577473495)}{0.9631250161}\cdot\left(1+\frac{0.09}{2}\right)$$

$$\mathrm{DUR} = 5.0537011279$$

Modified Duration

$$\mathrm{MD} = \frac{\mathrm{DUR}}{1+\dfrac{Y}{F}} = \frac{5.0537011279}{1+\dfrac{0.09}{2}} = 4.8360776344$$

Price Value of 0.01 (Basis Point Value)

$$\mathrm{PV01Y} = \frac{\left|\dfrac{dP}{dY}\right|}{100} = \frac{4.6577473495}{100} = 0.0465774735$$

Second Derivative of Price with Respect to Yield

Using the General Price/Yield Formula

$$\frac{d^2P}{dY^2} = P'' = -\frac{DF}{F^2}\cdot\left(1+\frac{Y}{F}\right)^{-2}\cdot P_{FULL}\cdot(DF-1) - 2\cdot\frac{DF}{F}\cdot\left(1+\frac{Y}{F}\right)^{-1}\cdot P'$$

$$+\left(1+\frac{Y}{F}\right)^{-DF}\left\{\frac{2C}{Y^3}\left[1-\frac{1}{\left(1+\dfrac{Y}{F}\right)^{n}}\right] - \frac{2C}{Y^2}\cdot\frac{n}{F}\cdot\left(1+\frac{Y}{F}\right)^{-n-1} - \frac{C}{Y}\cdot\frac{n}{F^2}\right.$$

$$\cdot(n+1)\cdot\left(1+\frac{Y}{F}\right)^{-n-2}+\frac{1}{F^2}\cdot(n+LDF)\cdot(n+1+LDF)$$

$$\left.\cdot\left(RV+\frac{C}{F}\cdot LCF\right)\cdot\left(1+\frac{Y}{F}\right)^{-n-2-LDF}\right\}$$

$$\frac{d^2P}{dY^2}=P''=-\frac{97}{2^2\cdot 184}\cdot\left(1+\frac{0.09}{2}\right)^{-2}\cdot 0.9631250161\cdot\left(\frac{97}{184}-1\right)-2\cdot\frac{97}{2\cdot 184}$$

$$\cdot\left(1+\frac{0.09}{2}\right)^{-1}\cdot(-4.6577473495)+\left(1+\frac{0.09}{2}\right)^{-\frac{97}{184}}\left\{\frac{2\cdot 0.08}{0.09^3}\left[1-\frac{1}{\left(1+\frac{0.09}{2}\right)^{12}}\right]\right.$$

$$-\frac{2\cdot 0.08}{0.09^2}\cdot\frac{12}{2}\cdot\left(1+\frac{0.09}{2}\right)^{-12-1}-\frac{0.08}{0.09}\cdot\frac{12}{2^2}\cdot(12+1)\cdot\left(1+\frac{0.09}{2}\right)^{-12-2}+\frac{1}{2^2}$$

$$\left.\cdot\left(12+\frac{61}{182}\right)\cdot\left(12+1+\frac{61}{182}\right)\cdot\left(1+\frac{0.08}{2}\cdot\frac{61}{182}\right)\cdot\left(1+\frac{0.09}{2}\right)^{-12-2-\frac{61}{182}}\right\}$$

$$\frac{d^2P}{dY^2}=P''=28.4314047333$$

By Approximation

$$\frac{d^2P}{dY^2}=P''\approx\frac{P(Y+\Delta Y)+P(Y-\Delta Y)-2P(Y)}{(\Delta Y)^2}$$

$$\frac{d^2P}{dY^2}=P''\approx\frac{P(0.09+0.0001)+P(0.09-0.0001)-2P(0.09)}{(0.0001)^2}$$

$$\frac{d^2P}{dY^2}=P''\approx\frac{0.9515724270+0.9525039765-2\cdot 0.9520380596}{(0.0001)^2}$$

$$\frac{d^2P}{dY^2} = P'' \approx 28.43$$

By Summation

$$\frac{d^2P}{dY^2} = P'' = \frac{1}{F^2} \cdot \left\{ \frac{\frac{C}{F} \cdot FCF \cdot DF \cdot (DF+1)}{\left(1+\frac{Y}{F}\right)^{DF+2}} + \sum_{t=1}^{n} \left[\frac{\frac{C}{F} \cdot (DF+t) \cdot (DF+t+1)}{\left(1+\frac{Y}{F}\right)^{DF+t+2}} \right] + \frac{(DF+n+LDF) \cdot (DF+n+LDF+1) \cdot \left(RV + \frac{C}{F} \cdot LCF\right)}{\left(1+\frac{Y}{F}\right)^{DF+n+LDF+2}} \right\}$$

$$\frac{d^2P}{dY^2} = P'' = \frac{1}{2^2} \left\{ \frac{\frac{0.08}{2} \cdot \frac{148}{184} \cdot \frac{97}{184} \cdot \left(\frac{97}{184}+1\right)}{\left(1+\frac{0.09}{2}\right)^{\frac{97}{184}+2}} + \sum_{t=1}^{12} \left[\frac{\frac{0.08}{2} \cdot \left(\frac{97}{184}+t\right) \cdot \left(\frac{97}{184}+t+1\right)}{\left(1+\frac{0.09}{2}\right)^{\frac{97}{184}+t+2}} \right] + \frac{\left(\frac{97}{184}+12+\frac{61}{182}\right)\left(\frac{97}{184}+12+\frac{61}{182}+1\right) \cdot \left(1+\frac{0.08}{2} \cdot \frac{61}{182}\right)}{\left(1+\frac{0.09}{2}\right)^{\frac{97}{184}+12+\frac{61}{182}+2}} \right\}$$

$$\frac{d^2P}{dY^2} = P'' = 28.4314047333$$

Convexity

$$\text{CONV} = \frac{\frac{d^2P}{dY^2}}{P_{\text{FULL}}} = \frac{28.4314047333}{0.9631250161} = 29.5199525063$$

Percentage Change in Full Price per Y

Here, $\Delta Y = 0.01\% = 1\text{bp}$ change in yield.

Predicted by Modified Duration and Convexity

$$\left(\frac{\Delta P}{P}\right)_{\text{FULL}} \approx -\text{MD} \cdot \Delta Y + \frac{1}{2} \cdot \text{CONV} \cdot (\Delta Y)^2$$

$$= -4.8360776344 \cdot 0.0001 + \frac{1}{2} \cdot 29.5199525063 \cdot (0.0001)^2$$

$$= -0.00048360776344 + 0.0000001476$$

$$= -0.0004834602 \approx -0.04834602\%$$

Actual

$$\left(\frac{\Delta P}{P}\right)_{\text{FULL}} = \frac{P_{\text{FULL}}(Y + \Delta Y) - P_{\text{FULL}}(Y - \Delta Y)}{2 \cdot P_{\text{FULL}}} \cdot 100$$

$$= \frac{P_{\text{FULL}}(0.09 + 0.0001) - P_{\text{FULL}}(0.09 - 0.0001)}{2 \cdot P_{\text{FULL}}(0.09)} \cdot 100$$

$$= \frac{0.9626593835 - 0.9635909330}{2 \cdot 0.9631250161} \cdot 100 = -0.0483607\%$$

Percentage Change in Full Price Not Explained by Modified Duration and Convexity Residual

$$\text{RES} = \left(\frac{\Delta P}{P}\right)_{\text{FULL (actual)}} - \left(\frac{\Delta P}{P}\right)_{\text{FULL (predicted)}} = -0.0483607 + 0.04834602 = -0.00001468\%$$

Yield Value of 0.01

$$\text{YV01P} = \frac{1}{100 \cdot \left|\frac{dP}{dY}\right|} = \frac{1}{100 \cdot \left|-4.6577473495\right|} = 0.0021469606$$

Chapter 5

Determining Coupon Dates for Periodic Payment Fixed Income Securities

This chapter describes how to determine coupon dates for periodic payment fixed income securities under various coupon period scenarios.

In the illustrations that follow it is assumed that coupon payments are semiannual.

All Coupon Periods Are Normal

End-Of-Month (EOM) Rule in Effect

If the maturity date is at the end of the month (including 2/29 in a leap year), all coupon dates are at the end of month.

Example	Maturity Date	Coupon Dates
1	3/31	3/31 and 9/30
2	11/30	11/30 and 5/31
3	2/28 (non–leap year)	2/28 (2/29 in leap year) and 8/31
4	2/29 (leap year)	2/28 (2/29 in leap year) and 8/31

If maturity date is on any day of the month, except the end of the month, coupon dates are on the same day of the month.

Example	Maturity Date	Coupon Dates
1	7/13	7/13 and 1/13
2	10/30	10/30 and 4/30

3	8/28	8/28 and 2/28 (in a leap year, too)
4	2/28 (leap year)	2/28 (in a leap year, too) and 8/28

Note the following special cases.

Special Case Example	Maturity Date	Coupon Dates
1	8/29	8/29 and 2/28 (2/29 in leap year)
2	8/30	8/30 and 2/28 (2/29 in leap year)

End-Of-Month Rule Not in Effect

Maturity date and all coupon dates are on the same day of the month.

Example	Maturity Date	Coupon Dates
1	5/18	5/18 and 11/18
2	9/30	9/30 and 3/30
3	2/28	2/28 and 8/28

Short or Long First Coupon Period

If there is a short or long first coupon period (but normal last coupon period), then the first coupon date must be given (in addition to maturity date) and the rules under section "All Coupon Periods are Normal" should be applied to the first coupon date (not to the maturity date).

End-Of-Month Rule in Effect

Example	Maturity Date	First Coupon Date	Coupon Dates
1	7/15	1/15	1/15 and 7/15
2	4/30	4/30	4/30 and 10/31

End-Of-Month Rule Not in Effect

Example	Maturity Date	First Coupon Date	Coupon Dates
1	3/30	9/30	9/30 and 3/30
2	7/31	1/31	1/31 and 7/31

Short or Long Last Coupon Period

If there is a short or long last coupon period (but normal first coupon period), then the last coupon date must be given (in addition to the maturity date) and the rules under section "All Coupon Periods Are Normal" should be applied to the last coupon date (not to the maturity date).

End-Of-Month Rule in Effect

Example	Maturity Date	Last Coupon Date	Coupon Dates
1	6/30	11/30	11/30 and 5/31
2	4/30	2/28 (2/29 in a leap year)	2/28 (2/29 in a leap year) and 8/31

End-Of-Month Rule Not in Effect

Example	Maturity Date	Last Coupon Date	Coupon Dates
1	10/5	2/28 (non–leap year or leap year)	2/28 (in a leap year, too) and 8/28
2	12/1	4/30	4/30 and 10/30

Both First and Last Coupon Dates Are Given

If both the first and last coupon dates are given, they must be on each other's anniversary and rules under the section "Short or Long Last Coupon Period" apply.

End-Of-Month Rule in Effect

Example	Maturity Date	First Coupon Date	Last Coupon Date	Coupon Dates
1	5/1	3/31	9/30	9/30 and 3/31
2	4/10	8/31	2/28 (non–leap year)	2/28 (2/29 in leap year) and 8/31

End-Of-Month Rule Not in Effect

Example	Maturity Date	First Coupon Date	Last Coupon Date	Coupon Dates
1	12/15	4/30	10/30	10/30 and 4/30
2	10/1	8/28	2/28 (non–leap year)	2/28 (in a leap year, too) and 8/28

Sometimes there are exceptions, and if you want to be sure, check the corresponding announcement of auction or prospectus.

Chapter 6

Cash Flow Calculations

Cash Flow Calculations

Settlement Date Not in Last Coupon Period

Number of cash flows: $n + 2$

$$CF_1 = \frac{C(1 - TX)}{F} \cdot FCF \cdot EXF$$

$$CF_i = \frac{C(1 - TX)}{F} \qquad i = 2, 3, \ldots, n + 1$$

$$CF_{n+2} = RV - TXG(RV1 - P0) + \frac{C(1 - TX)}{F} \cdot LCF$$

Settlement Date in Last Coupon Period

Number of cash flows: 1

$$CF = RV - TXG(RV1 - P0) + \frac{C(1 - TX)}{F} \cdot LCF \cdot EXF$$

where EXF is the ex-dividend factor, which is 0, when it is ex-dividend trading, or 1 otherwise.
All other variables are explained in Chapter 1.

Time in Years to Each Cash Flow

Settlement Date Not in Last Coupon Period

Number of cash flows: n + 2

$$t_i = \frac{1}{F} \cdot (DF + i - 1) \qquad i = 1, 2, \ldots, n + 1$$

t_1 corresponds to the first cash flow after a settlement date.

t_2 corresponds to the second cash flow, and so on.

For cash flow at maturity:

$$t_{n+2} = \frac{1}{F} \cdot \left(DF + n + LDF\right)$$

Settlement Date in Last Coupon Period

Number of cash flows: 1

$$t = \frac{DF}{F}$$

All variables are explained in Chapter 1.

Example 1: U.K. Gilt

Maturity Date:	11/15/2004
Settlement Date:	11/12/2002
Nominal Annual Coupon Rate:	10%
Frequency of Coupon Payments per Year:	2
Day Count Method:	ACT/ACT (in period)
Redemption Value:	100%
Tax Rate for Interest Income:	0%
Tax Rate for Capital Gains:	0%

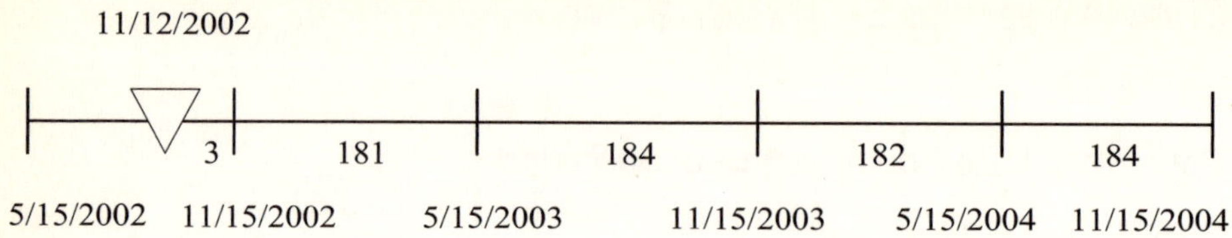

This is ex-dividend trading. The ex-dividend date is 11/6/2002.

EXF = 0	FCF = 1
n = 3	DF = 3/184
LCF = 1	LDF = 1

Number of cash flows: 5

<u>Date</u>	<u>Cash Flow (per 1£ of face value)</u>	<u>Time (in years)</u>
11/15/2002	$CF_1 = \frac{0.10 \cdot (1-0)}{2} \cdot 1 \cdot 0 = 0$	$t_1 = \frac{1}{2}\left(\frac{3}{184} + 1 - 1\right) = 0.00815217$
5/15/2003	$CF_2 = \frac{0.10 \cdot (1-0)}{2} = 0.05$	$t_2 = \frac{1}{2}\left(\frac{3}{184} + 2 - 1\right) = 0.50815217$
11/15/2003	$CF_3 = \frac{0.10 \cdot (1-0)}{2} = 0.05$	$t_3 = \frac{1}{2}\left(\frac{3}{184} + 3 - 1\right) = 1.00815217$
5/15/2004	$CF_4 = \frac{0.10 \cdot (1-0)}{2} = 0.05$	$t_4 = \frac{1}{2}\left(\frac{3}{184} + 4 - 1\right) = 1.50815217$
11/15/2004	$CF_5 = 1 - 0 \cdot (1 - P0) + \frac{0.10 \cdot (1-0)}{2} \cdot 1 = 1.05$	$t_5 = \frac{1}{2}\left(\frac{3}{184} + 3 + 1\right) = 2.00815217$

Example 2: Greek Government Bond

Maturity Date:	10/31/2004
Dated Date:	10/31/1997
Settlement Date:	5/18/2001

Coupon Rate: 8.9%

Frequency of Coupon Payments per Year: 1

Day Count Method: 30E/360

Redemption Value: 100%

Tax Rate for Interest Income: 7.5%

Tax Rate for Capital Gains: 0%

$FCF = 1 \qquad DF = \frac{172}{360} \qquad EXF = 1 \qquad LCF = 1 \qquad LDF = 1 \qquad n = 2$

Number of cash flows: 4

Date	Cash Flow (per 1 Drachma of face value) for after tax yield (issued in 1997)	Time (in years)
10/31/2001	$CF_1 = 0.089 \cdot 0.925 = 0.082325$	$t_1 = \frac{172}{360} = 0.477778$
10/31/2002	$CF_2 = 0.082325$	$t_2 = 1.477778$
10/31/2003	$CF_3 = 0.082325$	$t_3 = 2.477778$
10/31/2004	$CF_4 = 1.082325$	$t_4 = 3.477778$

Example 3: U.S. Corporate Bond

Short first and last coupon periods.

Maturity Date: 10/1/2004

Settlement Date: 7/3/1999

First Coupon Date: 8/25/1999

Dated Date: 6/5/1999

End-of-Month rule is in effect.

Nominal Annual Coupon Rate: 6%

Redemption Value: 100%

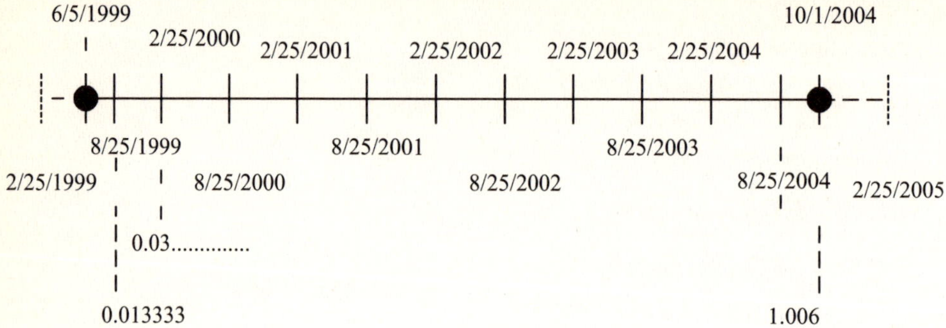

$$FCF = \frac{80}{180} \qquad DF = \frac{52}{180} \qquad LCF = \frac{36}{180} \qquad LDF = \frac{36}{180} \qquad n = 10$$

Number of cash flows: 12

Date	Cash Flow (per $1 of face value)	Time (in years)
08/25/1999	$CF_1 = \frac{0.06}{2} \cdot \frac{80}{180} = 0.013333$	$t_1 = \frac{1}{2} \cdot \frac{52}{180} = 0.144444$
02/25/2000 . . . 08/25/2004	$CF_i = \frac{0.06}{2} = 0.03$, $i = 2, 3, \ldots, 11$	$t_2 = 0.644444$ ⋮ $t_{11} = 5.144444$
10/1/2004	$CF_{12} = 1 + \frac{0.06}{2} \cdot \frac{36}{180} = 1.006$	$t_{12} = 5.244444$

Chapter 7

Forward Pricing Analysis

Introduction

The forward price of security represents its price at some future date (*termination date*). The assumption is that we borrowed money and purchased security with that money at the settlement date. At the termination date, we will sell the security for the forward price. The forward price will be the price of the security, at termination date, which satisfies the following equation:

> Full price at settlement date + cost of financing from settlement date to termination date
> = forward price + income (interest and principal payments) from settlement date (not inclusive) to termination date (inclusive)
> + reinvestment of income until termination date
> + accrued interest at termination date

In other words, the forward price equalizes expenses and income at the termination date.

Three methods are used to calculate forward price. They differ in the calculation of financing cost on borrowed money and on the reinvestment of any payments received between the settlement date (not inclusive) and the termination date (inclusive).

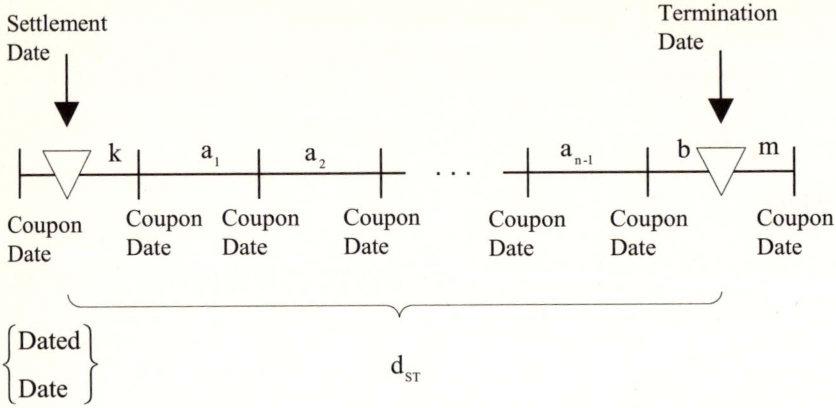

Each of these three methods can be used without reinvesting the payments received between the settlement date (not inclusive) and the termination date (inclusive).

The fourth method is the continuous compounding method, which uses current yield.

Forward Price Formulas

In all three methods we assume that there are no principal payments between the settlement date (not inclusive) and the termination date (inclusive).

Proceeds Method

The financing cost on the full price is calculated with simple interest from the settlement date to the termination date.

Reinvestment of payments is calculated with simple interest from one payment date to the following payment date, starting with the first payment date after the settlement date, until we reach the termination date.

$$\left(P_S + AI_S\right)\left(1 + R_B \frac{d_{ST}}{D}\right) = P_F + AI_T + CAR + \frac{\frac{C\cdot\left(1-TX\right)}{F}\cdot LCF}{1 + R_B \cdot \frac{m}{D}} \cdot EXF$$

$$P_F = (P_S + AI_S)\left(1 + R_B \frac{d_{ST}}{D}\right) - AI_T - CAR - \frac{\frac{C(1-TX)}{F} \cdot LCF}{1 + R_B \cdot \frac{m}{D}} \cdot EXF$$

P_F is the **F**orward **P**rice (price at termination date) per one currency unit of face value.

P_S is the **P**rice at **S**ettlement date per one currency unit of face value.

AI_S is the **A**ccrued **I**nterest at the **S**ettlement date per one currency unit of face value.

R_B is the **B**reak-even **R**epo rate, expressed as a decimal, where **$R_B = R + S$**.

R is the **R**epo rate, expressed as a decimal.

S is the **S**pread-over repo rate, expressed as a decimal.

d_{ST} is the actual number of **d**ays between the **S**ettlement date and the **T**ermination date.

D is the number of **D**ays in a year, which is the base for the repo rate.

AI_T is the **A**ccrued **I**nterest at **t**ermination date per one currency unit of face value.

CAR is the **C**oupons **A**nd **R**einvestments of coupons per one currency unit of face value.

C is the Nominal annual **C**oupon rate, expressed as a decimal.

F is the **F**requency of payments per year.

LCF is the **L**ast **C**oupon **F**actor (explained in Chapter 1).

TX is the **TaX** rate for interest income, expressed as a decimal.

m is the actual number of days from the termination date to the coupon date just after the termination date.

EXF is the **EX**-dividend **F**actor.

Cum-dividend trading at termination date: EXF = 0

Ex-dividend trading at the settlement date and ex-dividend trading at the termination date, when the settlement and termination dates are within the same coupon period (i.e., n = 0): **EXF = 0**.

Cum-dividend trading at the settlement date and ex-dividend trading at the termination date

or

Ex-dividend trading at the settlement date and ex-dividend trading at the termination date, when settlement date is not in the same coupon period as termination date (n ≥ 1): **EXF = 1**.

Note that the termination date must be *after* the settlement date and *before* the maturity date.

$$\text{CAR} = \frac{C(1-TX)}{F} \cdot \left(1 + R_B \cdot \frac{b}{D}\right) \left\{ \text{FCF} \prod_{i=1}^{n-1} \left(1 + R_B \cdot \frac{a_i}{D}\right) + \sum_{i=2}^{n-1} \left[\prod_{j=i}^{n-1} \left(1 + R_B \cdot \frac{a_j}{D}\right) \right] + 1 \right\}, \text{ for } n \geq 2$$

$$\text{CAR} = \frac{C(1-TX)}{F} \cdot \text{FCF}\left(1 + R_B \cdot \frac{b}{D}\right), \text{ for } n = 1$$

CAR = 0, for n = 0

b	is the actual number of days between the last coupon date on or before termination date and the termination date.
FCF	is the **F**irst **C**oupon **F**actor (explained in Chapter 1).
a_i i = 1, 2, . . . , n 1	is the actual number of days between consecutive coupon dates, (within the period between settlement date and termination date), starting with the first coupon date after the settlement date.
n	is the **n**umber of coupon payments between the settlement date (not inclusive) and the termination date (inclusive).

<u>NOTE:</u> $\sum_{i=k}^{n} x_i = 0$ **for k > n**

Another way to look at the forward-price formula:

$$\left(P_S + AI_S\right)\left(1 + R_B \frac{d_{ST}}{D}\right) = P_F + CAR + AI_T + \frac{\frac{C}{F}\left(1 - TX\right)LCF}{1 + R_B \frac{m}{D}} \cdot EXF$$

$$P_S + AI_S + \left(P_S + AI_S\right)R_B \frac{d_{ST}}{D} = P_F + CAR + AI_T + \frac{\frac{C}{F}\left(1 - TX\right)LCF}{1 + R_B \frac{m}{D}} \cdot EXF$$

$$P_F = P_S - \left\{\left[CAR + AI_T + \frac{\frac{C}{F}\left(1 - TX\right)LCF}{1 + R_B \frac{m}{D}} \cdot EXF - AI_S\right] - \left(P_S + AI_S\right)R_B \frac{d_{ST}}{D}\right\}$$

$$CI = \text{Coupon Income} = CAR + AI_T + \frac{\frac{C}{F}\left(1 - TX\right)LCF}{1 + R_B \frac{m}{D}} \cdot EXF - AI_S$$

$$COF = \text{Cost Of Financing} = \left(P_S + AI_S\right) \cdot R_B \frac{d_{ST}}{D}$$

$$P_F = P_S - \left(CI - COF\right)$$

$$COC = \text{Cost Of Carry} = CI - COF$$

$$P_F = P_S - COC$$

To clarify the CAR formula when $n \geq 2$, we fully expand the formula for the following example:

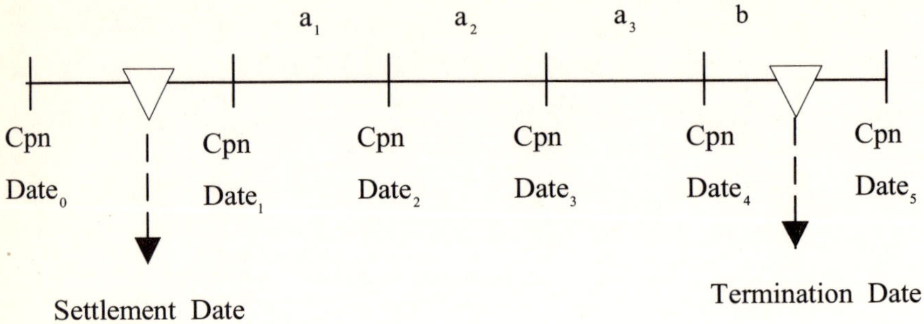

$$\text{CAR} = \frac{C(1-TX)}{F} \cdot \text{FCF}\left(1+R_B \cdot \frac{a_1}{D}\right)\left(1+R_B \cdot \frac{a_2}{D}\right)\left(1+R_B \cdot \frac{a_3}{D}\right)\left(1+R_B \cdot \frac{b}{D}\right) \quad \textbf{(1)}$$

$$+\frac{C(1-TX)}{F}\left(1+R_B \cdot \frac{a_2}{D}\right)\left(1+R_B \cdot \frac{a_3}{D}\right)\left(1+R_B \cdot \frac{b}{D}\right) \quad \textbf{(2)}$$

$$+\frac{C(1-TX)}{F}\left(1+R_B \cdot \frac{a_3}{D}\right)\left(1+R_B \cdot \frac{b}{D}\right) \quad \textbf{(3)}$$

$$+\frac{C(1-TX)}{F}\left(1+R_B \cdot \frac{b}{D}\right) \quad \textbf{(4)}$$

(1) Represents the first net coupon payment adjusted by the First Coupon Factor $\left[\frac{C}{F} \cdot \text{FCF}(1-TX)\right]$ received at **Cpn Date$_1$** (just after the settlement date), reinvested at simple interest at rate $\mathbf{R_B}$ for full coupon periods $\mathbf{a_1}$, $\mathbf{a_2}$, $\mathbf{a_3}$, and final partial period, **b**, from the coupon payment date (just prior to the termination date), to the termination date.

(2) Represents the normal net coupon payment $\left[\frac{C}{F}(1-TX)\right]$ received at **Cpn Date$_2$**, reinvested at simple interest rate $\mathbf{R_B}$ for full coupon periods $\mathbf{a_2}$, $\mathbf{a_3}$, and the final partial period, **b**.

(3) Represents the normal net coupon payment $\left[\frac{C}{F}(1-TX)\right]$ received at **Cpn Date$_3$**, reinvested at simple interest at rate $\mathbf{R_B}$ for full coupon period $\mathbf{a_3}$ and final partial period, **b**.

(4) Represents the normal net coupon payment $\left[\frac{C}{F}(1-TX)\right]$ received at **Cpn Date$_4$**, reinvested at simple interest rate $\mathbf{R_B}$ for final partial period, **b**.

CD Method

The financing cost on the full price is calculated with simple interest from the settlement date to the first payment date after the settlement date, then from that payment date to the following payment date, and so on, until we reach the termination date.

The reinvestment of payments is calculated with simple interest from one payment date to the following payment date, starting with the first payment date after the settlement date, until we reach the termination date.

$$P_F = (P_S + AI_S)\left(1 + R_B \cdot \frac{k}{D}\right)\left(1 + R_B \cdot \frac{b}{D}\right)\prod_{i=1}^{n-1}\left(1 + R_B \cdot \frac{a_i}{D}\right)$$

$$- AI_T - CAR - \frac{\frac{C(1-TX)}{F} \cdot LCF}{1 + R_B \cdot \frac{m}{D}} \cdot EXF, n \geq 2$$

$$P_F = (P_S + AI_S)\left(1 + R_B \frac{k}{D}\right)\left(1 + R_B \frac{b}{D}\right)$$

$$- AI_T - CAR - \frac{\frac{C(1-TX)}{F} \cdot LCF}{1 + R_B \frac{m}{D}} \cdot EXF, \quad n = 1$$

$$P_F = (P_S + AI_S)\cdot\left(1 + R_B\frac{d_{ST}}{D}\right) - AI_T - \frac{\frac{C(1-TX)}{F}\cdot LCF}{1 + R_B\frac{m}{D}}\cdot EXF,\ n = 0$$

k is the actual number of days between the settlement date and the first coupon date after the settlement date.

CAR is the same as described in the proceeds method.

Scientific Method

The financing cost on the full price is calculated by compounding interest from the settlement date to the termination date.

Coupon reinvestment is calculated by compounding interest from one payment date to the following payment date, starting with the first payment date after the settlement date, until we reach the termination date.

$$P_F = (P_S + AI_S)\left(1 + \frac{R_B}{F}\right)^{\frac{F\cdot d_{ST}}{D}} - AI_T - CAR - \frac{\frac{C(1-TX)}{F}\cdot LCF}{\left(1 + \frac{R_B}{F}\right)^{\frac{F\cdot m}{D}}}\cdot EXF$$

CAR =

$$\frac{C(1-TX)}{F}\left(1 + \frac{R_B}{F}\right)^{\frac{F\cdot b}{D}}\left\{FCF\prod_{i=1}^{n-1}\left(1 + \frac{R_B}{F}\right)^{\frac{F\cdot a_i}{D}} + \sum_{i=2}^{n-1}\left[\prod_{j=i}^{n-1}\left(1 + \frac{R_B}{F}\right)^{\frac{F\cdot a_j}{D}}\right] + 1\right\},$$

$n \geq 2$

$$CAR = \frac{C(1-TX)}{F}\cdot FCF\left(1 + \frac{R_B}{F}\right)^{\frac{F\cdot b}{D}},\quad n = 1$$

$CAR = 0$, for $n = 0$.

Without reinvesting the payments between the settlement date (not inclusive) and the termination date (inclusive), everything is the same, except that the coupon and reinvestment of coupons for all three methods is:

$$CAR = n \cdot \frac{C(1 - TX)}{F}, \quad \text{for } n \geq 0$$

Continuous Compounding Method

$$P_F = P_S e^{\left(R_B - \frac{C}{P_S}\right)\frac{d_{ST}}{D}}$$

$\frac{C}{P_S}$ is the current yield.

Other Calculations

Drop

$$\text{Drop} = P_S - P_F$$

Invoice Payment at the Settlement Date

$$IP_S = P_S + AI_S$$

Invoice Payment at the Termination Date

$$IP_T = P_F + AI_T$$

Net Profit/Loss

$$P/L = P_F - P_{Fo}$$

where $\mathbf{P_{FO}}$ is the forward price with spread-over repo rate equal to zero ($S = 0$).

Forward Yield

This is the yield-to-maturity of a bond where the settlement date is equal to the termination date, and the price is equal to the forward price.

Note that, for all three methods, every coupon payment date between settlement date (not inclusive) and termination date (inclusive) and one just after termination date, which is not on a business day, can be moved to the next business day. In that case, **k**, $\mathbf{a_i}$, **b**, and **m** may change.

Calculation of Breakeven Repo Rate Given Forward Price

R_B is determined through a series of iterations. Given **F**orward **P**rice as a function of the breakeven repo rate, that is:

$$P_F = f(R_B)$$

Note that the formula for $\mathbf{P_F}$ to be used depends on the method chosen; i.e., Proceeds, CD, or Scientific.

1. The initial guess for the breakeven repo rate is the actual repo rate R:

   $$R_{B1} = R$$

2. The forward price for this guess is a function of R_{B1}:

   $$P_{F1} = f(R_{B1})$$

3. The calculated forward price is compared to the given forward price by comparing the absolute value of the difference between the prices to a defined level of accuracy:

   $$|P_F - P_{F1}| \quad \begin{cases} \le 10^{-k}; \text{stop iterations, } R_{B1} \text{ is a solution.} \\ > 10^{-k}; \text{continue with step 4.} \end{cases}$$

   k can be adjusted to the desired level of accuracy.

4. Calculate the approximate first derivative of the forward price with respect to the breakeven repo rate:

   $$P'_{F1} \approx \frac{P_F(R_{B1} + \Delta R_B) - P_F(R_{B1} - \Delta R_B)}{2 \cdot \Delta R_B}, \qquad \Delta R_B = 0.00001 = 10^{-5}$$

5. The adjustment for $\mathbf{R_{B1}}$ is:

$$\Delta R_{B1} = \frac{P_F - P_{F1}}{P'_{F1}}$$

6. The next guess for $\mathbf{R_B}$ is:

$$R_{B2} = R_{B1} + \Delta R_{B1}$$

7. Continue with step 2, giving $\mathbf{R_{B1}}$ the value of $\mathbf{R_{B2}}$ and calculating a new $\mathbf{P_{F1}}$.

Forward Price for Treasury Bills

$$P_F = P_S \left(1 + R \frac{d_{ST}}{D} \right)$$

Example 1

U.S. Treasury Bond

The settlement date is in the short first coupon period.

Maturity Date:	5/15/2004
Settlement Date:	8/25/2001
Dated Date:	5/17/2001
First Coupon Date:	11/15/2001
Nominal Annual Coupon Rate:	4.25%
Price at Settlement Date:	100.09375%
Repo Rate:	3.1%
Spread-over Repo Rate:	4.4 bp
Termination Date:	8/26/2002
Frequency of Payments per Year:	2
Tax Rate for Interest Income:	0%

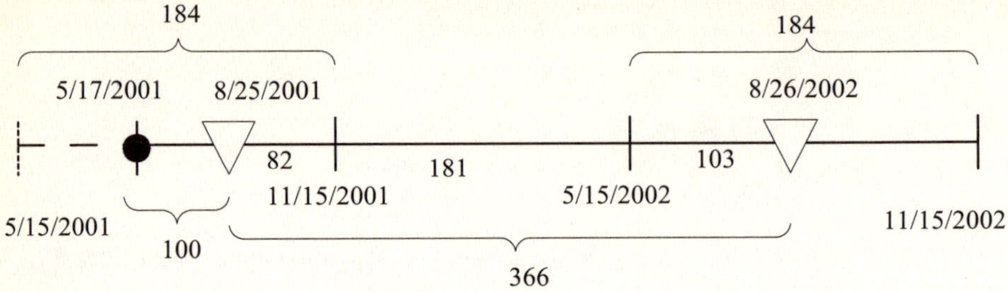

$n = 2$ $\qquad a_1 = 181$

$FCF = 182/184$ $\qquad b = 103$

$D = 360$ $\qquad d_{ST} = 366$

$C = 4.25\%$ $\qquad R_B = 3.1 + 0.044 = 3.144\%$

$F = 2$ $\qquad TX = 0$

$k = 82$ $\qquad EXF = 0$

$$AI_S = \frac{0.0425}{2} \cdot \frac{100}{184} = 0.01154891$$

$$AI_T = \frac{0.0425}{2} \cdot \frac{103}{184} = 0.01189538$$

Proceeds Method

$$P_F = (1.0009375 + 0.01154891) \cdot \left(1 + 0.03144 \cdot \frac{366}{360}\right) - 0.01189538 - CAR - 0$$

$$CAR = \frac{0.0425}{2} \cdot \left(1 + 0.03144 \cdot \frac{103}{360}\right) \cdot \left[\frac{182}{184} \cdot \left(1 + 0.03144 \cdot \frac{181}{360}\right) + 1\right]$$

$$CAR = 0.04298449$$

$$P_F = 0.98996966$$

CD Method

$$P_F = (1.0009375 + 0.01154891)\cdot\left(1+0.03144\cdot\frac{82}{360}\right)\left(1+0.03144\cdot\frac{103}{360}\right)$$

$$\cdot\left(1+0.03144\cdot\frac{181}{360}\right) - 0.01189538 - CAR - 0$$

$$CAR = \frac{0.0425}{2}\cdot\left(1+0.03144\cdot\frac{103}{360}\right)\cdot\left[\frac{182}{184}\cdot\left(1+0.03144\cdot\frac{181}{360}\right)+1\right]$$

$$CAR = 0.04298449$$

$$P_F = 0.9902945$$

Scientific Method

$$P_F = (1.0009375 + 0.01154891)\left(1+\frac{0.03144}{2}\right)^{\frac{2\cdot 366}{360}}$$

$$-0.01189538 - CAR - 0$$

$$CAR = \frac{0.0425}{2}\cdot\left(1+\frac{0.03144}{2}\right)^{\frac{2\cdot 103}{360}}\left[\frac{182}{184}\cdot\left(1+\frac{0.03144}{2}\right)^{\frac{2\cdot 181}{360}}+1\right]$$

$$CAR = 0.04298322$$

$$P_F = 0.99023382$$

No Reinvestments of Coupons (Proceeds Method Only)

$$P_F = (1.0009375 + 0.01154891)\left(1+0.03144\frac{366}{360}\right) -$$

$$-0.01189538 - CAR - 0$$

$$CAR = 2\cdot\frac{0.0425}{2} = 0.0425$$

$$P_F = 0.990454145$$

Continuous Compounding Method

$$P_F = 1.0009375\cdot e^{\left(0.03144-\frac{0.0425}{1.0009375}\right)\frac{366}{360}} = 0.989785721$$

Other Calculations (Proceeds Method Only)

Drop

Drop = 1.0009375 – 0.98996966 = 0.01096784

Invoice Payments

At Settlement Date:

$IP_S = 1.0009375 + 0.01154891 = 1.01248641$

At Termination Date:

$IP_T = 0.98996966 + 0.01189538 = 1.00186504$

Net Profit/Loss

$$P_{FO} = (1.0009375 + 0.01154891) \cdot \left(1 + 0.031 \cdot \frac{366}{360}\right) - 0.01189538 - CAR - 0$$

$$CAR = \frac{0.0425}{2} \cdot \left(1 + 0.031 \cdot \frac{103}{360}\right) \left[\frac{182}{184} \cdot \left(1 + 0.031 \cdot \frac{181}{360}\right) + 1\right]$$

$$CAR = 0.04297443$$

$$P_{FO} = 0.9895267948$$

$$P/L = 0.98996966 - 0.9895267948 = 0.0004428652$$

Example 2

U.S. Treasury Bond, where the settlement date is in a short first coupon period; the termination date coincides with the coupon date.

Maturity Date:	5/31/2006
Settlement Date:	10/26/2001
Dated Date:	6/1/2001
First Coupon Date	11/30/2001
Nominal Annual Coupon Rate:	5.375%
Price at Settlement Date:	102.5%
Repo Rate:	3.125%

Spread-over Repo Rate:	37.5 bp
Termination Date:	5/31/2002
Frequency of Payments per Year:	2
Tax Rate for Interest Income:	0%

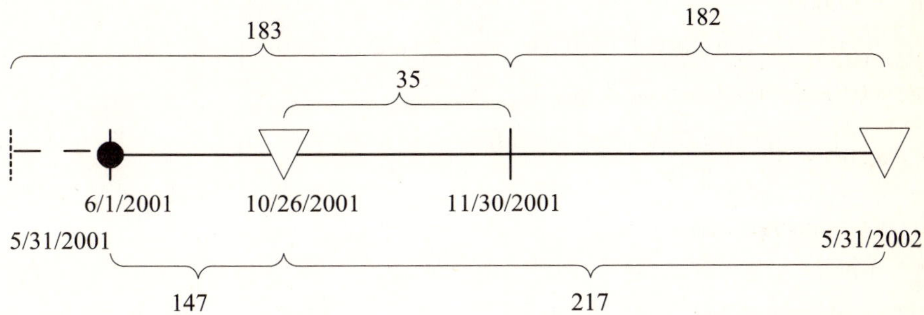

$n = 2$ $\qquad a_1 = 182$

$FCF = 182/183$ $\qquad b = 0$

$D = 360$ $\qquad d_{ST} = 217$

$C = 5.375\%$ $\qquad R_B = 3.125 + 0.375 = 3.5\%$

$F = 2$ $\qquad TX = 0$

$k = 35$ $\qquad EXF = 0$

$$AI_S = \frac{0.05375}{2} \cdot \frac{147}{183} = 0.02158812$$

$$AI_T = 0$$

Proceeds Method

$$P_F = (1.025 + 0.02158812)\left(1 + 0.035 \cdot \frac{217}{360}\right) - 0 - CAR - 0$$

$$\text{CAR} = \frac{0.05375}{2} \cdot \left(1 + 0.035 \cdot \frac{0}{360}\right)\left[\frac{182}{183}\left(1 + 0.035 \cdot \frac{182}{360}\right) + 1\right]$$

$$\text{CAR} = 0.054076082$$

$$P_F = 1.014592135$$

CD Method

$$P_F = (1.025 + 0.02158812)\left(1 + 0.035 \cdot \frac{35}{360}\right)\left(1 + 0.035 \cdot \frac{0}{360}\right)$$

$$\cdot \left(1 + 0.035 \cdot \frac{182}{360}\right) - 0 - \text{CAR} - 0$$

$$\text{CAR} = 0.05407608$$

$$P_F = 1.014655150$$

Scientific Method

$$P_F = (1.025 + 0.02158812)\left(1 + \frac{0.035}{2}\right)^{\frac{2 \cdot 217}{360}} - 0 - \text{CAR} - 0$$

$$\text{CAR} = \frac{0.05375}{2} \cdot \left(1 + \frac{0.035}{2}\right)^{\frac{2 \cdot 0}{360}}\left[\frac{182}{183} \cdot \left(1 + \frac{0.035}{2}\right)^{\frac{2 \cdot 182}{360}} + 1\right]$$

$$\text{CAR} = 0.05407613$$

$$P_F = 1.0146316$$

Other calculations (Proceeds method only)

Drop

$$\text{DROP} = 1.025 - 1.0145921 = 0.01040787$$

Invoice Payments

At Settlement date:

$$IP_S = 1.025 + 0.02158812 = 1.0465881$$

At Termination date:

$$IP_T = 1.0145921 + 0 = 1.0145921$$

Net Profit/Loss

$$P_{FO} = (1.025 + 0.02158812)\left(1 + 0.03125 \cdot \frac{217}{360}\right) - 0 - CAR - 0$$

$$CAR = \frac{0.05375}{2} \cdot \left(1 + 0.03125 \cdot \frac{0}{360}\right)\left[\frac{182}{183}\left(1 + 0.03125 \cdot \frac{182}{360}\right) + 1\right]$$

$$CAR = 0.054025410$$

$$P_{FO} = 1.012277082$$

$$P / L = 1.014592135 - 1.012277082 = 0.002315053$$

Example 3

Spanish Government Bond

Maturity Date:	1/31/2008
Settlement Date:	6/29/2001
Coupon Rate:	6%
Price at Settlement Date:	106%
Repo Rate:	4%
Spread-over Repo Rate:	0 bp
Termination Date:	9/4/2002
Frequency of Payments per Year:	1
Tax Rate for Interest Income:	0%

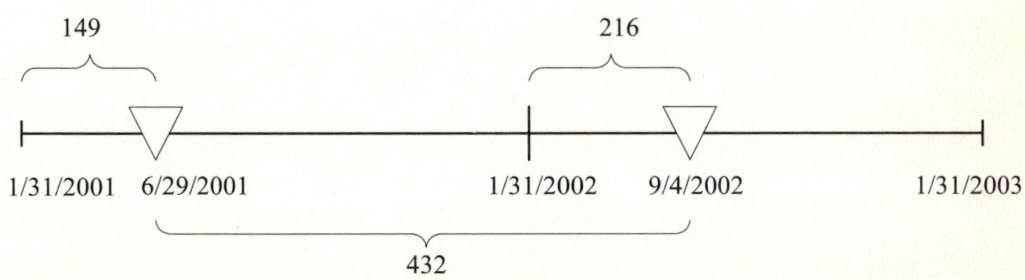

$n = 1$	$d_{ST} = 432$
$FCF = 1$	$R_B = 4\%$
$D = 360$	$TX = 0\%$
$C = 6\%$	$EXF = 0$
$F = 1$	

$$AI_S = 0.06 \cdot \frac{149}{365} = 0.024493151$$

$$AI_T = 0.06 \cdot \frac{216}{365} = 0.035506849$$

Proceeds Method

$$P_F = (1.06 + 0.024493151)\left(1 + 0.04 \cdot \frac{432}{360}\right) - 0.035506849 - CAR$$

$$CAR = 0.06 \cdot \left(1 + 0.04 \cdot \frac{216}{360}\right) = 0.06144$$

$$P_F = 1.039601973$$

Example 4

French Government O. A. T.

Maturity Date:	4/25/2009
Settlement Date:	6/29/2001
Coupon Rate:	4%
Price at Settlement Date:	93%
Repo Rate:	4%
Termination Date:	11/4/2002

Frequency of Payments per Year:	1
Tax Rate for Interest Income:	0%

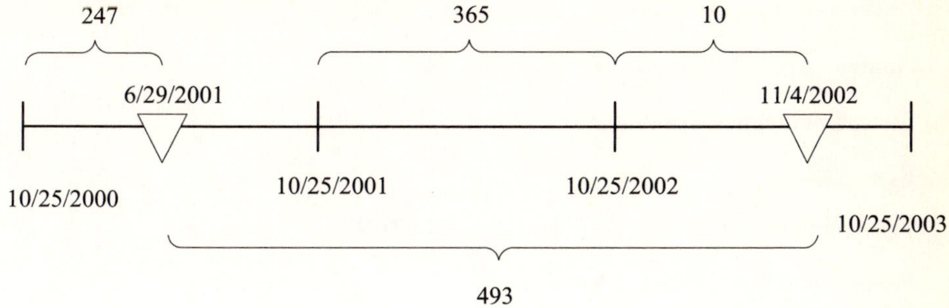

$n = 2$	$EXF = 0$	$FCF = 1$
$b = 10$	$a_1 = 365$	
$D = 360$	$d_{ST} = 493$	
$C = 4\%$	$R_B = 4\%$	
$F = 1$	$TX = 0\%$	

$$AI_S = 0.04 \cdot \frac{247}{365} = 0.027068493 \approx 0.02707$$

$$AI_T = 0.04 \cdot \frac{10}{365} = 0.00109589 \approx 0.00110$$

Proceeds Method

$$P_F = (0.93 + 0.02707)\left(1 + 0.04 \cdot \frac{493}{360}\right) - 0.00110 - CAR$$

$$CAR = 0.04 \cdot \left(1 + 0.04 \cdot \frac{10}{360}\right)\left[\left(1 + 0.04 \cdot \frac{365}{360}\right) + 1\right]$$

$$CAR = 0.081712914$$

$$P_F = 0.926683254$$

Example 5

Australian Government Bond

Maturity Date:	7/15/2009
Settlement Date:	8/12/2001
Nominal Annual Coupon Rate:	7%
Price at Settlement Date:	104%
Repo Rate:	5%
Termination Date:	7/10/2002
Frequency of Payments per Year:	2
Days in the Year:	365

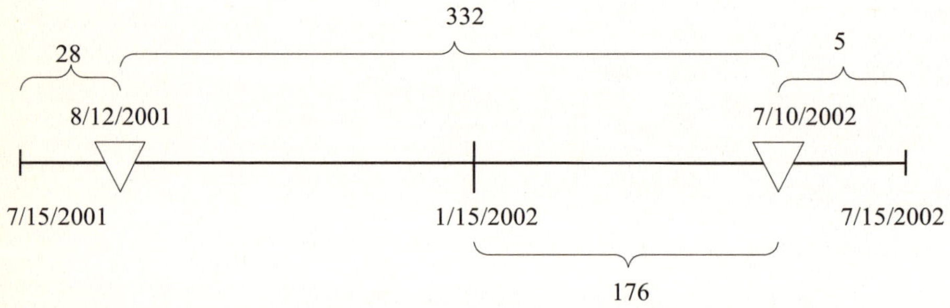

n = 1

EXF = 1 (Cum-dividend trading at the settlement date and ex-dividend trading at the termination date when settlement date is not in the same coupon period as the termination date).

$$AI_S = \frac{0.07}{2} \cdot \frac{28}{184} = 0.05326086 \approx 0.00533$$

$$AI_T = \frac{0.07}{2} \cdot \left(-\frac{5}{181}\right) = -0.00096685 \approx -0.00097$$

Proceeds Method

$$CAR = \frac{0.07}{2} \cdot \left(1 + 0.05\frac{176}{365}\right) = 0.035843835$$

$$P_F = (1.04 + 0.00533)\left(1 + 0.05\frac{332}{365}\right) + 0.00097 - 0.035843835 - \frac{\frac{0.07}{2}}{1 + 0.05\frac{5}{365}}$$

$$P_F = 1.023021157$$

Example 6

U.S. Government Note

Settlement date coincides with the coupon date.

Maturity Date:	5/15/2002
Settlement Date:	11/15/99
Nominal Annual Coupon Rate:	6.125%
Price at Settlement Date:	100.15625%
Repo Rate:	5.5%
Spread-over Repo Rate:	0
Termination Date:	12/14/99
Frequency of Payments per Year:	2
Tax Rate for Interest Income:	0

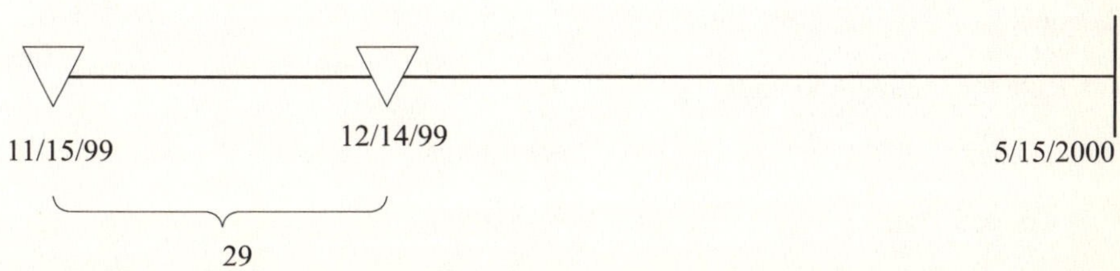

n = 0 (The coupon date of 11/15/99, which falls on settlement date is not included)

$D = 360$

$AI_S = 0$

$$AI_T = \frac{0.06125}{2} \cdot \frac{29}{182} = 0.00487981$$

Proceeds Method

$CAR = 0$

$$P_F = (1.0015625 + 0)\left(1 + 0.055\frac{29}{360}\right) - 0.00487981$$

$P_F = 1.001120168$

Example 7

Canadian Government Bond

The settlement date is in the short first coupon period.

Maturity Date:	9/15/2002
Settlement Date:	6/26/2000
Nominal Annual Coupon Rate:	6.25%
Price at Settlement Date:	99.85%
Repo Rate:	4.75%
Spread-over Repo Rate:	0
Termination Date:	12/16/2000
Frequency of Payments per Year:	2
Tax Rate for Interest Income:	0
Dated Date:	6/17/2000
First Coupon Date:	9/15/2000

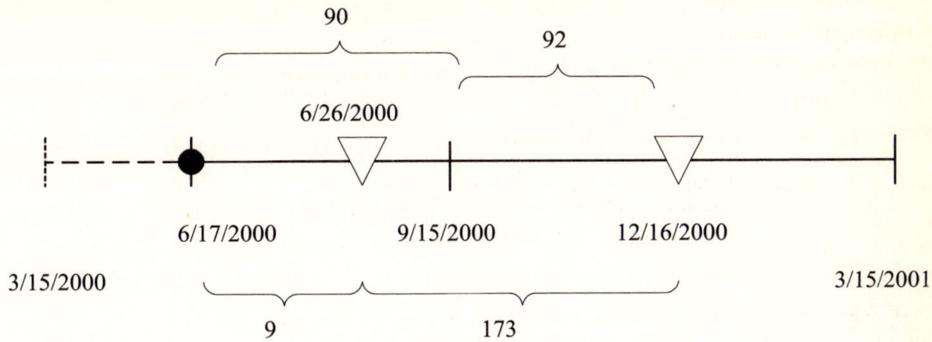

n = 1 b = 92 EXF = 0

$$FCF = \frac{90}{182.5} \qquad d_{ST} = 173$$

D = 365 $R_B = 4.75\%$

$$AI_S = \frac{0.0625}{2} \cdot \frac{9}{182.5} = 0.001541095$$

$$AI_T = \frac{0.0625}{2} \cdot \frac{92}{182.5} = 0.015753424$$

Proceeds Method

$$P_F = (0.9985 + 0.001541095)\left(1 + 0.0475\frac{173}{365}\right) - 0.015753424 - CAR$$

$$CAR = \frac{0.0625}{2} \cdot \frac{90}{182.5}\left(1 + 0.0475\frac{92}{365}\right) = 0.015595468$$

$$P_F = (0.9985 + 0.001541095)\left(1 + 0.0475\frac{173}{365}\right)$$

$$- 0.015753424 - 0.015595468 = 0.991206827$$

Example 8

U.S. Treasury Bond
The termination date is on the coupon date.

Maturity Date:	10/15/2010
Settlement Date:	1/24/2001
Nominal Annual Coupon Rate:	6.5%
Price at Settlement Date:	99.46875%
Repo Rate:	5.5%
Termination Date:	4/15/2001
Frequency of Payments per Year:	2
Days in Year:	360

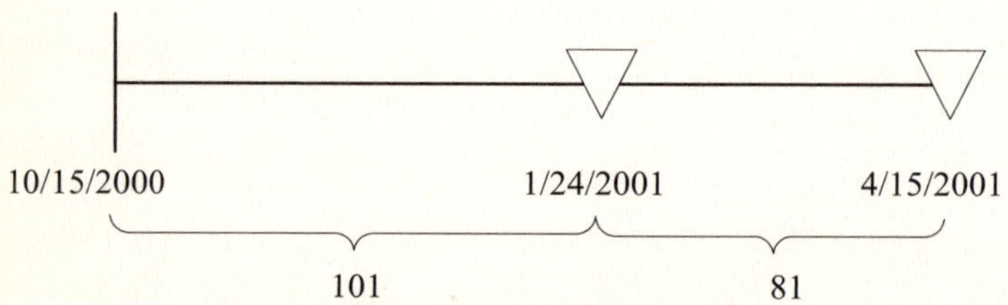

n = 1 (The coupon date of 4/15/2001, which falls on the termination date, is included.)

$$AI_S = \frac{0.065}{2} \cdot \frac{101}{182} = 0.018035714$$

$$AI_T = 0$$

$$CAR = \frac{0.065}{2} = 0.0325$$

$$P_F = (0.9946875 + 0.018035714)\left(1 + 0.055\frac{81}{360}\right) - 0 - 0.0325$$

$$P_F = 0.992755663$$

Example 9

South African Government Bond

Maturity Date:	8/15/2008
Settlement Date:	8/10/2001
Nominal Annual Coupon Rate:	13%
Price at Settlement Date:	110%
Repo Rate:	11%
Termination Date:	2/11/2002
Frequency of Payments per Year:	2
Days in Year:	365

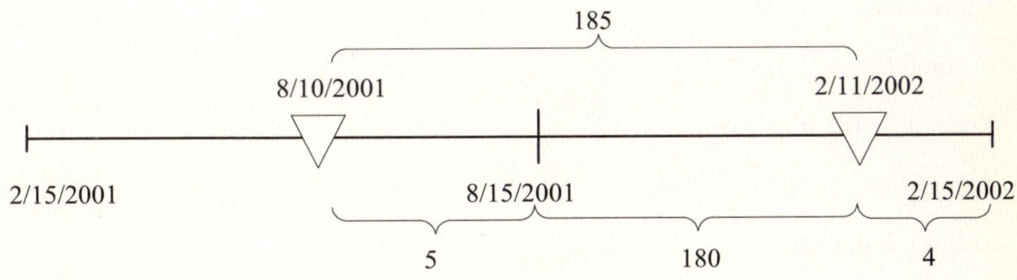

$n = 1$ $\qquad d_{ST} = 185$

$\text{FCF} = 0 \qquad\qquad \text{LCF} = 1$

$b = 180$

EXF = 1 (Ex-dividend trading at the settlement date and ex-dividend trading at the termination date, when settlement and termination dates are not in the same coupon period.)

$$\text{AI}_S = -\frac{0.13}{2}\cdot\frac{5}{182.5} = -0.001780822 \approx -0.0017808$$

$$\text{AI}_T = -\frac{0.13}{2}\cdot\frac{4}{182.5} = -0.001424658 \approx -0.0014247$$

Proceeds Method

$$P_F = (1.1 - 0.0017808)\left(1 + 0.11\frac{185}{365}\right) + 0.0014247 - \text{CAR} - \frac{\frac{0.13}{2}}{1 + 0.11\frac{4}{365}}$$

$\text{CAR} = 0$

$P_F = 1.095951643 \approx 1.0959516$

Example 10

Greek Government Bond

Maturity Date:	6/19/2007
Settlement Date:	2/5/99
Dated Date:	6/19/97
Coupon Rate:	8.8%
Price at Settlement Date:	96%
Repo Rate:	5%
Termination Date:	8/10/99
Frequency of Payments per Year:	1

Days in Year: 360

Tax Rate for Interest Income: 7.5%

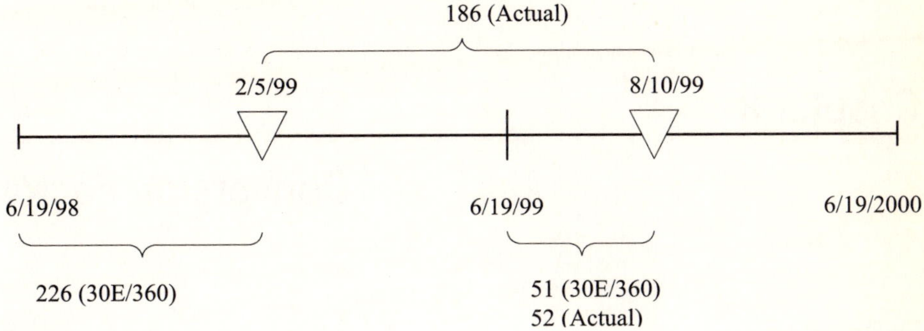

Gross

$$AI_S = 0.088 \cdot \frac{226}{360} = 0.055244444$$

$$AI_T = 0.088 \cdot \frac{51}{360} = 0.012466667$$

$$CAR = 0.088\left(1 + 0.05 \cdot \frac{52}{360}\right) = 0.088635556$$

$$(0.96 + 0.055244444)\left(1 + 0.05 \cdot \frac{186}{360}\right) = P_F + 0.012466667 + 0.088635556$$

$$P_F = 0.940369369$$

Net

$$AI_S = 0.088 \cdot \frac{226}{360} \cdot 0.925 = 0.051101111$$

$$AI_T = 0.088 \cdot \frac{51}{360} \cdot 0.925 = 0.011531666$$

$$CAR = 0.088 \cdot 0.925\left(1 + 0.05 \cdot \frac{52}{360}\right) = 0.081987889$$

$$(0.96 + 0.051101111)\left(1 + 0.05 \cdot \frac{186}{360}\right) = P_F + 0.011531666 + 0.081987889$$

$$P_F = 0.943701668$$

Chapter 8

Conversion Factor

Definitions

The conversion factor is a price per one currency unit of face value. This means that we will use the general price/yield formula for periodic payment fixed income securities for a particular country, in order to calculate the conversion factor.

Notional yield to maturity (or next call) is different for different countries and futures contracts.

The following is valid for all countries and futures contracts [these are the variables in the general price/yield formula for periodic payment fixed income securities (see Chapter 1)]:

- Redemption value = RV = 1 (even if conversion factor is calculated to the next call date).
- First coupon factor = FCF = 1.

  Exceptions:

  For ex-dividend trading, FCF = 0.

  For the United Kingdom, Euro contracts trading on MATIF, German, and Spanish futures contracts where it should be calculated if the settlement date is in the odd first coupon period.

  For Spanish government bonds when delivery date is before dated date, FCF = 0.
- Last coupon factor = LCF = 1.
- Last discount factor = LDF = 1.

Exception: For Spanish government bonds, when maturity is on a nonbusiness day, where it should be calculated after moving maturity date to the next business day.

- Tax rate for interest income = TX = 0.
- Tax rate for capital gains = TXG = 0.

Conventions

Canadian 10-Year Government Bond Futures Contract (on MSE Montreal Stock Exchange)

- Everything is the same as for U.S. Treasury Bond Futures Contract (on CBOT).

Canadian 5-Year Government Bond Futures Contract (on MSE)

- Everything is the same as for U.S. 5-Year Treasury note Futures Contract (on CBOT).

Euro 2-Year, 5-Year, and 10-Year Bond Futures Contract (on MATIF Marché A Terme International de France, Paris)

- Y = 3.5%
- The settlement date (it is called the Repartition Day) is one business day before the third Wednesday of the delivery month.
- The conversion factor is rounded to six decimal places.

E-Bond 30-Year Bond Futures Contract (on MATIF)

- Y = 5.5%
- Everything else is the same as for the Euro 10-Year Bond Futures Contract.

German 2-Year (SCHATZ), 5-Year (BOBL), 10-Year (BUND), and 30-Year (BUXL) Government Bond Futures Contract (on EUX- Eurex Frankfurt)

- Y = 6%
- The settlement date is the tenth calendar day of delivery month. If the tenth calendar day of delivery month is a nonbusiness day, then the settlement date is the next business day.
- Conversion Factor is rounded to six decimal places.

German 10-Year Government Bond Futures Contract (BUND) (on LIFFE London International Financial Futures & Options Exchange)

- Everything is the same as for German 10-Year Government Bond Futures Contract on EUX, except that the settlement date is the tenth calendar day of delivery month even if it is a nonbusiness day.

Italian 10-Year Government Bond Futures Contract (on MIF Mercato Italiano Futures, Milan)

- Y = 6% (compounded semiannually), gross yield
- The settlement date is the delivery date. The delivery date is the tenth calendar day of delivery month.
- The conversion factor is calculated with actual/ actual (in period) day count method. The conversion factor is rounded to six decimal places.

Japanese 5-Year, 10-Year, and 20-Year Government Bond Futures Contract (On TSE Tokyo Stock Exchange) and 10-Year (on LIFFE)

- Y = 6%
- Compound discounting
- The settlement date is the 20th of the delivery month (even if it is a nonbusiness day)
- Time from settlement date to the next coupon date is truncated to the nearest complete month.

- Discount Factor (DF) is the number of complete months from the settlement date to the next coupon date, divided by 6. Note that, if DF = 0, then make DF = 1 and decrease n by 1.
- Accrued-Interest Factor = AIF = 1 – DF.
- If the maturity date is not on the 20th of a month, we assume that it is on the 20th of a month (LCF = 1, LDF = 1).
- The conversion factor is truncated to six decimal places.

Spanish 10-Year Futures Contract (on MEFF RENTA FIJA, Barcelona)

- Y = 4%
- The settlement date is equal to the delivery date. Delivery date is the third Wednesday of the delivery month. If the third Wednesday is a nonbusiness day, the delivery date is the next business day.
- The conversion factor is rounded to seven decimal places.

Swiss 10-Year Government Bond Futures Contract (on Eurex Zurich)

- Y = 6%
- The settlement date is the delivery date. Delivery date is the 10th of the delivery month.

  If the 10th of the delivery month is a nonbusiness day, then the delivery date is the next business day.
- Time from settlement date to the next coupon date is truncated to the nearest complete month.
- If the bond is callable, then the next call date should be substituted for the maturity date.
- The Discount Factor (DF) is the number of complete months from the settlement date to the next coupon date, divided by 12.

  Note that if DF = 0, then make DF = 1 and decrease n by 1.
- Accrued-Interest Factor = AIF = 1 – DF
- The conversion factor is rounded to six decimal places.

U.K. Long GILT (10-Year) Futures Contract (on LIFFE)

- Y = 7%
- The settlement date is the first day of the delivery month.
- If GILT is in ex-dividend period on the first day of delivery month, the conversion factor is the ex-dividend price.
- Ex-dividend period is six business days prior to the coupon date.
- Conversion factor is rounded to seven decimal places.

U.S. Treasury Bond (20-Year) and 10-Year Treasury Note Futures Contract (on CBOT Chicago Board of Trade)

- Y = 6%
- The settlement date is the first day of the delivery month.
- Time from settlement date to the next coupon date is truncated to the nearest complete quarter.
- The Discount Factor (DF) is the number of months from the settlement date to the next coupon date (number of complete quarters times 3) divided by 6.

  Note that, if DF = 0, then make DF = 1 and decrease n by 1.
- Accrued-Interest Factor = AIF = 1 – DF.
- The conversion factor is rounded to four decimal places.

U.S. 2-Year and 5-Year Treasury Note Futures Contract (on CBOT)

- The same as for U.S. Treasury Bond Futures Contract, except that time from the settlement date to the next coupon date is truncated to the nearest complete month.

U.S. Index-Linked Note Futures Contract

- Y = 3%
- Everything else is the same as for the U.S. Treasury Bond Futures Contract.

Examples

1. Canadian 10-Year Government Bond

Maturity Date: 6/1/2010

Settlement Date: 9/1/2001 (The first day of the delivery month.)

$C = 5.5\%$

$Y = 6\%$

$F = 2$

$$DF = \frac{3}{6} = 0.5, \qquad n = 16, \qquad AIF = 1 - 0.5 = 0.5$$

$$CF = \left(1 + \frac{0.06}{2}\right)^{-0.5} \left\{ \frac{0.055}{2} \cdot 1 + \frac{0.055}{0.06} \left[1 - \frac{1}{\left(1 + \frac{0.06}{2}\right)^{16}} \right] + \left(1 + \frac{0.055}{2} \cdot 1\right)\left(1 + \frac{0.06}{2}\right)^{-16-1} \right\}$$

$$-\frac{0.055}{2} \cdot 0.5$$

$CF = 0.9662$

2. Euro 10-Year Notional Bond (French Government Bond on MATIF)

Maturity Date: 4/25/2009

Settlement Date: 3/14/2000 (Repartition date)

$C = 4\%$

$Y = 3.5\%$

$F = 1$

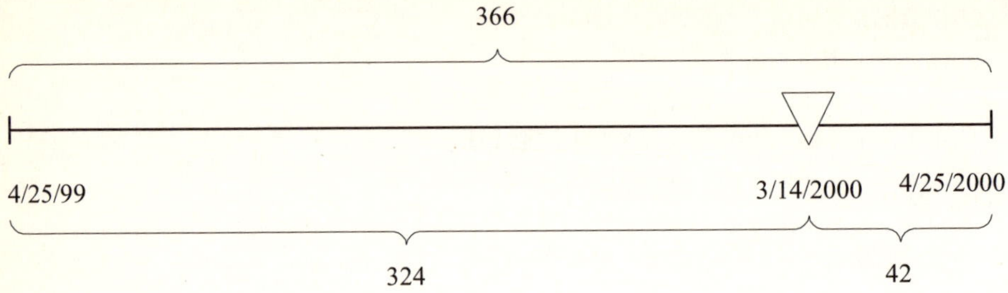

$$AIF = \frac{324}{366}, \qquad FCF = 1, \qquad DF = \frac{42}{366}, \qquad n = 8$$

$$CF = \left(1+0.035\right)^{-\frac{42}{366}} \left\{ 0.04 + \frac{0.04}{0.035}\left[1 - \frac{1}{\left(1+0.035\right)^{8}}\right] + \left(1+0.04\right)\left(1+0.035\right)^{-8-1} \right\}$$

$$-0.04 \cdot \frac{324}{366}$$

$$CF = 1.038381$$

3. Euro 10-Year Notional Bond (German Government Bond on MATIF)

Long First Coupon Period

Maturity Date:	1/4/2011
Settlement Date:	6/19/2001
Dated Date:	10/20/2000
First Coupon Date:	1/4/2002

$C = 5.25\%$

$Y = 3.5\%$

$F = 1$

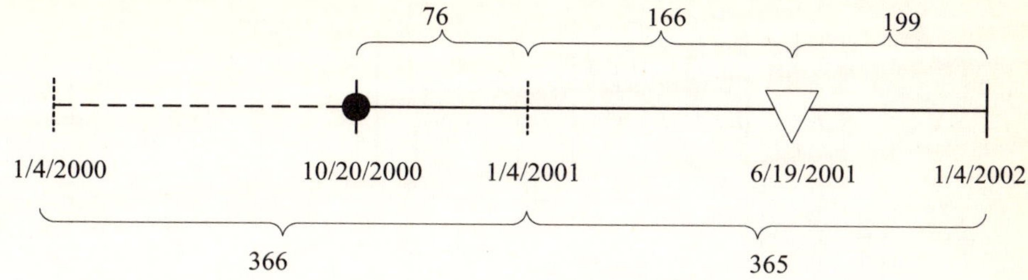

$$AIF = \frac{76}{366} + \frac{166}{365}, \qquad FCF = 1 + \frac{76}{366}, \qquad DF = \frac{199}{365}, \qquad n = 8$$

$CF = 1.139525$

4. Italian 10-Year Government Bond

Maturity Date: 5/1/2009

Settlement Date: 3/10/2000

$C = 4.5\%$

$Y = 6\%$

$F = 2$

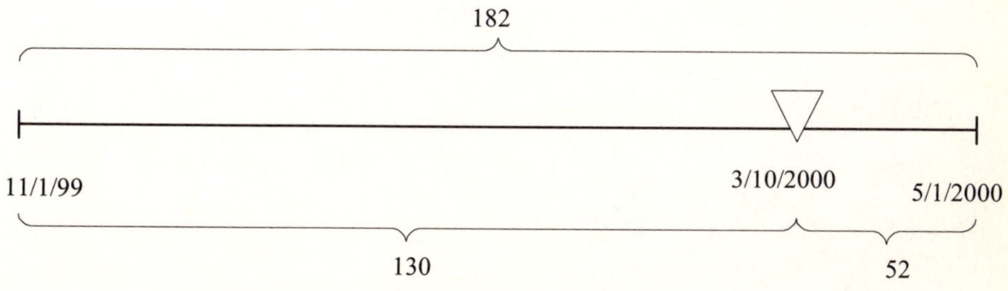

$$AIF = \frac{130}{182}, \qquad FCF = 1, \qquad DF = \frac{52}{182}, \qquad n = 17$$

$$CF = \left(1+\frac{0.06}{2}\right)^{-\frac{52}{182}} \left\{ \frac{0.045}{2} + \frac{0.045}{0.06}\left[1-\frac{1}{\left(1+\frac{0.06}{2}\right)^{17}}\right] + \left(1+\frac{0.045}{2}\right)\left(1+\frac{0.06}{2}\right)^{-17-1} \right\}$$

$$-\frac{0.045}{2}\cdot\frac{130}{182}$$

$$CF = 0.895546$$

5. Japanese 10-Year Government Bond

Maturity Date:	3/20/2009
Settlement Date:	6/20/2001 (The twentieth day of the delivery month.)

$C = 1.9\%$

$Y = 6\%$

$F = 2$

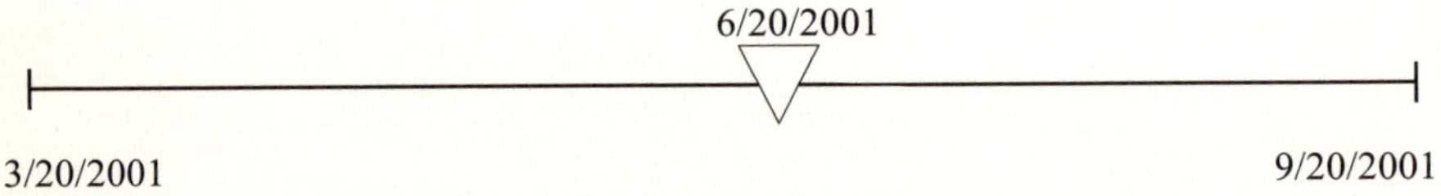

$DF = 0.5,\quad AIF = 0.5,\quad FCF = 1,\quad n = 14$

$$CF = \left(1+\frac{0.06}{2}\right)^{-0.5} \left\{ \frac{0.019}{2} + \frac{0.019}{0.06}\left[1-\frac{1}{\left(1+\frac{0.06}{2}\right)^{14}}\right] + \left(1+\frac{0.019}{2}\right)\left(1+\frac{0.06}{2}\right)^{-14-1} \right\}$$

$$-\frac{0.019}{2}\cdot 0.5$$

$$CF = 0.748802$$

6. Japanese 5-Year Government Bond

Maturity Date: 11/20/2003

Settlement Date: 3/20/2000 (The twentieth day of the delivery month.)

C = 1.4%

Y = 6%

F = 2

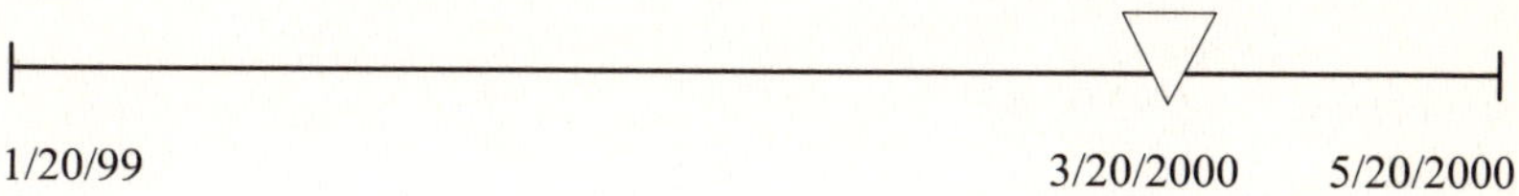

$$DF = \frac{2}{6}, \quad AIF = \frac{4}{6}, \quad FCF = 1, \qquad n = 6$$

CF = 0.850568

7. Spanish 10-Year Government Bond

Maturity Date: 7/30/2011

Settlement Date: 9/19/2001 (Third Wednesday of delivery month)

C = 5.4%

Y = 4%

F = 1

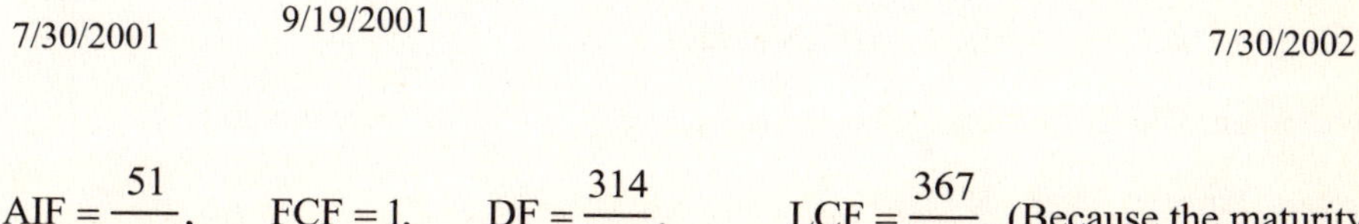

$AIF = \frac{51}{365}, \qquad FCF = 1, \qquad DF = \frac{314}{365}, \qquad LCF = \frac{367}{365}$ (Because the maturity date is a nonbusiness day and it is moved to the next business day).

n = 8

CF = 1.1119727

8. Spanish 10-Year Government Bond

The Dated Date is after the Delivery Date.

Maturity Date:	10/31/2011
Settlement Date:	9/19/2001 (Third Wednesday of the delivery month.)
Dated Date:	10/31/2001
First Coupon Date:	10/31/2002

C = 5.35%

Y = 4%

F = 1

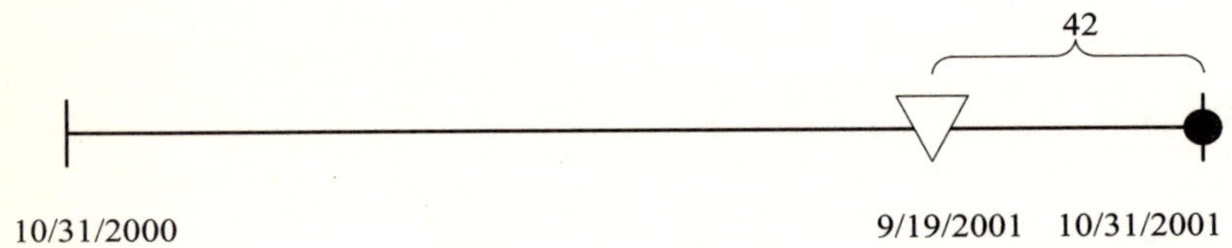

$$AIF = 0, \qquad FCF = 0, \qquad DF = \frac{42}{365}, \qquad n = 9$$

CF = 1.1045011

9. Spanish 10-Year Government Bond

Short First Coupon Period

Maturity Date:	1/31/2010 (Sunday)
Settlement Date:	12/15/99 (Third Wednesday of the delivery month.)
Dated Date:	5/11/99
First Coupon Date:	1/31/2000

C = 4%

Y = 4%

F = 1

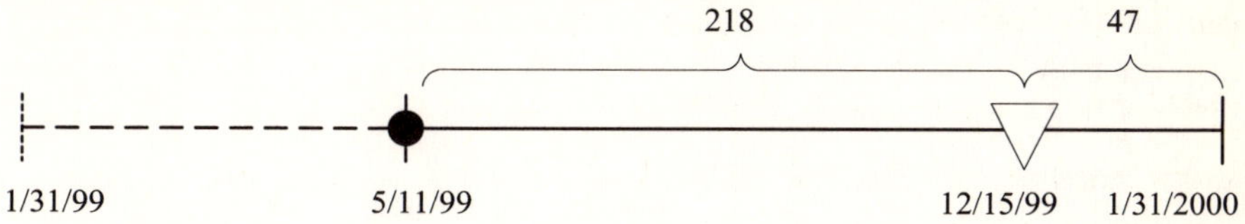

$$AIF = \frac{218}{365}, \quad FCF = \frac{265}{365}, \quad DF = \frac{47}{365}, \quad LCF = 1, \quad LDF = \frac{366}{365}, \quad n = 9$$

CF = 0.9998917

10. Swiss Government Bond

Maturity Date: 6/10/2011

Settlement Date: 9/10/2001 (Delivery Date)

C = 4%

Y = 6%

F = 1

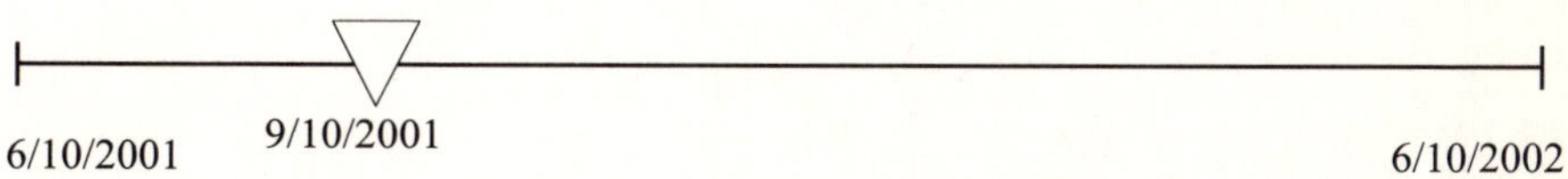

$$DF = \frac{9}{12}, \quad n = 8, \quad AIF = 1 - \frac{9}{12} = \frac{3}{12}$$

$$CF = \left(1 + \frac{0.06}{1}\right)^{-\frac{9}{12}} \left\{ \frac{0.04}{1} \cdot 1 + \frac{0.04}{0.06}\left[1 - \frac{1}{\left(1 + \frac{0.06}{1}\right)^{8}}\right] + \left(1 + \frac{0.04}{1} \cdot 1\right)\left(1 + \frac{0.06}{1}\right)^{-8-1} \right\}$$

$$- \frac{0.04}{1} \cdot \frac{3}{12}$$

$$CF = 0.855312$$

11. Swiss Government Bond

Maturity Date: 6/10/2012

Settlement Date: 12/10/2000 (12/10/2000 is a nonbusiness day, so 12/11/2000 is the delivery date)

$C = 2.75\%$

$Y = 6\%$

$F = 1$

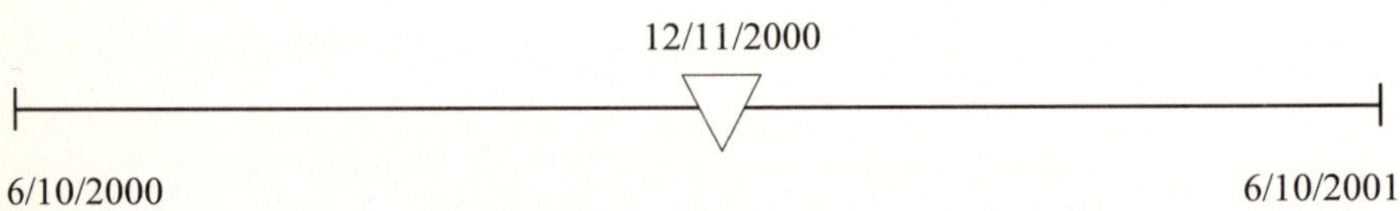

$$DF = \frac{5}{12}, \quad n = 10, \quad AIF = 1 - \frac{5}{12} = \frac{7}{12}$$

$$CF = 0.736637$$

12. U.K. Long GILT

Maturity Date: 8/6/2012

Settlement Date: 3/1/2001 (The first day of the delivery month.)

$C = 9\%$

$Y = 7\%$

$F = 2$

$$AIF = \frac{23}{181}, \qquad DF = \frac{158}{181} \qquad n = 21$$

$$CF = \left(1 + \frac{0.07}{2}\right)^{\frac{158}{181}} \left\{ \frac{0.09}{2} + \frac{0.09}{0.07}\left[1 - \frac{1}{\left(1 + \frac{0.07}{2}\right)^{21}}\right] + \left(1 + \frac{0.09}{2}\right)\left(1 + \frac{0.07}{2}\right)^{-21-1} \right\}$$

$$- \frac{0.09}{2} \cdot \frac{23}{181}$$

$CF = 1.1555512$

13. U.S. 2-Year Treasury Note

Maturity Date:	1/31/2002
Delivery Date:	4/3/2000
Settlement Date:	3/1/2000 (The first day of the delivery month.)

$C = 6.25\%$

$Y = 6\%$

$F = 2$

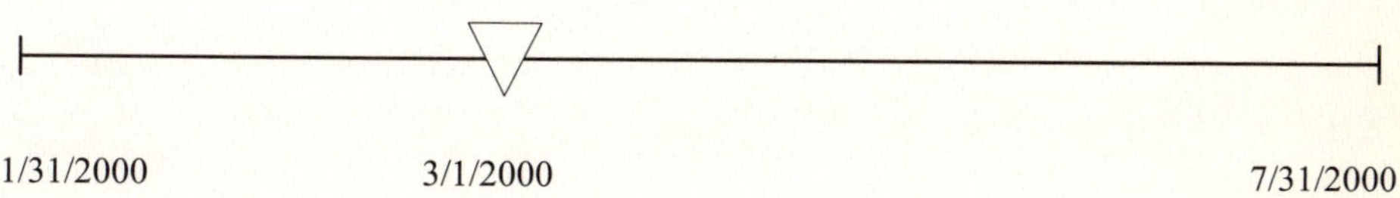

$$DF = \frac{4}{6}, \qquad n = 2, \qquad AIF = 1 - \frac{4}{6} = \frac{2}{6}$$

$$CF = \left(1+\frac{0.06}{2}\right)^{-\frac{4}{6}} \left\{ \frac{0.0625}{2}\cdot 1 + \frac{0.0625}{0.06}\left[1-\frac{1}{\left(1+\frac{0.06}{2}\right)^{2}}\right] + \left(1+\frac{0.0625}{2}\cdot 1\right)\left(1+\frac{0.06}{2}\right)^{-2-1} \right\}$$

$$-\frac{0.0625}{2}\cdot\frac{2}{6}$$

$CF = 1.0042$

14. U.S. 10-Year Treasury Note

Maturity Date: 2/15/2008

Settlement Date: 6/1/2001 (The first day of the delivery month.)

$C = 5.5\%$

$Y = 6\%$

$F = 2$

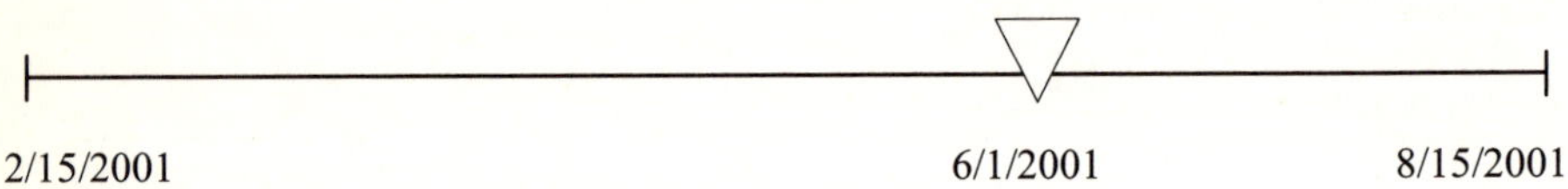

$DF = 0,$ $n = 12$

Because $DF = 0$, we make $DF = 1$ and decrease n by 1 to $n = 11$.

$AIF = 1 - 1 = 0$

$$CF=\left(1+\frac{0.06}{2}\right)^{-1}\left\{\frac{0.055}{2}\cdot 1+\frac{0.055}{0.06}\left[1-\frac{1}{\left(1+\frac{0.06}{2}\right)^{11}}\right]+\left(1+\frac{0.055}{2}\cdot 1\right)\left(1+\frac{0.06}{2}\right)^{-11-1}\right\}$$

$$-\frac{0.055}{2}\cdot 0$$

$$CF=0.9734$$

15. U.S. Treasury Bond

Maturity Date: 5/15/2021

Settlement Date: 6/1/2001 (The first day of the delivery month.)

$C = 8.125\%$

$Y = 6\%$

$F = 2$

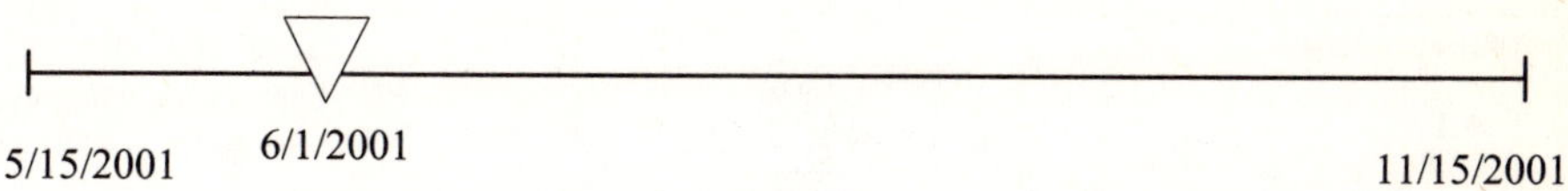

$$DF=\frac{3}{6},\qquad AIF=\frac{3}{6},\qquad n=38$$

$$CF=\left(1+\frac{0.06}{2}\right)^{-\frac{3}{6}}\left\{\frac{0.08125}{2}\cdot 1+\frac{0.08125}{0.06}\left[1-\frac{1}{\left(1+\frac{0.06}{2}\right)^{38}}\right]+\left(1+\frac{0.08125}{2}\cdot 1\right)\left(1+\frac{0.06}{2}\right)^{-38-1}\right\}$$

$$-\frac{0.08125}{2}\cdot\frac{3}{6}$$

$$CF = 1.2438$$

Chapter 9

Futures Analytics

Futures Calculations

Futures calculations are very similar to the proceeds method in forward pricing.

Futures Calculations for $n \geq 2$

In this scenario, there are two or more coupon payments between the settlement date (not inclusive) and the delivery date (inclusive).

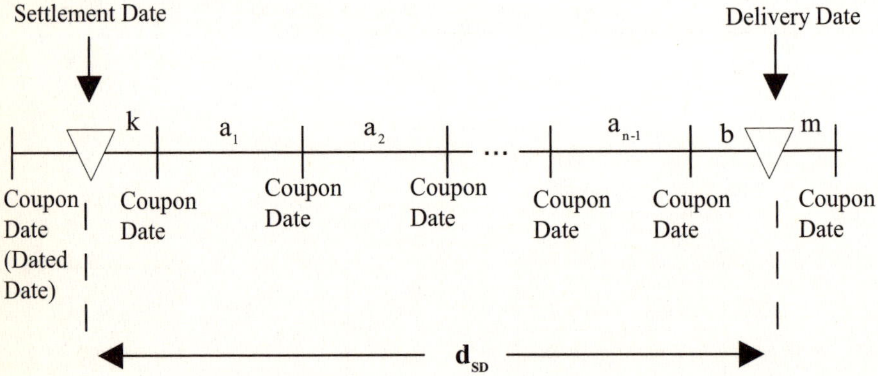

$$\left(BP + AI_S\right)\left(1 + R_{impl} \cdot \frac{d_{SD}}{D}\right) = FP \cdot CF + \frac{C\left(1 - TX\right)}{F}\left(1 + R_{impl} \cdot \frac{b}{D}\right)$$

$$\cdot\left\{FCF\prod_{i=1}^{n-1}\left(1 + R_{impl} \cdot \frac{a_i}{D}\right) + \sum_{i=2}^{n-1}\left[\prod_{j=i}^{n-1}\left(1 + R_{impl} \cdot \frac{a_j}{D}\right)\right] + 1\right\}$$

$$+AI_D + \frac{\frac{C}{F} \cdot LCF\left(1 - TX\right)}{1 + R_{impl} \cdot \frac{m}{D}} \cdot EXF \qquad (1)$$

BP	is the **B**ond **P**rice at settlement date per one currency unit of face value.
FP	is the **F**utures contract **P**rice, expressed as a decimal.
CF	is the **C**onversion **F**actor of a bond.
C	is the Nominal annual **C**oupon rate, expressed as a decimal.
F	is the **F**requency of coupon payments per year.
TX	is the **Tax** rate for interest income, expressed as a decimal.
$\mathbf{R_{impl}}$	is the **Impl**ied repo **R**ate, expressed as a decimal.
b	is the actual number of days **b**etween the last coupon date on or before delivery date and delivery date.
D	is the Number of **D**ays in a year, which is the base for repo rate.
FCF	is the **F**irst **C**oupon **F**actor (explained with the general price/yield formula).
$\mathbf{a_i}$	is the **a**ctual number of days between consecutive coupon payment dates, starting with the first coupon payment date after the settlement date.
$\mathbf{AI_D}$	is the **A**ccrued **I**nterest at delivery date per one currency unit of face value.
LCF	is the **L**ast **C**oupon **F**actor (explained with the general price/yield formula).
m	is the Actual number of days from delivery date to the coupon payment date just after delivery date.

EXF is the **Ex**-dividend **F**actor explained with forward pricing analysis.

AI_S is the **A**ccrued **I**nterest at **S**ettlement date per one currency unit of face value.

d_{SD} is the actual number of **d**ays between the **S**ettlement date and the **D**elivery date.

Futures Calculations for n = 1

In this scenario, there is one coupon payment between the settlement date (not inclusive) and the delivery date (inclusive).

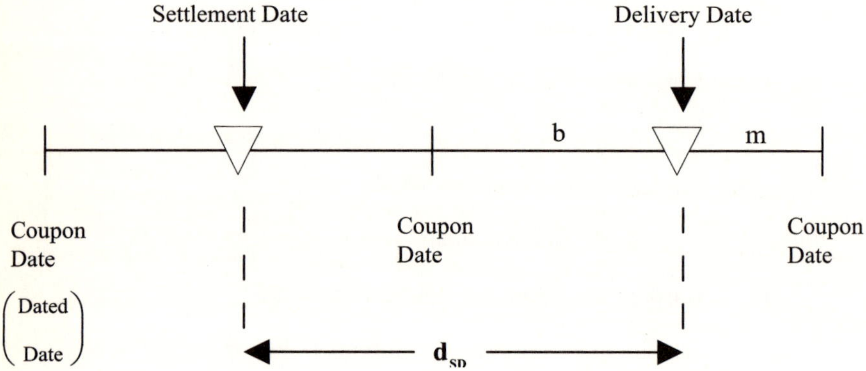

$$\left(BP + AI_S\right)\left(1 + R_{impl} \cdot \frac{d_{SD}}{D}\right) = FP \cdot CF + \frac{C}{F} \cdot FCF\left(1 - TX\right)\left(1 + R_{impl} \cdot \frac{b}{D}\right)$$

$$+AI_D + \frac{\frac{C}{F} \cdot LCF \cdot \left(1 - TX\right)}{1 + R_{impl} \cdot \frac{m}{D}} \cdot EXF$$

Futures Calculations for n = 0

In this scenario, there are no coupon payments between the settlement date (not inclusive) and the delivery date (inclusive).

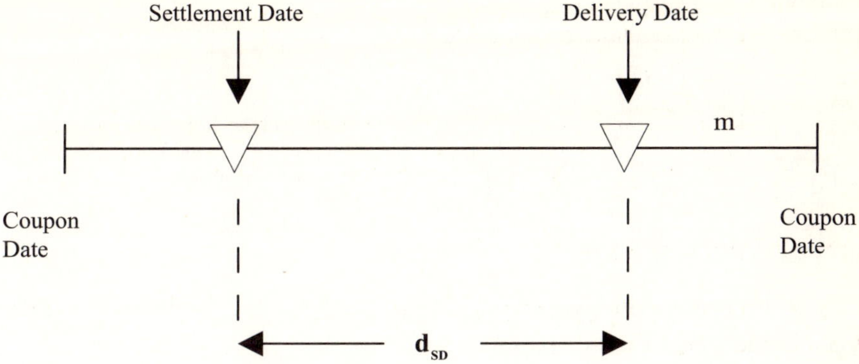

$$(BP + AI_S)\left(1 + R_{impl} \cdot \frac{d_{SD}}{D}\right) = FP \cdot CF + AI_D + \frac{\frac{C}{F} \cdot LCF \cdot (1 - TX)}{1 + R_{impl} \cdot \frac{m}{D}} \cdot EXF$$

Another way to look at formula (1):

If we do the same transformations as with forward price formula, we will get:

$FP \cdot CF = BP - COC$

$BP - FP \cdot CF = COC$

$GB = COC$

$NB = GB - COC = 0$

This is true when we use the implied repo rate, but if we use the actual repo rate, the net basis will not be zero.

Calculation of Implied Repo Rate by Iterations

Usually, the values of **BP** and **FP** are given; therefore, we can calculate $\mathbf{R_{impl}}$ by an iterative method. We use the Newton-Raphson (Tangent) method. Equation (1) can be written as follows:

$$BP = \frac{\dfrac{FP \cdot CF + \dfrac{C}{F} \cdot FCF(1-TX)\left(1+R_{impl} \cdot \dfrac{b}{D}\right)}{1+R_{impl} \cdot \dfrac{d_{SD}}{D}}}{\cdot\left\{FCF\prod_{i=1}^{n-1}\left(1+R_{impl} \cdot \dfrac{a_i}{D}\right)+\sum_{i=2}^{n-1}\left[\prod_{j=i}^{n-1}\left(1+R_{impl} \cdot \dfrac{a_j}{D}\right)\right]+1\right\}}$$

$$\frac{+AI_D + \dfrac{\dfrac{C}{F} \cdot LCF \cdot (1-TX)}{1+R_{impl} \cdot \dfrac{m}{D}} \cdot EXF}{} - AI_S$$

or

$$BP = f\left(R_{impl}\right)$$

1. First guess for implied repo rate:

   $$R_{impl1} = R$$

   R is the actual repo rate.

2. $BP_1 = f\left(R_{impl1}\right)$

3. We now compare the given bond price **BP** with the calculated bond price $\mathbf{BP_1}$:

   $$\left|BP - BP_1\right| \begin{cases} \le 10^{-k} & \text{Stop iterations. } \mathbf{R_{impl1}} \text{ is the solution.} \\ > 10^{-k} & \text{Continue with } \textbf{step 4}. \end{cases}$$

   We should give the value of **k** according to the desired accuracy.

4. $$BP_1' \approx \frac{BP\left(R_{impl1} + \Delta R\right) - BP\left(R_{impl1} - \Delta R\right)}{2 \cdot \Delta R}$$

   $$\Delta R = 0.00001 = 10^{-5}$$

5. The correction for $\mathbf{R_{impl1}}$ is:

   $$\Delta R_{impl1} = \frac{BP - BP_1}{BP_1'}$$

6. The new value for $\mathbf{R_{impl}}$ is:

$$R_{impl2} = R_{impl1} + \Delta R_{impl1}$$

7. Continue with **step 2**, giving $\mathbf{R_{impl1}}$, the value of $\mathbf{R_{impl2}}$ and calculating a new $\mathbf{BP_1}$.

Cost of Financing

$$COF = \left(BP + AI_S\right) \cdot R \cdot \frac{d_{SD}}{D}$$

R is the actual **r**epo rate, expressed as a decimal.

Coupon Income

$$CI = \frac{C}{F}(1 - TX)\left(1 + R \cdot \frac{b}{D}\right)\left\{FCF\prod_{i=1}^{n-1}\left(1 + R \cdot \frac{a_i}{D}\right)\right.$$

$$\left. + \sum_{i=2}^{n-1}\left[\prod_{j=i}^{n-1}\left(1 + R \cdot \frac{a_j}{D}\right)\right] + 1\right\} + AI_D$$

$$+ \frac{\frac{C}{F} \cdot LCF\left(1 - TX\right)}{1 + R \cdot \frac{m}{D}} \cdot EXF - AI_S$$

CI is the **C**oupon **I**ncome per one currency unit of face value.

Gross Basis

$$GB = BP - \left(FP \cdot CF\right)$$

GB is the **G**ross **B**asis per one currency unit of face value.

Gross Basis in 32nds

$$\text{GB32} = \text{GB} \cdot 32$$

GB32 is the **G**ross **B**asis in **32**nds per one currency unit of face value.

Cost of Carry

$$\text{COC} = \text{CI} - \text{COF}$$

COC is the **C**ost **Of** **C**arry per one currency unit of face value.

Net Basis

$$\text{NB} = \text{GB} - \text{COC}$$

NB is the **N**et **B**asis per one currency unit of face value.

Net Basis in 32nds

$$\text{NB32} = \text{NB} \cdot 32$$

NB32 is the **N**et **B**asis in **32**nds per one currency unit of face value.

Example 1

U.S. Treasury Bond

Maturity Date:	8/15/2020
Settlement Date:	9/21/2000
Nominal Annual Coupon Rate:	8.75%
Price at Settlement Date:	129%
Delivery Date:	12/29/2000

Frequency of Payments per Year:	2
Tax Rate for Interest Income:	0%
Repo Rate:	6.4%
Futures Price:	98%
Days in Year:	360

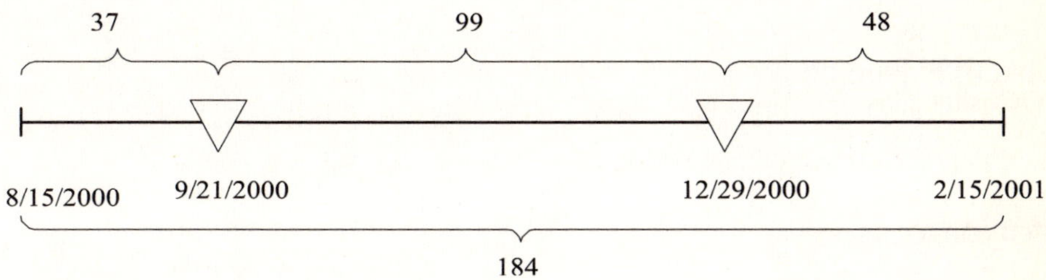

$n = 0$	$TX = 0$
$EXF = 0$	
$m = 48$	$R = 6.4\%$
$FP = 98\%$	$D = 360$
$d_{SD} = 99$	$F = 2$
$C = 8.75\%$	$CF = 1.3136$

$$AI_S = \frac{0.0875}{2} \cdot \frac{37}{184} = 0.008797554$$

$$AI_T = \frac{0.0875}{2} \cdot \frac{136}{184} = 0.032336957$$

Implied Repo Rate

$$1.29 = \frac{0.98 \cdot 1.3136 + 0.032336957 + 0}{1 + R_{impl} \cdot \frac{99}{360}} - 0.008797554$$

$$R_{impl} = \left(\frac{0.98 \cdot 1.3136 + 0.032336957}{1.29 + 0.008797554} - 1 \right) \cdot \frac{360}{99}$$

$$R_{impl} = 0.058424398 \approx 5.84\%$$

Cost of Financing

$$COF = (1.29 + 0.008797554) \cdot 0.064 \cdot \frac{99}{360}$$

$$COF = 0.022858837$$

Coupon Income

$$CI = 0.032336957 - 0.008797554$$

$$CI = 0.023539403$$

Gross Basis

$$GB = 1.29 - (0.98 \cdot 1.3136)$$

$$GB = 0.002672$$

Gross Basis in 32nds

$$GB32 = GB \cdot 32$$

$$GB32 = 0.002672 \cdot 32 = 0.085504$$

Cost of Carry

$$COC = 0.023539403 - 0.022858837$$

$$COC = 0.000680566$$

Net Basis

$$NB = 0.002672 - 0.000680566$$

$$NB = 0.001991434$$

Net Basis in 32nds

$$NB32 = 0.001991434 \cdot 32 = 0.063725888$$

Example 2

U.S. Treasury Bond

Maturity Date:	5/15/2017
Settlement Date:	9/21/2000
Nominal Annual Coupon Rate:	8.75%
Price at Settlement Date:	126%
Delivery Date:	3/30/2001
Futures Price:	98%
Days in Year:	360
Conversion Factor:	1.2803

Calculate the Implied Repo Rate

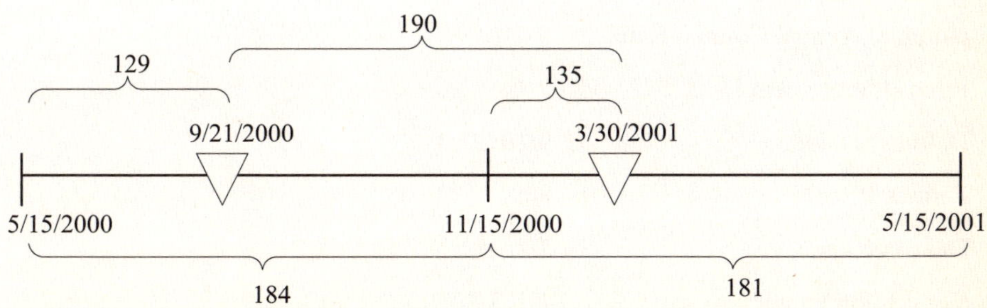

n = 1 (One coupon payment date between the settlement date and the delivery date.)

$$AI_S = \frac{0.0875}{2} \cdot \frac{129}{184} = 0.030672554$$

$$AI_D = \frac{0.0875}{2} \cdot \frac{135}{181} = 0.032631215$$

$$(1.26 + 0.030672554)\left(1 + R_{impl} \cdot \frac{190}{360}\right) =$$

$$= 0.98 \cdot 1.2803 + \frac{0.0875}{2}\left(1 + R_{impl} \cdot \frac{135}{360}\right) + 0.032631215$$

$$R_{impl} = \frac{0.98 \cdot 1.2803 + 0.04375 + 0.032631215 - (1.26 + 0.030672554)}{(1.26 + 0.030672554)\frac{190}{360} - 0.04375 \cdot \frac{135}{360}}$$

$$R_{impl} = 6.07758\%$$

Example 3

Spanish Government Bond, Dated Date after the Settlement Date

Maturity Date:	7/30/2011
Settlement Date:	9/28/2000
Dated Date:	7/30/2001
Issue Date:	9/19/2000
First Coupon Date:	7/30/2002
Nominal Annual Coupon Rate:	5.4%
Price at Settlement Date:	94%
Delivery Date:	9/19/2001
Futures Price:	86%
Days in Year:	360
Conversion Factor:	1.1119727
Repo Rate:	5%

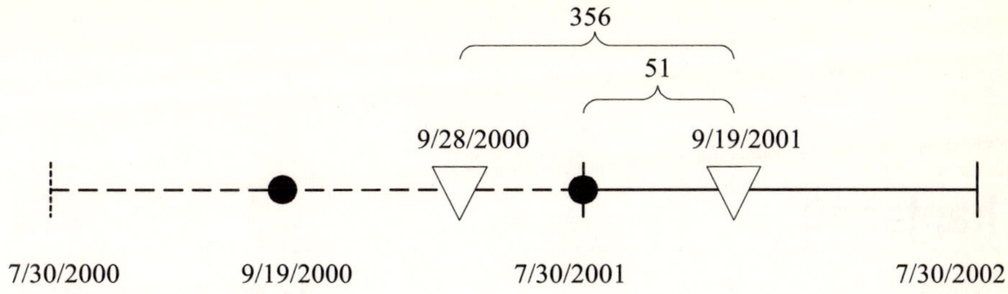

n = 0 (No coupon payments between the settlement date and the delivery date.)

$$AI_S = 0$$

$$AI_D = 0.054 \cdot \frac{51}{365} = 0.007545205$$

$$COF = 0.94 \cdot 0.05 \cdot \frac{356}{360} = 0.046477778$$

$$CI = 0.007545205$$

$$GB = 0.94 - 0.86 \cdot 1.1119727 = -0.016296522$$

$$COC = 0.007545205 - 0.046477778 = -0.038932573$$

$$NB = -0.016296522 + 0.038932573 = 0.022636051$$

$$R_{impl} = \left(\frac{0.86 \cdot 1.1119727 + 0.007545205}{0.94} - 1 \right) \frac{360}{356}$$

$$R_{impl} = 2.5648523\%$$

Chapter 10

U.S. Securities

Treasury Notes and Bonds

Conventions

- Quoted in prices
- Coupon payments are semiannual.
- The day count method is actual/actual (in period) for everything.
- The settlement date is one business day after the trade date.

In all examples that follow, we will assume that TX = 0, TXG = 0, and RV = 1.

Example 1

Normal last coupon period

The settlement date is in neither the first nor the last coupon period.

Maturity Date:	2/15/2010
Settlement Date:	6/5/2001
Nominal Annual Coupon Rate:	5.625%
Nominal Annual Yield to Maturity:	7%

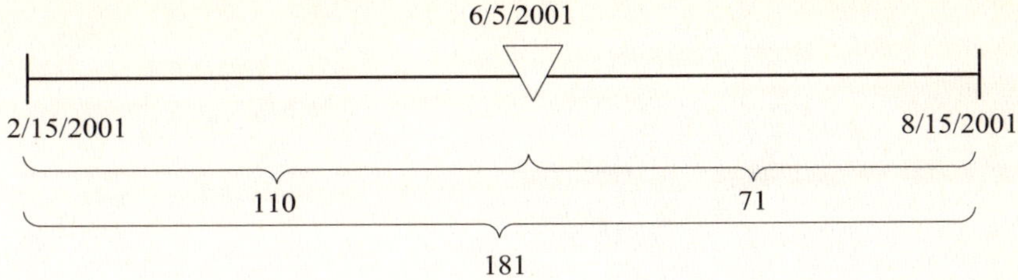

$$AIF = \frac{110}{181},\ FCF = 1,\ DF = \frac{71}{181},\ LCF = 1, \qquad LDF = 1,\ n = 16$$

$$AI = 0.0170925414$$

$$P = 0.9114396435$$

$$\frac{dP}{dY} = -6.0777659998$$

$$DUR = 6.7746578009$$

$$MD = 6.5455630926$$

$$CONV = 53.52252275$$

Example 2

Long First Coupon Period, Normal Last Coupon Period.

The settlement date is in the first coupon period, after the normal issue date.

Maturity Date:	11/15/2021
Settlement Date:	3/10/2002
Nominal Annual Coupon Rate:	15.75%
Nominal Annual Yield to Maturity:	12%
Dated Date:	10/7/2001
First Coupon Date:	5/15/2002

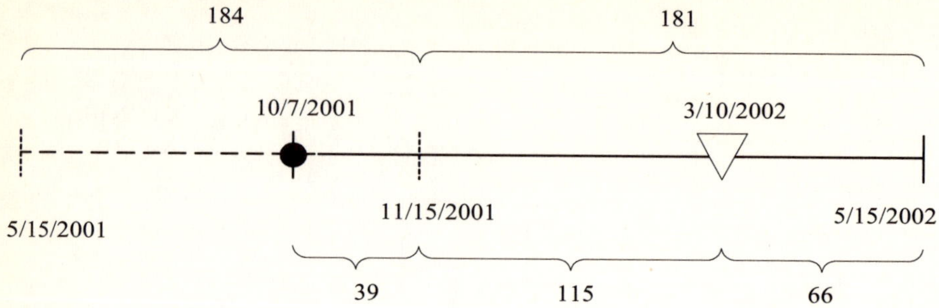

$$AIF = \frac{39}{184} + \frac{115}{181}$$

$$FCF = \frac{39}{184} + 1, \quad DF = \frac{66}{181}, \quad LCF = 1, \quad LDF = 1, n = 38$$

$$AI = \frac{0.1575}{2} \cdot \left(\frac{39}{184} + \frac{115}{181} \right) = 0.0667261065$$

$$P = 1.2800883773$$

$$\frac{dP}{dY} = -9.2557467957$$

$$DUR = 7.2846644593$$

$$MD = 6.8723249616$$

$$CONV = 82.99493648$$

Example 3

Normal Last Coupon Period.

The settlement date is in the last coupon period.

Maturity Date:	11/30/2001
Settlement Date:	6/5/2001
Nominal Annual Coupon Rate:	5.375%
Nominal Annual Yield to Maturity:	5.5%

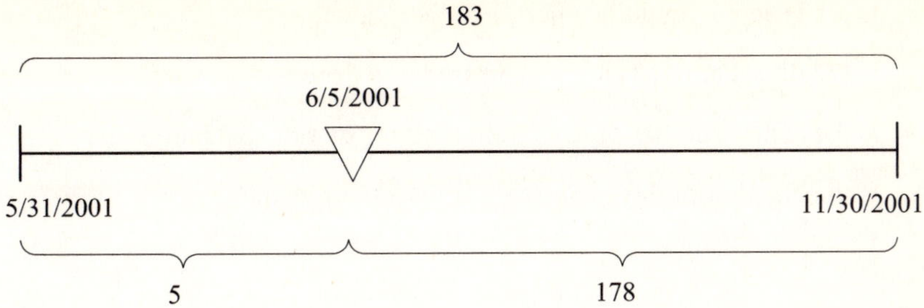

$$AIF = \frac{5}{183}, \quad LCF = 1, \quad DF = \frac{178}{183}$$

$$AI = \frac{0.05375}{2} \cdot \frac{5}{183} = 0.0007342896$$

$$P = \frac{1 + \frac{0.05375}{2}}{1 + \frac{0.055}{2} \cdot \frac{178}{183}} - 0.0007342896 = 0.9993887845$$

$$\frac{dP}{dY} = -0.4737271007$$

$$DUR = 0.4863387978$$

$$MD = 0.4736688044$$

$$CONV = 0.4487242725$$

Treasury Bills

Treasury bills are quoted in discount rates.

Discount in Dollars

$$D = d \cdot \frac{t_{SM}}{N_d}$$

D	is the **D**iscount in dollars per $1 of face value.
d	is the **d**iscount rate (yield), expressed as a decimal.
t_{SM}	is the actual number of days from **S**ettlement date to **M**aturity date.
N_d	is the **N**umber of **d**ays in a year for discount rate quote.

Price

$$P = 1 - D$$

P	is the **P**rice per $1 of face value.

Discount Rate

$$d = (1 - P) \cdot \frac{N_d}{t_{SM}}$$

Yields

1. 182 days or less from the settlement date to the maturity date.

- U.S. Treasury Yield

$$Y = \frac{N_{d1} \cdot d}{N_d - d \cdot t_{SM}}, \quad d = \frac{N_d \cdot Y}{N_{d1} + Y \cdot t_{SM}}$$

N_{d1} is the **N**umber of **d**ays in a year for yield calculation.

Note that for U.S. Treasury bills, $N_d = 360$ days and $N_{d1} = 365$ days. 366 should be used instead of 365 (for N_{d1}) if the issue date is after 2/28 of one year and before 3/1 of the next year that is a leap year.

- U.S. Government Bond equivalent yield (six months or less from the settlement date to the maturity date)

$$Y = \left(\frac{1}{P} - 1\right) \cdot \frac{2}{DF}, \quad P = \frac{1}{1 + \frac{Y}{2} \cdot DF}$$

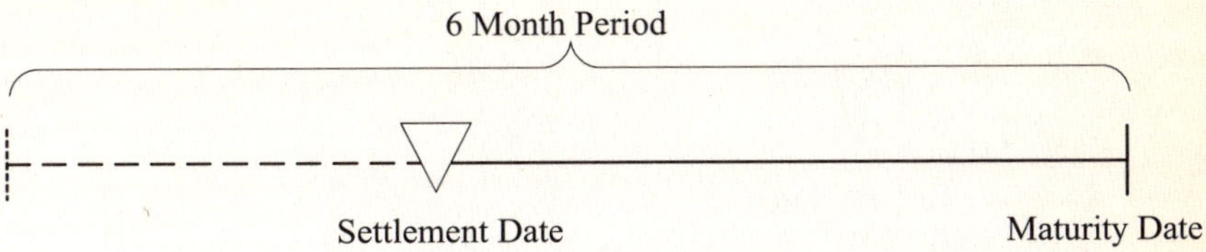

$$DF = \frac{\text{Actual number of days from settlement date to maturity date}}{\text{Actual number of days in a six - month period ending with maturity date}}$$

Note that the six-month period ending with maturity date means that the start of that period is the same day of the month, six months before maturity date or the end of month (if maturity date is end of month) six months before maturity date.

- Simple interest yield

$$Y = \frac{N_d \cdot d}{N_d - d \cdot t_{SM}} \quad , \quad d = \frac{N_d \cdot Y}{N_d + Y \cdot t_{SM}}$$

- Medium-term CD yield (six months or less from settlement date to maturity date).

$$Y = \frac{N_d \cdot d}{N_d - d \cdot t_{SM}} \quad , \quad d = \frac{N_d \cdot Y}{N_d + Y \cdot t_{SM}}$$

Other Calculations (with U.S. Treasury Yield Only)

- First derivative of price with respect to yield

$$\frac{dP}{dY} = P' = \frac{-N_{d1} \cdot t_{SM}}{\left(N_{d1} + Y \cdot t_{SM}\right)^2}$$

- Second derivative of price with respect to yield

$$\frac{d^2P}{dY^2} = P'' = \frac{2N_{d1} \cdot t_{SM}^2}{\left(N_{d1} + Y \cdot t_{SM}\right)^3}$$

- Duration

$$DUR = \frac{t_{SM}}{N_{d1}}$$

- Modified duration

$$MD = \frac{\left|\frac{dP}{dY}\right|}{P}$$

- Convexity

$$CONV = \frac{\frac{d^2P}{dY^2}}{P}$$

- Change in price (per \$100 of face value)
  per 1bp = 0.01% change in yield

$$PV01Y = \frac{\frac{dP}{dY}}{100}$$

per 1bp = 0.01% change in discount rate

$$PV01D = -\frac{t_{SM}}{100 \cdot N_d}$$

- Change in yield (as a percent)
  per 1bp = 0.01% change in price

$$YV01P = \frac{1}{10000 \cdot PV01Y}$$

per 1bp = 0.01% change in discount rate

$$YV01D = \frac{N_{d1} \cdot N_d}{100 \cdot \left(N_d - dt_{SM}\right)^2}$$

- Change in discount rate (as a percent)
  per 1bp = 0.01% change in price

$$DV01P = \frac{1}{10000 \cdot PV01D}$$

per 1bp = 0.01% change in yield

$$DV01Y = \frac{1}{10000 \cdot YV01D}$$

2. More than 182 days from the settlement date to the maturity date.

- U.S. Treasury Yield (street convention)

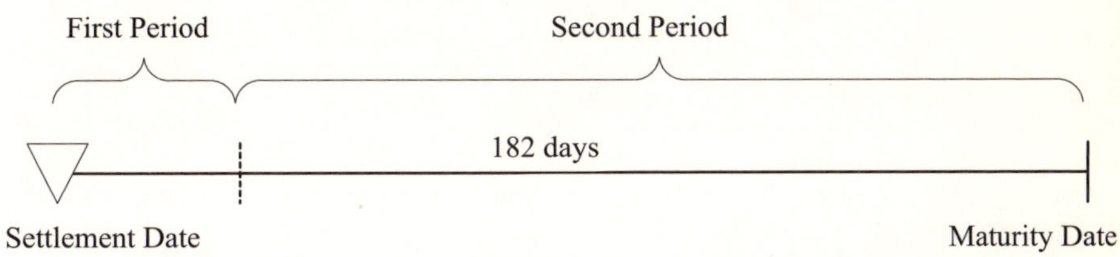

Simple interest in the first period, compound interest in the second period.

$$P = \frac{1}{\left(1+\frac{Y}{2}\right)\left[1+\frac{Y}{2}\left(\frac{2t_{SM}}{N_{d1}}-1\right)\right]}$$

$$Y = \frac{-\frac{2t_{SM}}{N_{d1}} + 2\sqrt{\left(\frac{t_{SM}}{N_{d1}}\right)^2 - \left(\frac{2t_{SM}}{N_{d1}}-1\right)\left(1-\frac{1}{P}\right)}}{\frac{2t_{SM}}{N_{d1}}-1}$$

Note that, for U.S. Treasury Bills, $N_{d1} = 365$ days. 366 should be used instead of 365 (for N_{d1}) if the issue date is after 2/28 of one year and before 3/1 of the next year that is a leap year.
Special Case: If $N_{d1} = 366$ and $t_{sm} = 183$, then use these formulas:

$$P = \frac{1}{1+\frac{Y}{2}}$$

$$Y = \left(\frac{1}{P}-1\right) \cdot 2$$

- U.S. government bond equivalent yield (more than six months from the settlement date to the maturity date)

$$Y = \left(\frac{1}{P^{\frac{1}{1+DF}}} - 1 \right) \cdot 2, \quad P = \frac{1}{\left(1 + \frac{Y}{2}\right)^{1+DF}}$$

- Simple interest yield

$$Y = \left(\frac{1}{P} - 1 \right) \cdot \frac{N_d}{t_{SM}}, \quad P = \frac{1}{1 + Y \frac{t_{SM}}{N_d}}$$

- Medium-term CD yield (more than six months from the settlement date to the maturity date).

$$Y = \frac{N_d \cdot \left[-(d_1 + d_2) + \sqrt{(d_1 + d_2)^2 - 4 \cdot d_1 \cdot d_2 \left(1 - \frac{1}{P}\right)} \right]}{2d_1d_2}$$

$$P = \frac{1}{\left(1 + Y \cdot \frac{d_1}{N_d}\right) \cdot \left(1 + Y \cdot \frac{d_2}{N_d}\right)}$$

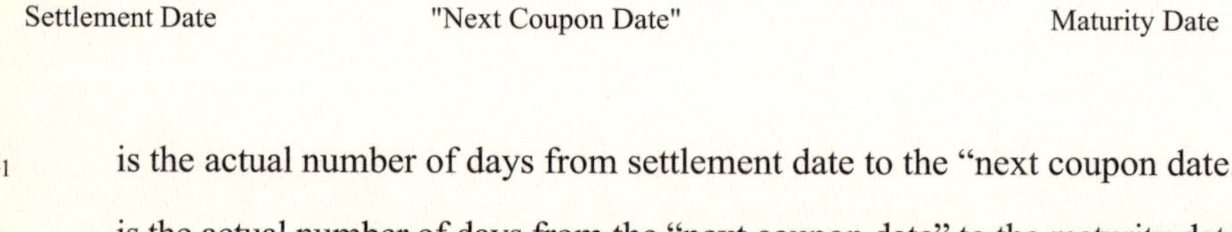

d_1 is the actual number of days from settlement date to the "next coupon date."

d_2 is the actual number of days from the "next coupon date" to the maturity date.

"Next Coupon Date" is the same day of the month, six months before maturity date or the end of the month (if the maturity date is at the end of the month), six months before the maturity date.

Other Calculations: (with U.S. Treasury Yield Only)

- First derivative of price with respect to yield

$$\frac{dP}{dY} = P' = -P^2\left[\frac{Y}{2}\left(\frac{2t_{SM}}{N_{d1}} - 1\right) + \frac{t_{SM}}{N_{d1}}\right]$$

- Second derivative of price with respect to yield

$$\frac{d^2P}{dY^2} = P'' = P'\left\{-\left(1+\frac{Y}{2}\right)^{-1} - \left[1+\frac{Y}{2}\left(\frac{2t_{SM}}{N_{d1}} - 1\right)\right]^{-1}\right.$$
$$\left.+\frac{1}{2}\left(\frac{2t_{SM}}{N_{d1}} - 1\right)\left[\frac{Y}{2}\left(\frac{2t_{SM}}{N_{d1}} - 1\right) + \frac{t_{SM}}{N_{d1}}\right]\right\}$$

- Duration

$$DUR = \frac{t_{SM}}{N_{d1}}$$

- Modified duration

$$MD = \frac{\left|\frac{dP}{dY}\right|}{P}$$

- Convexity

$$CONV = \frac{\frac{d^2P}{dY^2}}{P}$$

- Change in price (per \$100 of face value) per 1bp = 0.01% change in yield

$$PV01Y = \frac{\frac{dP}{dY}}{100}$$

per 1bp = 0.01% change in discount rate

$$\text{PV01D} = -\frac{t_{SM}}{100 \cdot N_d}$$

- Change in yield (as a percent)
  per 1bp = 0.01% change in price

$$\text{YV01P} = \frac{1}{10000 \cdot \text{PV01Y}}$$

per 1bp = 0.01% change in discount rate

$$\text{YV01D} = \frac{N_d \cdot t_{SM}}{100 \cdot \left(N_d - dt_{SM}\right)^2 \sqrt{\left(\frac{t_{SM}}{N_{d1}}\right)^2 - \left(\frac{2t_{SM}}{N_{d1}} - 1\right)\left(1 - \frac{1}{P}\right)}}$$

- Change in discount rate (as a percent)
  per 1bp = 0.01% change in price

$$\text{DV01P} = \frac{1}{10000 \cdot \text{PV01D}}$$

per 1bp = 0.01% change in yield

$$\text{DV01Y} = \frac{1}{10000 \cdot \text{YV01D}}$$

Example 1

Less than 182 days from the settlement date to the maturity date.

Maturity Date:	1/8/2002
Settlement Date:	8/6/2001
Discount Rate:	5.18%

$t_{SM} = 155$

$$P = 1 - 0.0518\frac{155}{360} = 0.9776972222$$

Treasury Yield

$$Y = \frac{365 \cdot 0.0518}{360 - 0.0518 \cdot 155} = 5.371749\%$$

U.S. government bond Equivalent Yield:

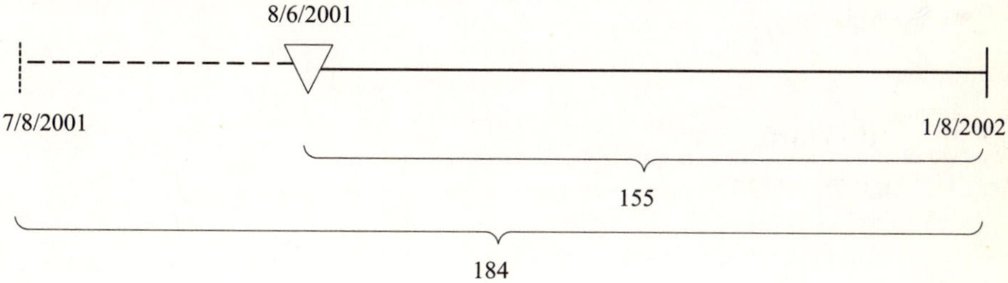

$$DF = \frac{155}{184}$$

$$Y = \left(\frac{1}{0.9776972222} - 1\right)\frac{2}{155} \cdot 184 = 5.415901\%$$

Simple Interest Yield:

$$Y = \frac{360 \cdot 0.0518}{360 - 0.0518 \cdot 155} = 5.29816\%$$

Medium-Term CD Yield:

$$Y = \frac{360 \cdot 0.0518}{360 - 0.0518 \cdot 155} = 5.29816\%$$

$$\frac{dP}{dY} = -\frac{365 \cdot 155}{(365 + 0.05371749 \cdot 155)^2} = -0.405927$$

$$\frac{d^2P}{dY^2} = \frac{2 \cdot 365 \cdot 155^2}{(365 + 0.05371749 \cdot 155)^3} = 0.3370705$$

$$\text{DUR} = \frac{155}{365} = 0.424658$$

$$\text{MD} = \frac{0.405927}{0.9776972222} = 0.4151868$$

$$\text{CONV} = \frac{0.3370705}{0.977697222} = 0.3447596$$

$$\text{PV01Y} = \frac{-0.405927}{100} = -0.00405927$$

$$\text{PV01D} = -\frac{155}{100 \cdot 360} = -0.00430556$$

$$\text{YV01P} = \frac{1}{10000(-0.00405927)} = -0.02463497$$

$$\text{YV01D} = \frac{365 \cdot 360}{100(360 - 0.0518 \cdot 155)^2} = 0.01060673$$

$$\text{DV01P} = \frac{1}{10000(-0.00430556)} = -0.02322578$$

$$\text{DV01Y} = \frac{1}{10000 \cdot 0.01060673} = 0.009427976$$

Example 2

More than 182 days from the settlement date to the maturity date.

Maturity Date: 7/23/2002

Settlement Date: 8/6/2001

Discount Rate: 5.23%

$t_{SM} = 351$

$$P = 1 - 0.0523 \frac{351}{360} = 0.9490075$$

Treasury Yield:

$$Y = \frac{-\frac{2 \cdot 351}{365} + 2\sqrt{\left(\frac{351}{365}\right)^2 - \left(\frac{2 \cdot 351}{365} - 1\right)\left(1 - \frac{1}{0.9490075}\right)}}{\frac{2 \cdot 351}{365} - 1}$$

$Y = 5.5145688\%$

U.S. government bond Equivalent Yield:

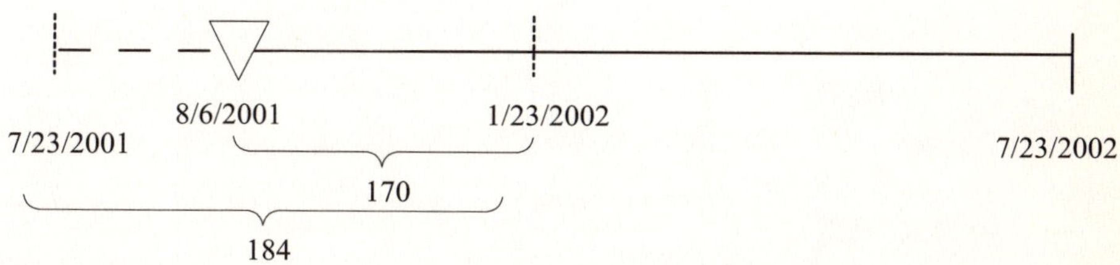

$$DF = \frac{170}{184}$$

$$Y = \left(\frac{1}{0.9490075^{\frac{1}{1+\frac{170}{184}}}} - 1 \right) \cdot 2 = 5.515529\%$$

Simple Interest Yield:

$$Y = \left(\frac{1}{0.9490075} - 1\right)\frac{360}{351} = 5.5110207\%$$

Medium-Term CD Yield:

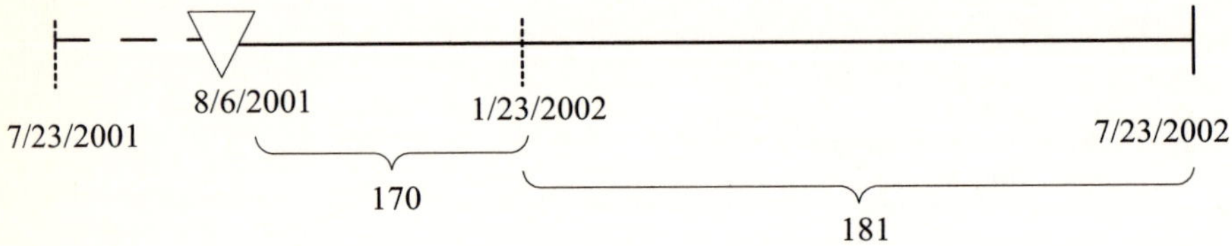

$$Y = \frac{360\left[-(170+181) + \sqrt{(170+181)^2 - 4\cdot 170\cdot 181\cdot\left(1 - \frac{1}{0.9490075}\right)}\right]}{2\cdot 170\cdot 181}$$

$$Y = 5.438984\%$$

$$\frac{dP}{dY} = -0.9490075^2\left[\frac{0.055145688}{2}\left(\frac{2\cdot 351}{365} - 1\right) + \frac{351}{365}\right]$$

$$\frac{dP}{dY} = -0.88899865$$

$$\frac{d^2P}{dY^2} = -0.88899865\left\{-\left(1 + \frac{0.055145688}{2}\right)^{-1}\right.$$

$$-\left[1 + \frac{0.055145688}{2}\left(\frac{2\cdot 351}{365} - 1\right)\right]^{-1}$$

$$\left. + \frac{1}{2}\left(\frac{2\cdot 351}{365} - 1\right)\left[\frac{0.055145688}{2}\left(\frac{2\cdot 351}{365} - 1\right) + \frac{351}{365}\right]\right\}$$

$$= 1.32696564$$

$$\mathrm{DUR} = \frac{351}{365} = 0.9616438$$

$$\mathrm{MD} = \frac{0.88899865}{0.9490075} = 0.9367667$$

$$\mathrm{CONV} = \frac{1.32696564}{0.9490075} = 1.3982668$$

$$\mathrm{PV01Y} = \frac{-0.88899865}{100} = -0.0088899865$$

$$\mathrm{PV01D} = -\frac{351}{100 \cdot 360} = -0.00975$$

$$\mathrm{YV01P} = \frac{1}{10000(-0.0088899865)} = -0.0112486$$

$$\mathrm{YV01D} = -\frac{360 \cdot 351}{100(360 - 0.0523 \cdot 351)^2 \sqrt{\left(\frac{351}{365}\right)^2 - \left(\frac{2 \cdot 351}{365} - 1\right)\left(1 - \frac{1}{0.9490075}\right)}}$$

$$\mathrm{YV01D} = 0.010967395$$

$$\mathrm{DV01P} = \frac{1}{10000(-0.00975)} = -0.0102564$$

$$\mathrm{DV01Y} = \frac{1}{10000 \cdot 0.010967395} = 0.009117934$$

STRIPS (Separately Traded Registered Interest and Principal Securities)

Everything is the same as for notes/bonds, with the coupon equal to zero.

Example 1

Maturity Date: 9/30/2004

Settlement Date: 10/14/2001

Nominal Annual Yield to Maturity: 6%

Yield Compounding Frequency: 2

$$DF = \frac{168}{182}, \qquad n = 4$$

$$P = \frac{1}{\left(1 + \frac{0.06}{2}\right)^{\frac{168}{182}+4+1}} = 0.839390656$$

Example 2

The settlement date is in the last coupon period.

Maturity Date: 2/15/2002

Settlement Date: 10/7/2001

Nominal Annual Yield to Maturity: 5%

Yield Compounding Frequency: 2

$$DF = \frac{131}{184}$$

$$P = \frac{1}{1 + \frac{0.05}{2} \cdot \frac{131}{184}} = 0.982512348$$

Corporate Securities

Bonds and Notes

Conventions

- Quoted in prices
- Coupon payments are semiannual.
- The day count method is 30/360 for everything.
- The settlement date is three business days after the trade date.

Combinations of Settlement Date, First and Last Coupon Periods for the Price/Yield, and Other Calculations

The numbers in the matrices below are numbers for the examples that follow.

- The settlement date coincides with the dated date:

		First Coupon Period		
		Normal	Short	Long
Last Coupon Period	Normal	1	2	3
	Short	4	5	6
	Long	7	8	9

- The settlement date is in the first coupon period:

<table>
<tr><td colspan="2" rowspan="3"></td><td colspan="5">First Coupon Period</td></tr>
<tr><td rowspan="2">Normal</td><td rowspan="2">Short</td><td colspan="3">Long</td></tr>
<tr><td>Sett'l before normal issue</td><td>Sett'l on normal issue</td><td>Sett'l after normal issue</td></tr>
<tr><td rowspan="3">Last Coupon Period</td><td>Normal</td><td>10</td><td>11</td><td>12</td><td>13</td><td>14</td></tr>
<tr><td>Short</td><td>15</td><td>16</td><td>17</td><td>18</td><td>19</td></tr>
<tr><td>Long</td><td>20</td><td>21</td><td>22</td><td>23</td><td>24</td></tr>
</table>

- The settlement date is in neither the first nor the last coupon period.

  The first coupon period is not important for calculation.

  25. Normal last coupon period
  26. Short last coupon period
  27. Long last coupon period

- The settlement date coincides with the coupon date (except the last coupon date).

  The first coupon period is not important for calculation.

  28. Normal last coupon period
  29. Short last coupon period
  30. Long last coupon period

- The settlement date is in the last coupon period and coincides with the last coupon date.

  The first coupon period is not important for calculation.

  31. Normal last coupon period
  32. Short last coupon period
  33. Long last coupon period

- The settlement date is in the last coupon period and does not coincide with the last coupon date.

  The first coupon period is not important for calculation.

  34. Normal last coupon period
  35. Short last coupon period
  36. Long last coupon period, settlement date is before normal maturity date
  37. Long last coupon period, settlement date coincides with normal maturity date
  38. Long last coupon period, settlement date is after normal maturity date

- The coupon date is on 2/28 (or 2/29 in a leap year). The settlement date is on:

  39. 8/29, leap year
  40. 8/30, leap year
  41. 8/31, leap year
  42. 2/27, leap year
  43. 2/28, leap year
  44. 2/29, leap year
  45. 2/28, non–leap year
  46. 3/1, non–leap year

In all examples that follow, we will assume that **TX = 0**, **TXG = 0** and **RV = 1**.

Example 1

Normal first and last coupon period and settlement date coincides with dated date.

Maturity Date:	5/31/2007
Settlement Date:	11/30/2000
Dated Date:	11/30/2000
Nominal Annual Coupon Rate:	9%
Nominal Annual Yield to Maturity:	10%

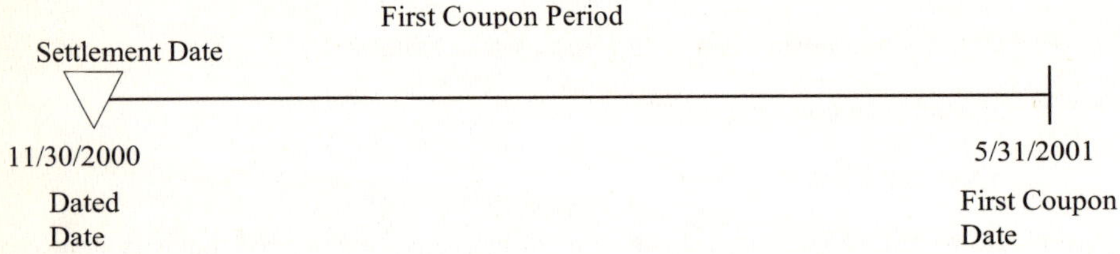

AIF = 0

FCF = 1

DF = 1

LCF = 1

LDF = 1

n = 11

AI = 0

P = 0.9530321351

$$\frac{dP}{dY} = -4.555402014$$

DUR = 5.018899089

MD = 4.779903894

CONV = 28.99989745

Example 2

Short first coupon period, normal last coupon period, and settlement date coincides with dated date.

Maturity Date: 6/30/2007

Settlement Date: 9/29/2000

Dated Date: 9/29/2000

First Coupon Date: 12/31/2000

Nominal Annual Coupon Rate: 9%

Nominal Annual Yield to Maturity: 10%

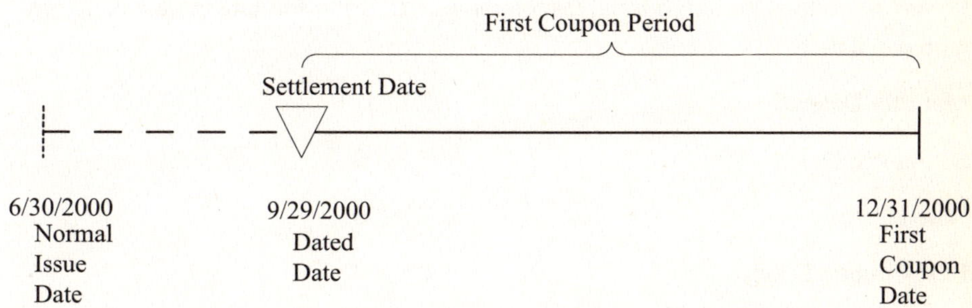

$$\text{AIF} = 0$$

$$\text{FCF} = \frac{92}{180}$$

$$\text{DF} = \frac{92}{180}$$

$$\text{LCF} = 1$$

$$\text{LDF} = 1$$

$$n = 12$$

$$\text{AI} = 0$$

$$P = 0.9519936038$$

$$\frac{dP}{dY} = -4.674909931$$

$$\text{DUR} = 5.156185302$$

$$\text{MD} = 4.910652668$$

$$\text{CONV} = 30.76355268$$

Example 3

Long first coupon period, normal last coupon period, and settlement date coincides with dated date.

Maturity Date:	7/20/2010
Settlement Date:	6/7/2000
Dated Date:	6/7/2000
First Coupon Date:	1/20/2001
Nominal Annual Coupon Rate:	9%
Nominal Annual Yield to Maturity:	10%

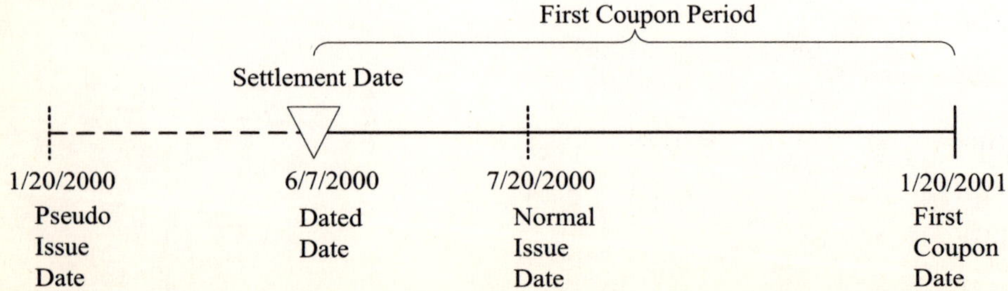

$$AIF = 0$$

$$FCF = \frac{43}{180} + 1 = \frac{223}{180}$$

$$DF = \frac{43}{180} + 1 = \frac{223}{180}$$

$$LCF = 1$$

$$LDF = 1$$

$$n = 18$$

$$AI = 0$$

$$P = 0.9369426861$$

$$\frac{dP}{dY} = -6.009195762$$

$$DUR = 6.734302582$$

$$MD = 6.413621506$$

$$CONV = 55.45428482$$

Example 4

Normal first coupon period, short last coupon period, and settlement date coincides with dated date.

Maturity Date:	6/15/2008
Settlement Date:	4/30/2000
Dated Date:	4/30/2000
Last Coupon Date:	4/30/2008

Nominal Annual Coupon Rate: 9%

Nominal Annual Yield to Maturity: 10%

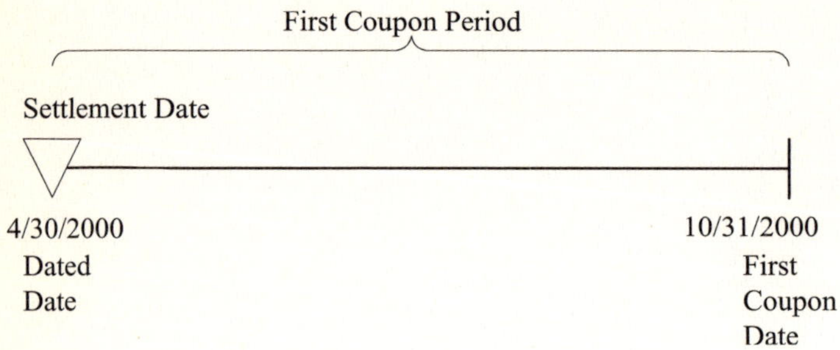

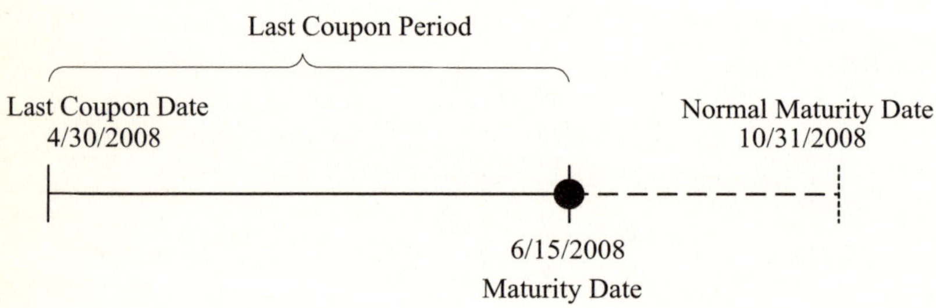

$$\text{AIF} = 0$$

$$\text{FCF} = 1$$

$$\text{DF} = 1$$

$$\text{LCF} = \frac{45}{180}$$

$$\text{LDF} = \frac{45}{180}$$

$$n = 15$$

$$AI = 0$$

$$P = 0.9453485322$$

$$\frac{dP}{dY} = -5.276990941$$

$$DUR = 5.861161570$$

$$MD = 5.582058638$$

$$CONV = 40.59121113$$

Example 5

Short first coupon period, short last coupon period, and settlement date coincides with dated date.

Maturity Date:	6/15/2008
Settlement Date:	7/20/2000
Dated Date:	7/20/2000
First Coupon Date:	10/31/2000
Last Coupon Date:	4/30/2008
Nominal Annual Coupon Rate:	9%
Nominal Annual Yield to Maturity:	10%

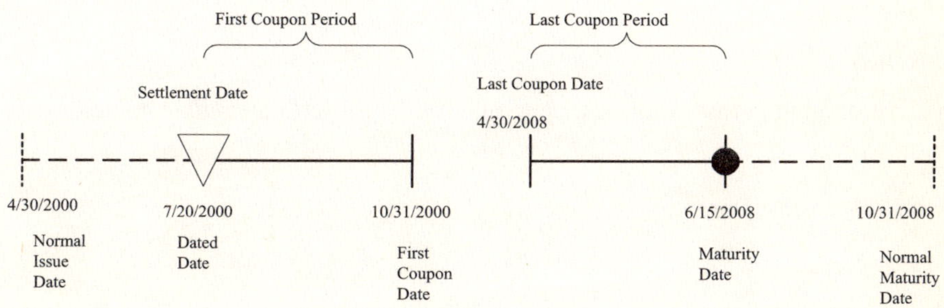

$$AIF = 0$$

$$FCF = \frac{101}{180}$$

$$DF = \frac{101}{180}$$

$$LCF = \frac{45}{180}$$

$$LDF = \frac{45}{180}$$

$$n = 15$$

$$AI = 0$$

$$P = 0.9465933656$$

$$\frac{dP}{dY} = -5.184224320$$

$$DUR = 5.750553230$$

$$MD = 5.476717362$$

$$CONV = 38.97363026$$

Example 6

Long first coupon period, short last coupon period, and settlement date coincides with dated date.

Maturity Date:	6/15/2008
Settlement Date:	3/22/2000
Dated Date:	3/22/2000
First Coupon Date:	10/31/2000

Last Coupon Date:	4/30/2008
Nominal Annual Coupon Rate:	9%
Nominal Annual Yield to Maturity:	10%

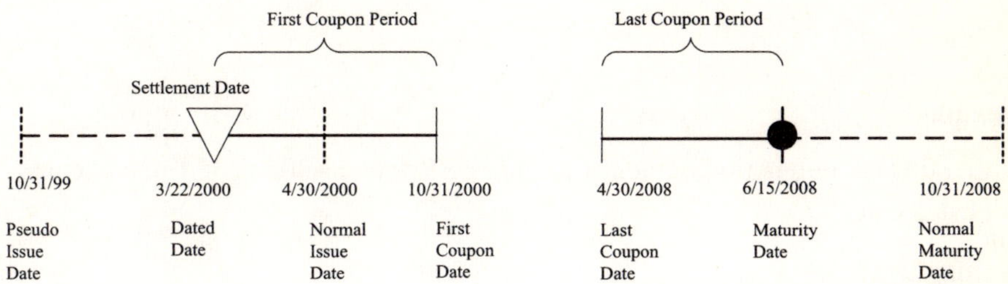

$$\text{AIF} = 0$$

$$\text{FCF} = \frac{38}{180} + 1 = \frac{218}{180}$$

$$\text{DF} = \frac{38}{180} + 1 = \frac{218}{180}$$

$$\text{LCF} = \frac{45}{180}$$

$$\text{LDF} = \frac{45}{180}$$

$$n = 15$$

$$\text{AI} = 0$$

$$P = 0.9446161858$$

$$\frac{dP}{dY} = -5.322141788$$

DUR = 5.915893631

MD = 5.634184411

CONV = 41.38127202

Example 7

Normal first coupon period, long last coupon period, and settlement date coincides with dated date.

Maturity Date:	6/15/2008
Settlement Date:	10/31/2000
Dated Date:	10/31/2000
Last Coupon Date:	10/31/2007
Nominal Annual Coupon Rate:	9%
Nominal Annual Yield to Maturity:	10%

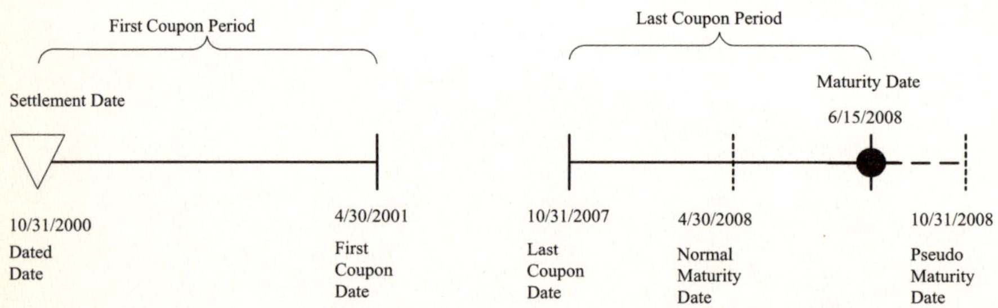

AIF = 0

FCF = 1

DF = 1

$$\text{LCF} = \frac{45}{180} + 1 = \frac{225}{180}$$

$$\text{LDF} = \frac{45}{180} + 1 = \frac{225}{180}$$

$$n = 13$$

$$\text{AI} = 0$$

$$P = 0.9473535374$$

$$\frac{dP}{dY} = -5.068837419$$

$$\text{DUR} = 5.618049736$$

$$\text{MD} = 5.350523558$$

$$\text{CONV} = 36.98523486$$

Example 8

Short first coupon period, long last coupon period, and settlement date coincides with dated date.

Maturity Date:	6/15/2008
Settlement Date:	7/20/2000
Dated Date:	7/20/2000
First Coupon Date:	10/31/2000
Last Coupon Date:	10/31/2007
Nominal Annual Coupon Rate:	9%
Nominal Annual Yield to Maturity:	10%

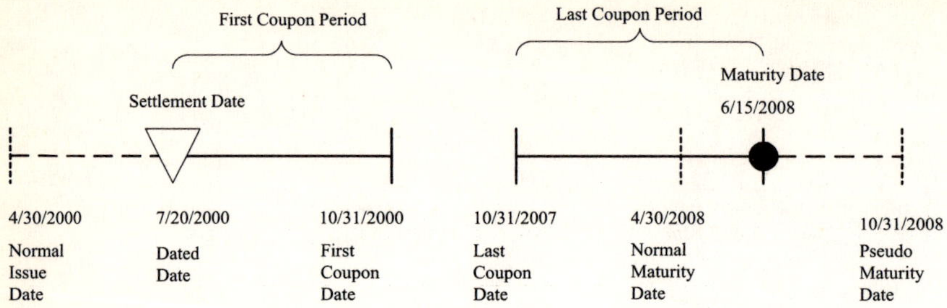

$$\text{AIF} = 0$$

$$\text{FCF} = \frac{101}{180}$$

$$\text{DF} = \frac{101}{180}$$

$$\text{LCF} = \frac{45}{180} + 1 = \frac{225}{180}$$

$$\text{LDF} = \frac{45}{180} + 1 = \frac{225}{180}$$

$$\text{n} = 14$$

$$\text{AI} = 0$$

$$\text{P} = 0.9463380309$$

$$\frac{\text{dP}}{\text{dY}} = -5.184809168$$

$$\text{DUR} = 5.752753718$$

$$\text{MD} = 5.478813065$$

$$\text{CONV} = 39.00872589$$

Example 9

Long first coupon period, long last coupon period, and settlement date coincides with dated date.

Maturity Date:	6/15/2008
Settlement Date:	3/22/2000
Dated Date:	3/22/2000
First Coupon Date:	10/31/2000
Last Coupon Date:	10/31/2007
Nominal Annual Coupon Rate:	9%
Nominal Annual Yield to Maturity:	10%

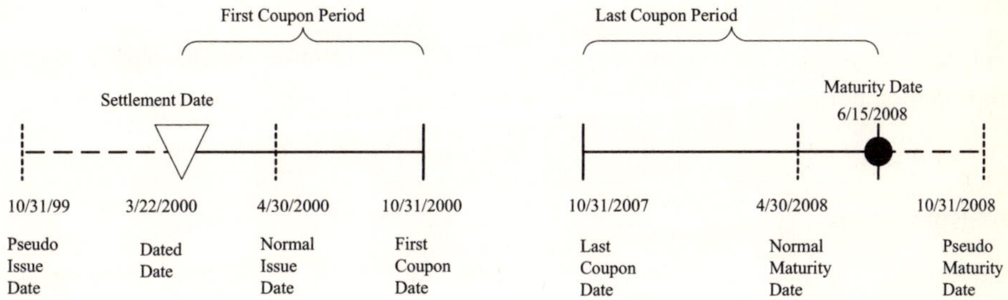

$$AIF = 0$$

$$FCF = \frac{38}{180} + 1 = \frac{218}{180}$$

$$DF = \frac{38}{180} + 1 = \frac{218}{180}$$

$$LCF = \frac{45}{180} + 1 = \frac{225}{180}$$

$$LDF = \frac{45}{180} + 1 = \frac{225}{180}$$

$$n = 14$$

$$AI = 0$$

$$P = 0.9443688216$$

$$\frac{dP}{dY} = -5.322631814$$

$$DUR = 5.917988054$$

$$MD = 5.636179099$$

$$CONV = 41.41628136$$

Example 10

Normal first coupon period, normal last coupon period, and settlement date is in the first coupon period.

Maturity Date:	4/30/2008
Settlement Date:	12/15/2000
Dated Date:	10/31/2000
Nominal Annual Coupon Rate:	9%
Nominal Annual Yield to Maturity:	10%

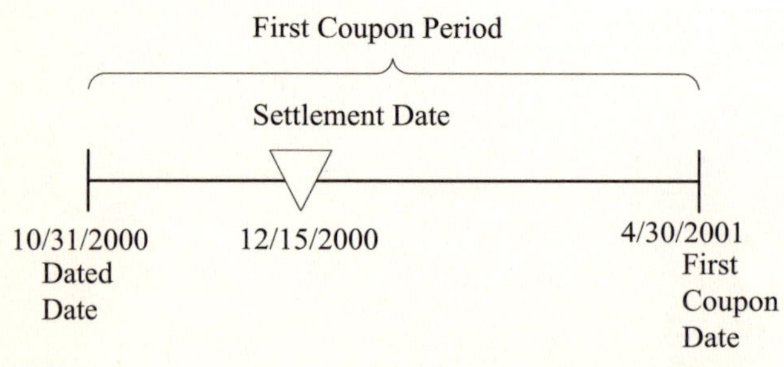

$$AIF = \frac{45}{180}$$

$$FCF = 1$$

$$DF = \frac{135}{180}$$

$$LCF = 1$$

$$LDF = 1$$

$$n = 13$$

$$AI = 0.01125$$

$$P = 0.9484870363$$

$$\frac{dP}{dY} = -4.961713607$$

$$DUR = 5.428361198$$

$$MD = 5.169867807$$

$$CONV = 34.75937694$$

Example 11

Short first coupon period, normal last coupon period, and settlement date is in the first coupon period.

Maturity Date:	10/31/2002
Settlement Date:	8/31/2000
Dated Date:	6/15/2000
First Coupon Date:	10/31/2000
Nominal Annual Coupon Rate:	11.25%
Nominal Annual Yield to Maturity:	11%

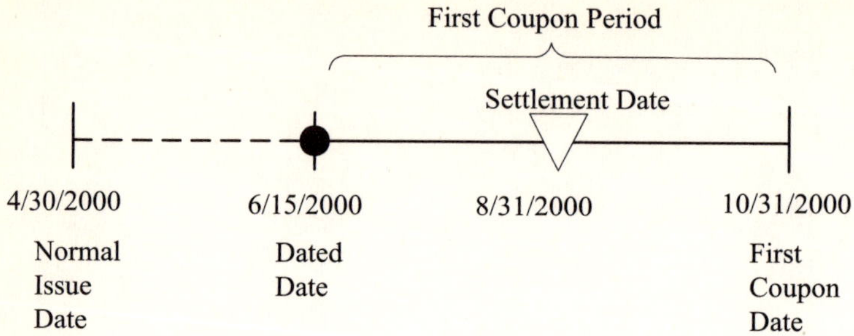

$$AIF = \frac{76}{180}$$

$$FCF = \frac{136}{180}$$

$$DF = \frac{60}{180}$$

$$LCF = 1$$

$$LDF = 1$$

$$n = 3$$

$$AI = 0.02375$$

$$P = 1.004613561$$

$$\frac{dP}{dY} = -1.888996191$$

$$DUR = 1.937924540$$

$$MD = 1.836895299$$

$$CONV = 4.500244269$$

Example 12

Long first coupon period, normal last coupon period, and settlement date is in the first coupon period before normal issue date.

Maturity Date:	10/31/2005
Settlement Date:	3/1/2001
Dated Date:	2/15/2001
First Coupon Date:	10/31/2001
Nominal Annual Coupon Rate:	9.875%
Nominal Annual Yield to Maturity:	11%

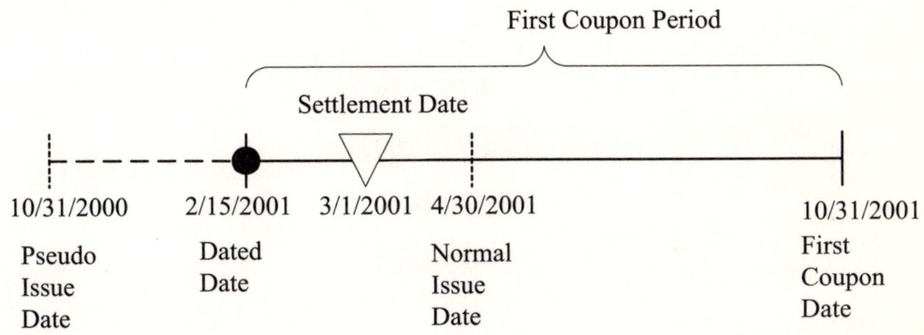

$$\text{AIF} = \frac{16}{180}$$

$$\text{FCF} = \frac{75}{180} + 1 = \frac{255}{180}$$

$$\text{DF} = \frac{59}{180} + 1 = \frac{239}{180}$$

$$\text{LCF} = 1$$

$$\text{LDF} = 1$$

$$n = 7$$

$$\text{AI} = 0.00438888889$$

$$P = 0.9589500975$$

$$\frac{dP}{dY} = -3.489775644$$

$$DUR = 3.821825293$$

$$MD = 3.622583216$$

$$CONV = 16.49895191$$

Example 13

Long first coupon period, normal last coupon period, and settlement date is on normal issue date.

Maturity Date:	5/15/2010
Settlement Date:	11/15/2002
Dated Date:	9/1/2002
First Coupon Date:	5/15/2003
Nominal Annual Coupon Rate:	8%
Nominal Annual Yield to Maturity:	7.5%

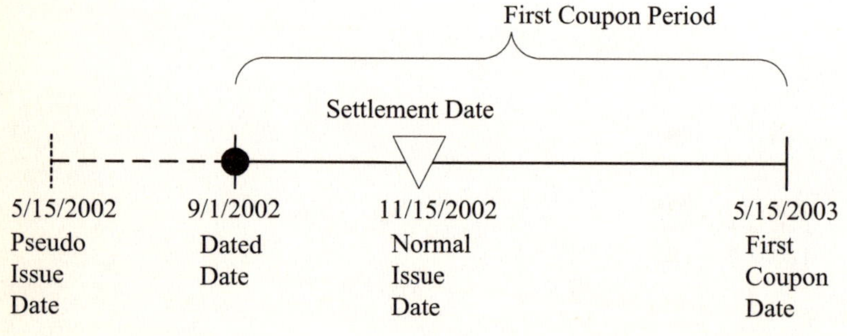

$$AIF = \frac{74}{180}$$

$$FCF = \frac{74}{180} + 1 = \frac{254}{180}$$

$$DF = 1$$

$$LCF = 1$$

$$LDF = 1$$

$$n = 13$$

$$AI = 0.01644444444$$

$$P = 1.027693863$$

$$\frac{dP}{dY} = -5.765028838$$

$$DUR = 5.728376573$$

$$MD = 5.521326817$$

$$CONV = 38.715899505$$

Example 14

Long first coupon period, normal last coupon period, and settlement date is in the first coupon period after normal issue date.

Maturity Date:	11/30/2003
Settlement Date:	7/10/2000
Dated Date:	3/15/2000
First Coupon Date:	11/30/2000
Nominal Annual Coupon Rate:	9.875%
Nominal Annual Yield to Maturity:	11%

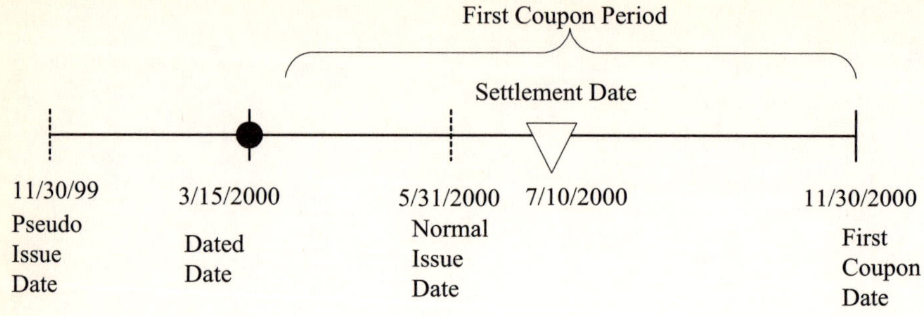

$$AIF = \frac{76}{180} + \frac{40}{180} = \frac{116}{180}$$

$$FCF = \frac{76}{180} + 1 = \frac{256}{180}$$

$$DF = \frac{140}{180}$$

$$LCF = 1$$

$$LDF = 1$$

$$n = 5$$

$$AI = 0.03181944444$$

$$P = 0.967797179$$

$$\frac{dP}{dY} = -2.721642223$$

$$DUR = 2.872433769$$

$$MD = 2.722686037$$

$$CONV = 9.537853627$$

Example 15

Normal first coupon period, short last coupon period, and settlement date is in the first coupon period.

Maturity Date:	6/15/2008
Settlement Date:	12/13/2000
Dated Date:	10/31/2000
Last Coupon Date:	4/30/2008
Nominal Annual Coupon Rate:	9%
Nominal Annual Yield to Maturity:	10%

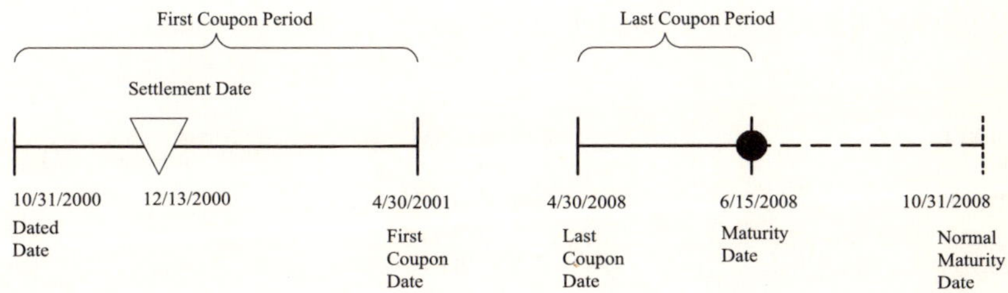

$$AIF = \frac{43}{180}$$

$$FCF = 1$$

$$DF = \frac{137}{180}$$

$$LCF = \frac{45}{180}$$

$$LDF = \frac{45}{180}$$

$$n = 14$$

$$AI = 0.01075$$

$$P = 0.9479754456$$

$$\frac{dP}{dY} = -5.018522102$$

$$DUR = 5.496305779$$

$$MD = 5.234576932$$

$$CONV = 35.692042065$$

Example 16

Short first and last coupon period, and settlement date is in the first coupon period.

Maturity Date:	11/1/2003
Settlement Date:	3/31/2001
Dated Date:	2/20/2001
First Coupon Date:	6/1/2001
Last Coupon Date:	6/1/2003
Nominal Annual Coupon Rate:	13.375%
Nominal Annual Yield to Maturity:	11%

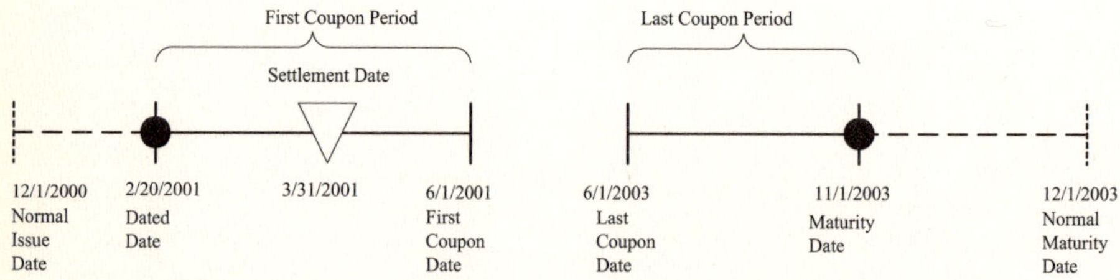

$$AIF = \frac{41}{180}$$

$$FCF = \frac{101}{180}$$

$$DF = \frac{60}{180}$$

$$LCF = \frac{150}{180}$$

$$LDF = \frac{150}{180}$$

$$n = 4$$

$$AI = 0.01523263889$$

$$P = 1.052487069$$

$$\frac{dP}{dY} = -2.268113691$$

$$DUR = 2.241093731$$

$$MD = 2.124259460$$

$$CONV = 5.934609807$$

Example 17

Long first coupon period, short last coupon period, and settlement date is in the first coupon period before the normal issue date.

Maturity Date:	7/20/2005
Settlement Date:	3/1/2001
Dated Date:	2/15/2001

First Coupon Date:	10/15/2001
Last Coupon Date:	4/15/2005
Nominal Annual Coupon Rate:	9.875%
Nominal Annual Yield to Maturity:	11%

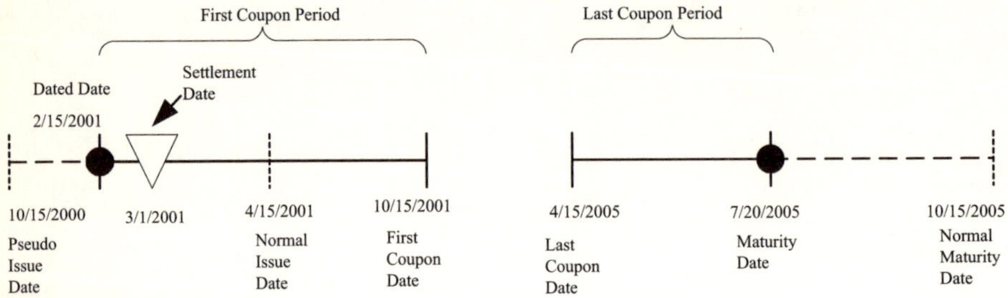

$$\text{AIF} = \frac{16}{180}$$

$$\text{FCF} = \frac{60}{180} + 1 = \frac{240}{180}$$

$$\text{DF} = \frac{44}{180} + 1 = \frac{224}{180}$$

$$\text{LCF} = \frac{95}{180}$$

$$\text{LDF} = \frac{95}{180}$$

$$n = 7$$

$$\text{AI} = 0.004388888889$$

$$\text{P} = 0.9612109221$$

$$\frac{dP}{dY} = -3.329221819$$

$$DUR = 3.637458272$$

$$MD = 3.447827746$$

$$CONV = 14.92715586$$

Example 18

Long first coupon period, short last coupon period, and settlement date is on the normal issue date.

Maturity Date:	4/1/2010
Settlement Date:	11/15/2002
Dated Date:	9/1/2002
First Coupon Date:	5/15/2003
Last Coupon Date:	11/15/2009
Nominal Annual Coupon Rate:	8%
Nominal Annual Yield to Maturity:	7.5%

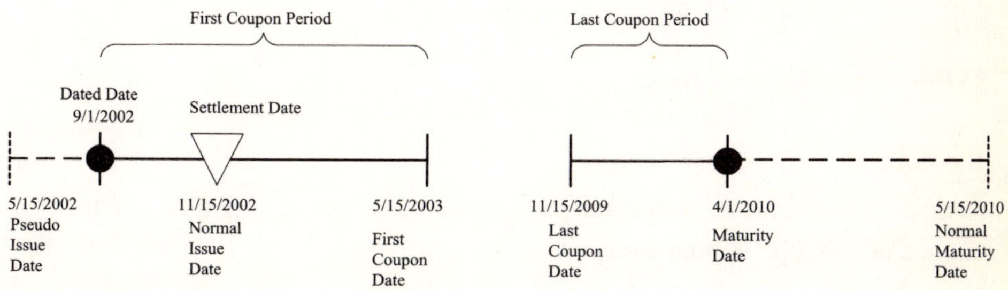

$$AIF = \frac{74}{180}$$

$$FCF = \frac{74}{180} + 1 = \frac{254}{180}$$

$$DF = 1$$

$$LCF = \frac{136}{180}$$

$$LDF = \frac{136}{180}$$

$$n = 13$$

$$AI = 0.01644444444$$

$$P = 1.027426175$$

$$\frac{dP}{dY} = -5.692595286$$

$$DUR = 5.657854049$$

$$MD = 5.453353300$$

$$CONV = 37.71052363$$

Example 19

Long first coupon period, short last coupon period, and settlement date is in the first coupon period after normal issue date.

Maturity Date:	7/20/2005
Settlement Date:	7/11/20001
Dated Date:	2/15/2001
First Coupon Date:	10/15/2001
Last Coupon Date:	4/15/2005

Nominal Annual Coupon Rate: 11%

Nominal Annual Yield to Maturity: 9.75%

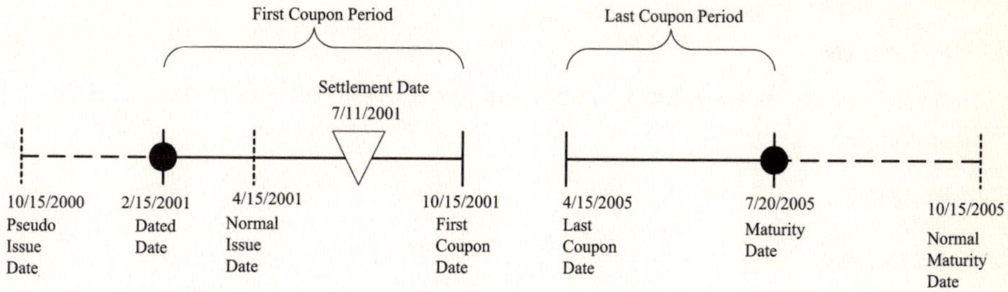

$$\text{AIF} = \frac{60}{180} + \frac{86}{180} = \frac{146}{180}$$

$$\text{FCF} = \frac{60}{180} + 1 = \frac{240}{180}$$

$$\text{DF} = \frac{94}{180}$$

$$\text{LCF} = \frac{95}{180}$$

$$\text{LDF} = \frac{95}{180}$$

$$n = 7$$

$$\text{AI} = 0.044611111$$

$$P = 1.040254147$$

$$\frac{dP}{dY} = -3.354129434$$

$$\text{DUR} = 3.242470176$$

MD = 3.091747487

CONV = 12.488453

Example 20

Normal first coupon period, long last coupon period, and settlement date is in the first coupon period.

Maturity Date:	6/15/2008
Settlement Date:	12/15/2000
Dated Date:	10/31/2000
Last Coupon Date:	10/31/2007
Nominal Annual Coupon Rate:	9%
Nominal Annual Yield to Maturity:	10%

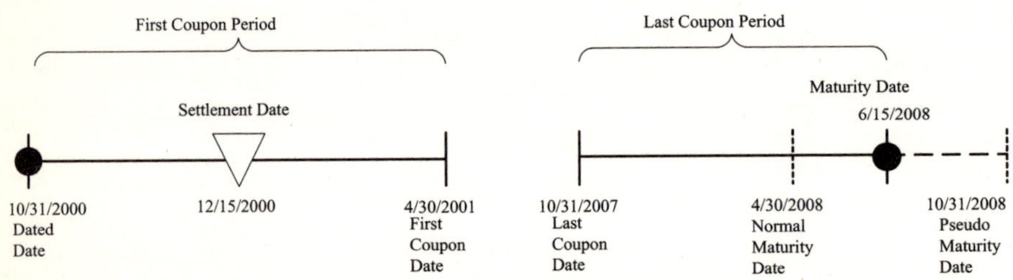

$$\text{AIF} = \frac{45}{180}$$

$$\text{FCF} = 1$$

$$\text{DF} = \frac{135}{180}$$

$$\text{LCF} = \frac{45}{180} + 1 = \frac{225}{180}$$

$$\text{LDF} = \frac{45}{180} + 1 = \frac{225}{180}$$

$$n = 13$$

$$\text{AI} = 0.01125$$

$$P = 0.9477296821$$

$$\frac{dP}{dY} = -5.016879132$$

$$\text{DUR} = 5.493049736$$

$$\text{MD} = 5.231475939$$

$$\text{CONV} = 35.66878367$$

Example 21

Short first coupon period, long last coupon period, and settlement date is in the first coupon period.

Maturity Date:	6/15/2009
Settlement Date:	9/13/2001
Dated Date:	7/20/2001
First Coupon Date:	10/31/2001
Last Coupon Date:	10/31/2008
Nominal Annual Coupon Rate:	9%
Nominal Annual Yield to Maturity:	10%

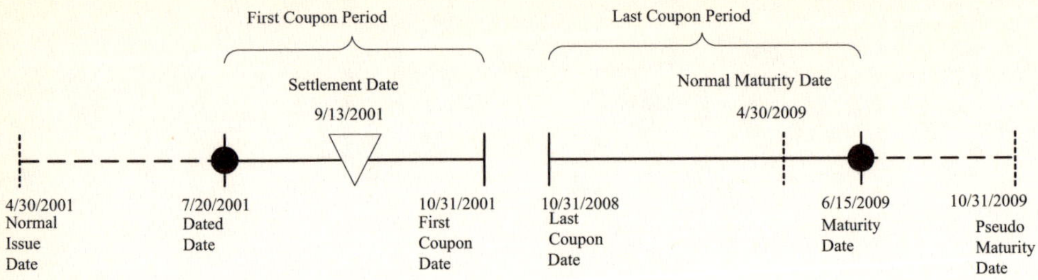

$$AIF = \frac{53}{180}$$

$$FCF = \frac{101}{180}$$

$$DF = \frac{48}{180}$$

$$LCF = \frac{45}{180} + 1 = \frac{225}{180}$$

$$LDF = \frac{45}{180} + 1 = \frac{225}{180}$$

$$n = 14$$

$$AI = 0.01325$$

$$P = 0.9467812390$$

$$\frac{dP}{dY} = -5.125224140$$

$$DUR = 5.605531496$$

$$MD = 5.338601425$$

$$CONV = 37.42523101$$

Example 22

Long first coupon period, long last coupon period, and settlement date is in the first coupon period before the normal issue date.

Maturity Date:	6/15/2009
Settlement Date:	4/11/2001
Dated Date:	3/22/2001
First Coupon Date:	10/31/2001
Last Coupon Date:	10/31/2008
Nominal Annual Coupon Rate:	9%
Nominal Annual Yield to Maturity:	10%

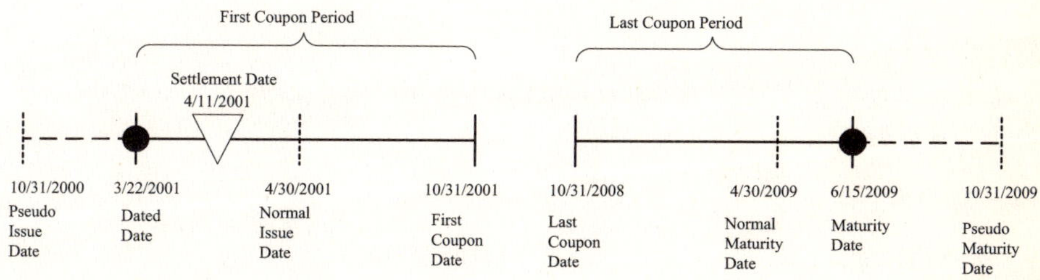

$$\text{AIF} = \frac{19}{180}$$

$$\text{FCF} = \frac{38}{180} + 1 = \frac{218}{180}$$

$$\text{DF} = \frac{19}{180} + 1 = \frac{199}{180}$$

$$\text{LCF} = \frac{45}{180} + 1 = \frac{225}{180}$$

$$\text{LDF} = \frac{45}{180} + 1 = \frac{225}{180}$$

n = 14

AI = 0.00475

P = 0.9444949353

$$\frac{dP}{dY} = -5.302401094$$

DUR = 5.865210276

MD = 5.585914548

CONV = 40.82827237

Example 23

Long first coupon period, long last coupon period, and settlement date is on the normal issue date.

Maturity Date:	7/1/2010
Settlement Date:	11/15/2002
Dated Date:	9/1/2002
First Coupon Date:	5/15/2003
Last Coupon Date:	11/15/2009
Nominal Annual Coupon Rate:	8%
Nominal Annual Yield to Maturity:	7.5%

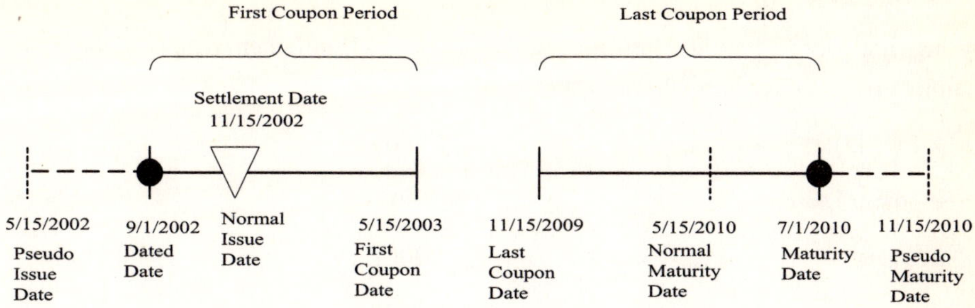

$$AIF = \frac{74}{180}$$

$$FCF = \frac{74}{180} + 1 = \frac{254}{180}$$

$$DF = 1$$

$$LCF = \frac{46}{180} + 1 = \frac{226}{180}$$

$$LDF = \frac{46}{180} + 1 = \frac{226}{180}$$

$$n = 13$$

$$AI = 0.01644444444$$

$$P = 1.027917253$$

$$\frac{dP}{dY} = -5.840407119$$

$$DUR = 5.802034295$$

$$MD = 5.592322212$$

$$CONV = 39.78343722$$

Example 24

Long first coupon period, long last coupon period, and settlement date is in the first coupon period after normal issue date.

Maturity Date:	6/15/2009
Settlement Date:	6/8/2001
Dated Date:	3/22/2001
First Coupon Date:	10/31/2001
Last Coupon Date:	10/31/2008
Nominal Annual Coupon Rate:	9%
Nominal Annual Yield to Maturity:	10%

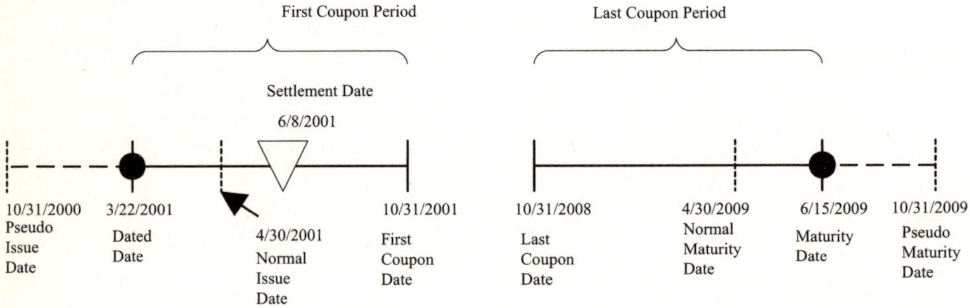

$$AIF = \frac{38}{180} + \frac{38}{180} = \frac{76}{180}$$

$$FCF = \frac{38}{180} + 1 = \frac{218}{180}$$

$$DF = \frac{142}{180}$$

$$LCF = \frac{45}{180} + 1 = \frac{225}{180}$$

$$\text{LDF} = \frac{45}{180} + 1 = \frac{225}{180}$$

$$n = 14$$

$$\text{AI} = 0.019$$

$$P = 0.9450248596$$

$$\frac{dP}{dY} = -5.239591660$$

$$\text{DUR} = 5.706876942$$

$$\text{MD} = 5.435120898$$

$$\text{CONV} = 39.09456370$$

Example 25

Normal last coupon period and settlement date is in neither the first nor the last coupon period.

Maturity Date:	3/15/2004
Settlement Date:	5/10/2001
Nominal Annual Coupon Rate:	9.75%
Nominal Annual Yield to Maturity:	11%

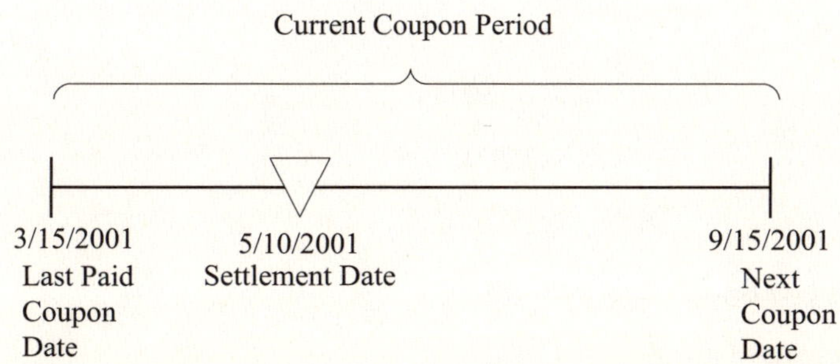

$$AIF = \frac{55}{180}$$

$$FCF = 1$$

$$DF = \frac{125}{180}$$

$$LCF = 1$$

$$LDF = 1$$

$$n = 4$$

$$AI = 0.01489583333$$

$$P = 0.9698613494$$

$$\frac{dP}{dY} = -2.346058485$$

$$DUR = 2.513403046$$

$$MD = 2.382372555$$

$$CONV = 7.266758784$$

Example 26

Short last coupon period and settlement date is in neither the first coupon period nor the last coupon period.

Maturity Date:	7/20/2003
Settlement Date:	1/3/2001
Last Coupon Date:	2/15/2003
Nominal Annual Coupon Rate:	9.75%
Nominal Annual Yield to Maturity:	11%

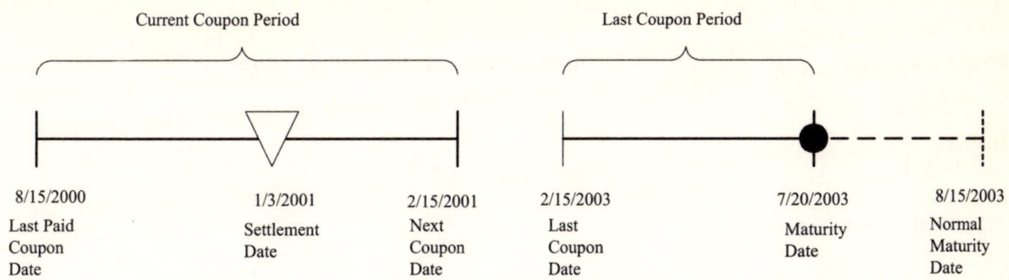

$$AIF = \frac{138}{180}$$

$$FCF = 1$$

$$DF = \frac{42}{180}$$

$$LCF = \frac{155}{180}$$

$$LDF = \frac{155}{180}$$

$$n = 4$$

$$AI = 0.037375$$

$$P = 0.972757196$$

$$\frac{dP}{dY} = -2.133787682$$

$$DUR = 2.228565739$$

$$MD = 2.112384587$$

$$CONV = 5.893043595$$

Example 27

Long last coupon period and settlement date is in neither the first nor the last coupon period.

Maturity Date:	6/15/2008
Settlement Date:	9/30/2000
Last Coupon Date:	10/31/2007
Nominal Annual Coupon Rate:	9%
Nominal Annual Yield to Maturity:	10%

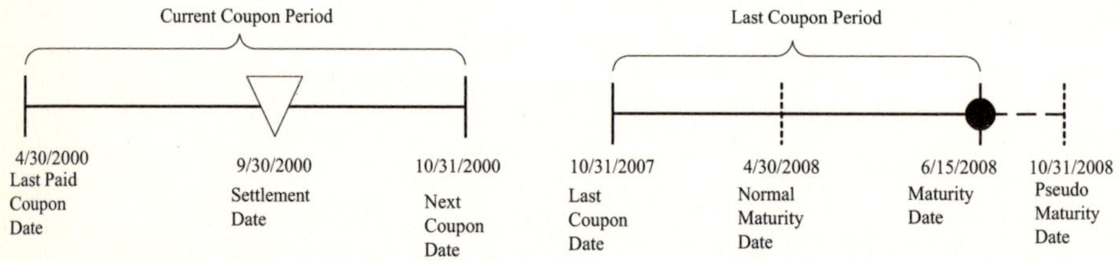

$$\text{AIF} = \frac{150}{180}$$

$$\text{FCF} = 1$$

$$\text{DF} = \frac{30}{180}$$

$$\text{LCF} = \frac{45}{180} + 1 = \frac{225}{180}$$

$$\text{LDF} = \frac{45}{180} + 1 = \frac{225}{180}$$

$$n = 14$$

$$\text{AI} = 0.0375$$

$$P = 0.9468167427$$

$$\frac{dP}{dY} = -5.105906694$$

$$DUR = 5.446622816$$

$$MD = 5.187259825$$

$$CONV = 36.16294360$$

Example 28

Normal last coupon period and settlement date coincides with a coupon date.

Maturity Date: 3/1/2004

Settlement Date: 3/1/2001

Nominal Annual Coupon Rate: 9%

Nominal Annual Yield to Maturity: 10%

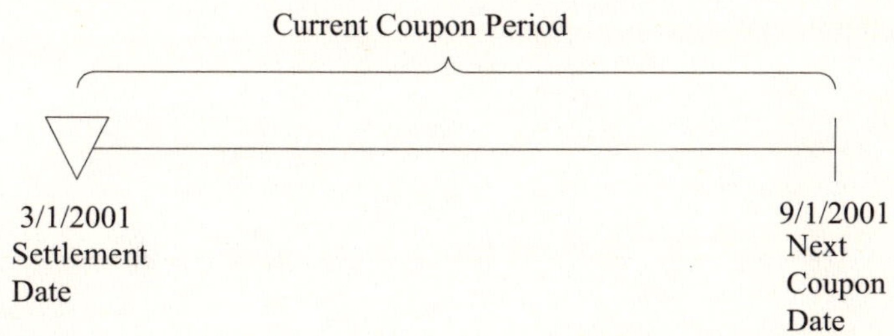

$$AIF = 0$$

$$FCF = 1$$

$$DF = 1$$

$$LCF = 1$$

$$LDF = 1$$

$$n = 4$$

$$AI = 0$$

$$P = 0.9746215397$$

$$\frac{dP}{dY} = -2.497265829$$

$$DUR = 2.690407521$$

$$MD = 2.562292877$$

$$CONV = 8.223826154$$

Example 29

Short last coupon period and settlement date coincides with a coupon date.

Maturity Date:	6/15/2008
Settlement Date:	10/31/2000
Last Coupon Date:	4/30/2008
Nominal Annual Coupon Rate:	9%
Nominal Annual Yield to Maturity:	10%

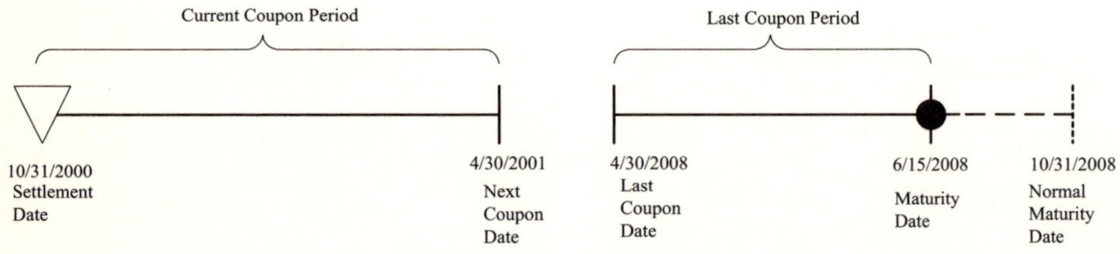

$$AIF = 0$$

$$FCF = 1$$

$$DF = 1$$

$$\text{LCF} = \frac{45}{180}$$

$$\text{LDF} = \frac{45}{180}$$

$$n = 14$$

$$\text{AI} = 0$$

$$P = 0.9476159588$$

$$\frac{dP}{dY} = -5.068166222$$

$$\text{DUR} = 5.615750224$$

$$\text{MD} = 5.348333546$$

$$\text{CONV} = 36.950087940$$

Example 30

Long last coupon period and settlement date coincides with a coupon date.

Maturity Date:	6/15/2008
Settlement Date:	10/31/2000
Last Coupon Date:	10/31/2007
Nominal Annual Coupon Rate:	9%
Nominal Annual Yield to Maturity:	10%

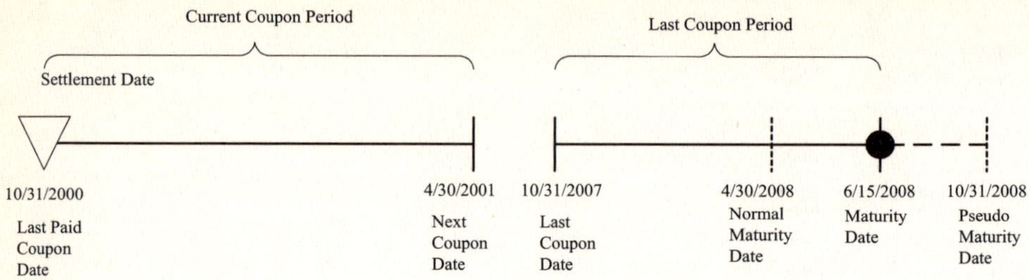

$$AIF = 0$$

$$FCF = 1$$

$$DF = 1$$

$$LCF = \frac{45}{180} + 1 = \frac{225}{180}$$

$$LDF = \frac{45}{180} + 1 = \frac{225}{180}$$

$$n = 13$$

$$AI = 0$$

$$P = 0.9473535374$$

$$\frac{dP}{dY} = -5.068837419$$

$$DUR = 5.618049736$$

$$MD = 5.350523558$$

$$CONV = 36.98523486$$

Example 31

Normal last coupon period and settlement date coincides with the last coupon date.

Maturity Date:	6/20/2002
Settlement Date:	12/20/2001
Nominal Annual Coupon Rate:	10%
Nominal Annual Yield to Maturity:	11%

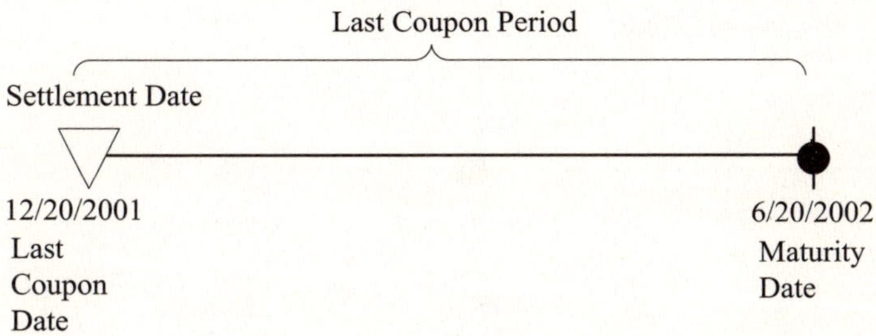

$$AIF = 0$$

$$DF = 1$$

$$LCF = 1$$

$$AI = 0$$

$$P = 0.9952606635$$

$$\frac{dP}{dY} = -0.4716875183$$

$$DUR = 0.500$$

$$MD = 0.4739336493$$

$$CONV = 0.4492262079$$

Example 32

Short last coupon period and settlement date coincides with the last coupon date.

Maturity Date:	12/13/2000
Settlement Date:	9/30/2000
Last Coupon Date:	9/30/2000
Nominal Annual Coupon Rate:	9%
Nominal Annual Yield to Maturity:	10%

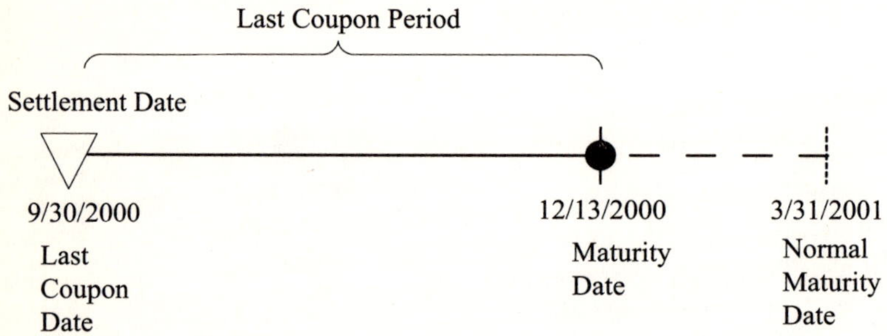

$$AIF = 0$$

$$DF = \frac{73}{180}$$

$$LCF = \frac{73}{180}$$

$$AI = 0$$

$$P = 0.9980125238$$

$$\frac{dP}{dY} = -0.1983526116$$

$$DUR = 0.2027777778$$

$$MD = 0.1987476178$$

$$CONV = 0.07900123112$$

Example 33

Long last coupon period and settlement date coincides with the last coupon date.

Maturity Date:	6/15/2001
Settlement Date:	9/30/2000
Last Coupon Date:	9/30/2000
Nominal Annual Coupon Rate:	9%
Nominal Annual Yield to Maturity:	10%

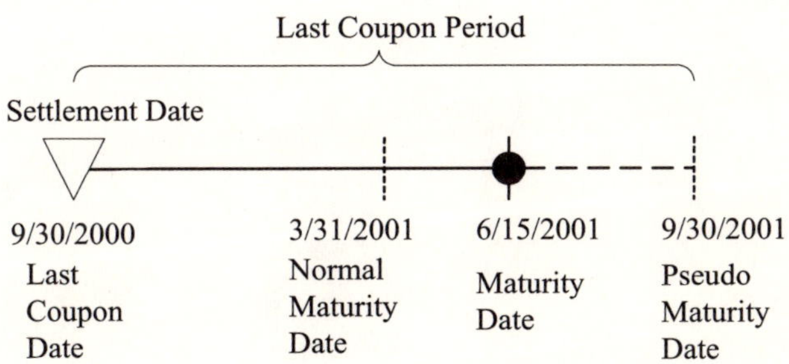

$$AIF = 0$$

$$DF = \frac{225}{180}$$

$$LCF = \frac{75}{180} + 1 = \frac{255}{180}$$

$$AI = 0$$

$$P = 0.9933852140$$

$$\frac{dP}{dY} = -0.6571030599$$

DUR = 0.7083333333

MD = 0.6614785992

CONV = 0.8751078745

Example 34

Normal last coupon period and settlement date is in the last coupon period.

Maturity Date:	9/15/2001
Settlement Date:	5/11/2001
Nominal Annual Coupon Rate:	9.875%
Nominal Annual Yield to Maturity:	11%

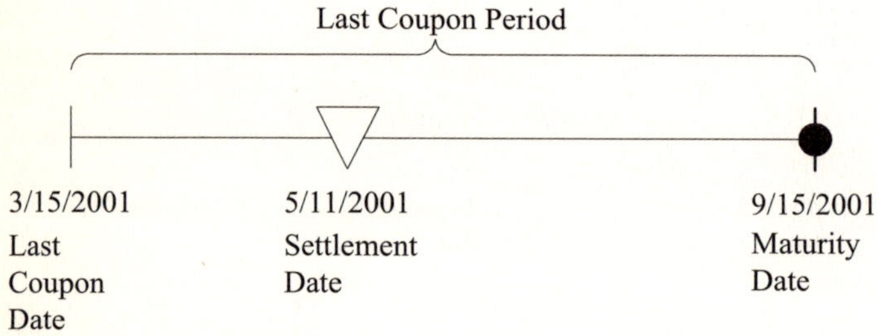

$$AIF = \frac{56}{180}$$

$$DF = \frac{124}{180}$$

LCF = 1

AI = 0.01536111111

P = 0.9957056912

$$\frac{dP}{dY} = -0.3355429919$$

$$DUR = 0.3444444444$$

$$MD = 0.3318702494$$

$$CONV = 0.2202757249$$

Example 35

Short last coupon period and settlement date is in the last coupon period.

Maturity Date:	7/31/2001
Settlement Date:	6/10/2001
Last Coupon Date:	5/15/2001
Nominal Annual Coupon Rate:	9.25%
Nominal Annual Yield to Maturity:	11%

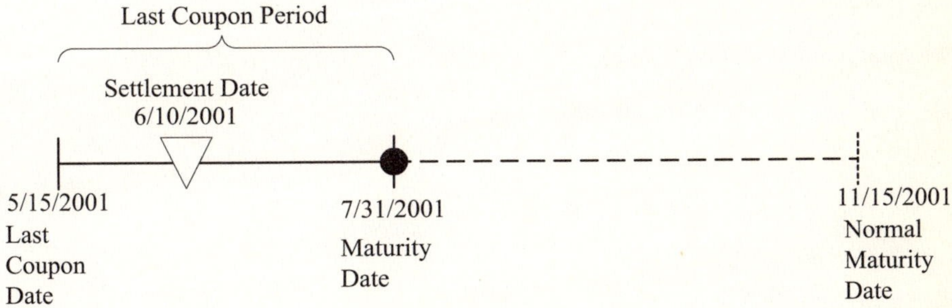

$$AIF = \frac{25}{180}$$

$$DF = \frac{51}{180}$$

$$LCF = \frac{76}{180}$$

$$AI = 0.006423611111$$

$$P = 0.9974603089$$

$$\frac{dP}{dY} = -0.1400346815$$

$$DUR = 0.1416666667$$

$$MD = 0.1394929023$$

$$CONV = 0.03891653957$$

Example 36

Long last coupon period and settlement date is in the last coupon period, before the normal maturity date.

Maturity Date:	5/31/2002
Settlement Date:	10/31/2001
Last Coupon Date:	8/15/2001
Nominal Annual Coupon Rate:	10%
Nominal Annual Yield to Maturity:	11%

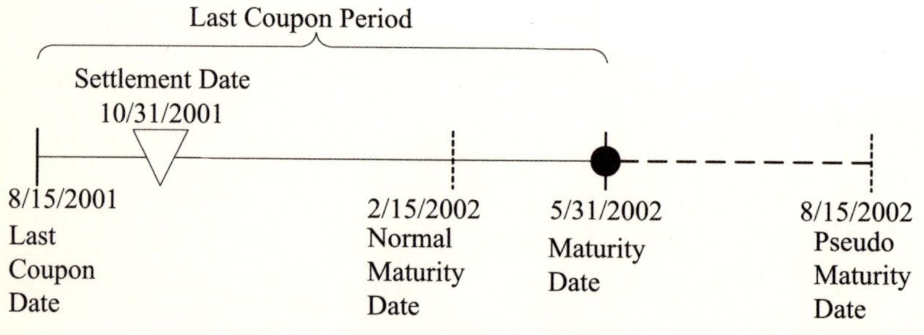

$$AIF = \frac{76}{180}$$

$$DF = \frac{210}{180}$$

$$LCF = 1 + \frac{106}{180} = \frac{286}{180}$$

$$AI = 0.02111111111$$

$$P = 0.9932454538$$

$$\frac{dP}{dY} = -0.5560294404$$

$$DUR = 0.5833333333$$

$$MD = 0.5481597494$$

$$CONV = 0.6009582218$$

Example 37

Long last coupon period and settlement date coincides with normal maturity date.

Maturity Date:	2/1/2002
Settlement Date:	1/1/2002
Last Coupon Date:	7/1/2001
Nominal Annual Coupon Rate:	11.125%
Price:	99%

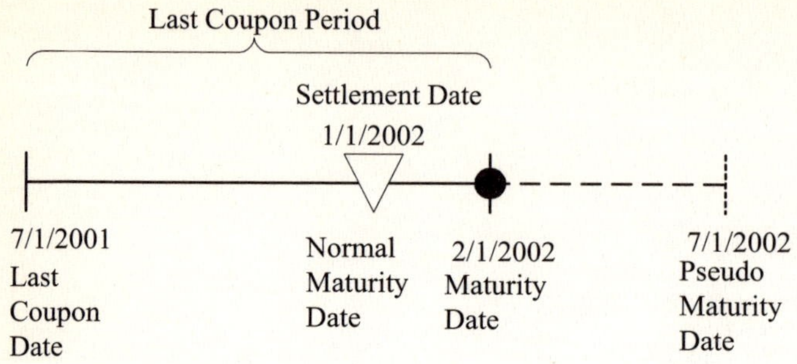

$$AIF = 1$$

$$DF = \frac{30}{180}$$

$$LCF = 1 + \frac{30}{180} = \frac{210}{180}$$

$$AI = 0.055625$$

$$Y = 22.11595935\%$$

$$\frac{dP}{dY} = -0.085558575$$

$$DUR = 0.08333333333$$

$$MD = 0.08182529590$$

$$CONV = 0.01339075810$$

Example 38

Long last coupon period and settlement date is in the last coupon period after normal maturity date.

Maturity Date:	5/31/2002
Settlement Date:	3/31/2002
Last Coupon Date:	8/15/2001

Nominal Annual Coupon Rate: 10%

Nominal Annual Yield to Maturity: 11%

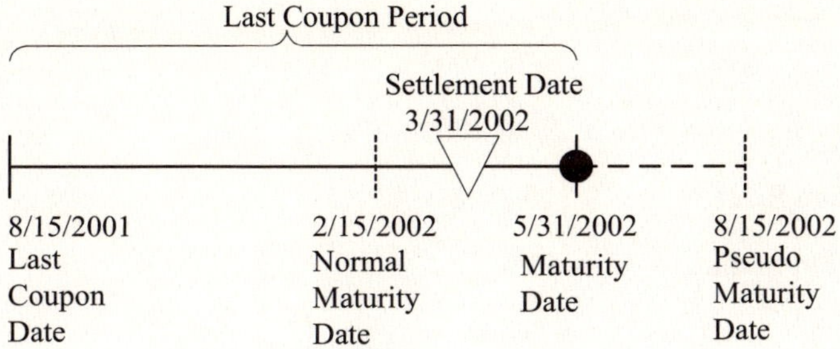

$$\text{AIF} = 1 + \frac{46}{180} = \frac{226}{180}$$

$$\text{DF} = \frac{60}{180}$$

$$\text{LCF} = 1 + \frac{106}{180} = \frac{286}{180}$$

$$\text{AI} = 0.06277777778$$

$$\text{P} = 0.9972331333$$

$$\frac{dP}{dY} = -0.1734878742$$

$$\text{DUR} = 0.1666666667$$

$$\text{MD} = 0.1636661211$$

$$\text{CONV} = 0.05357319840$$

Example 39

Normal last coupon period and settlement date is in neither the first nor the last coupon period. Coupon dates are on February 28th or 29th.

Maturity Date:	8/31/2003
Settlement Date:	8/29/2000
Nominal Annual Coupon Rate:	10.25%
Nominal Annual Yield to Maturity:	11%

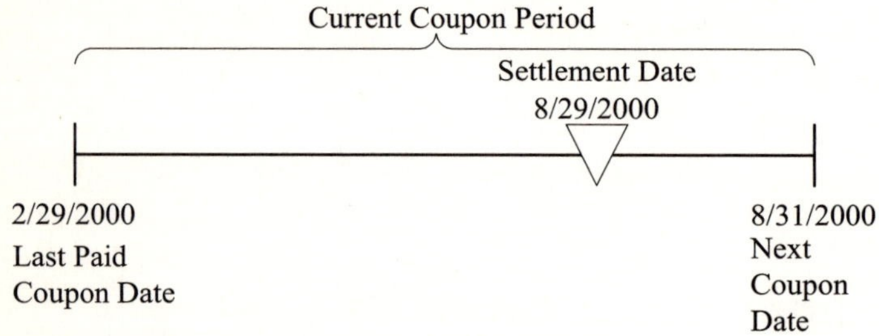

$$AIF = \frac{179}{180}$$

$$FCF = 1$$

$$DF = \frac{1}{180}$$

$$LCF = 1$$

$$LDF = 1$$

$$n = 5$$

$$AI = 0.05096527778$$

$$P = 0.9812444085$$

$$\frac{dP}{dY} = -2.4700588143$$

DUR = 2.524595616

MD = 2.392981627

CONV = 7.610836874

Example 40

Normal last coupon period and settlement date is in neither the first nor the last coupon period. Coupon dates are on February 28th or 29th.

Maturity Date:	8/31/2003
Settlement Date:	8/30/2000
Nominal Annual Coupon Rate:	10.25%
Nominal Annual Yield to Maturity:	11%

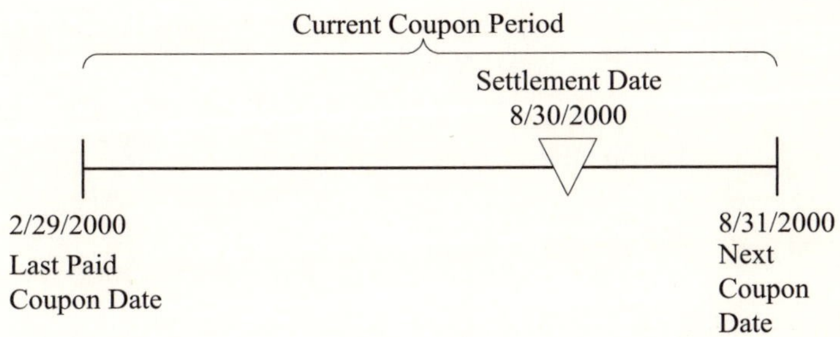

AIF = 1

FCF = 1

DF = 0

LCF = 1

LDF = 1

n = 5

AI = 0.05125

P = 0.9812667613

$$\frac{dP}{dY} = -2.468075059$$

DUR = 2.521817839

MD = 2.390348662

CONV = 7.596994683

Example 41

Normal last coupon period and settlement date coincides with a coupon date. Coupon dates are on February 28th or 29th.

Maturity Date:	8/31/2003
Settlement Date:	8/31/2000
Nominal Annual Coupon Rate:	10.25%
Nominal Annual Yield to Maturity:	11%

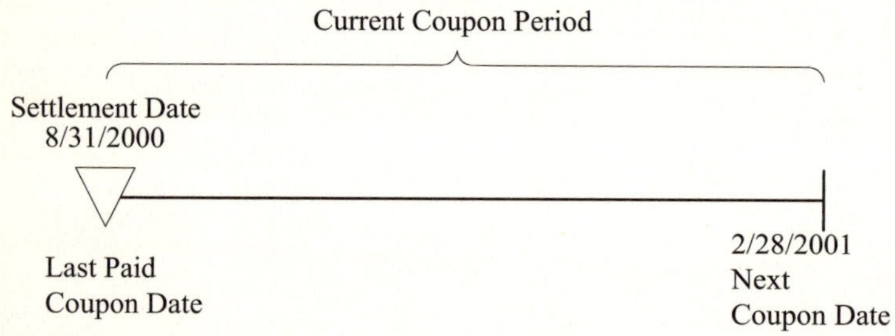

AIF = 0

FCF = 1

DF = 1

LCF = 1

LDF = 1

n = 4

$$AI = 0$$

$$P = 0.9812667613$$

$$\frac{dP}{dY} = -2.468075059$$

$$DUR = 2.653528368$$

$$MD = 2.515192766$$

$$CONV = 7.993773615$$

Example 42

Normal last coupon period and settlement date is in neither the first nor the last coupon period. Coupon dates are on February 28th or 29th.

Maturity Date:	8/31/2003
Settlement Date:	2/27/2000
Nominal Annual Coupon Rate:	10.25%
Nominal Annual Yield to Maturity:	11%

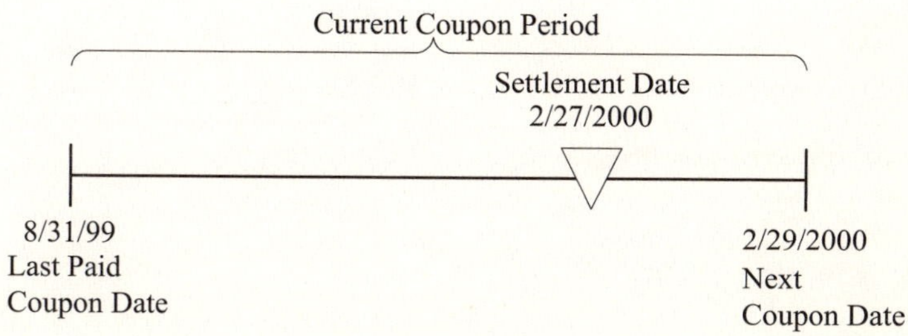

$$AIF = \frac{177}{180}$$

$$FCF = 1$$

$$DF = \frac{3}{180}$$

LCF = 1

LDF = 1

n = 6

AI = 0.05039583333

P = 0.9786243880

$$\frac{dP}{dY} = -2.808869004$$

DUR = 2.879784807

MD = 2.729653846

CONV = 9.845632612

Example 43

Normal last coupon period and settlement date is in neither the first nor the last coupon period. Coupon dates are on February 28th or 29th.

Maturity Date: 8/31/2003

Settlement Date: 2/28/2000

Nominal Annual Coupon Rate: 10.25%

Nominal Annual Yield to Maturity: 11%

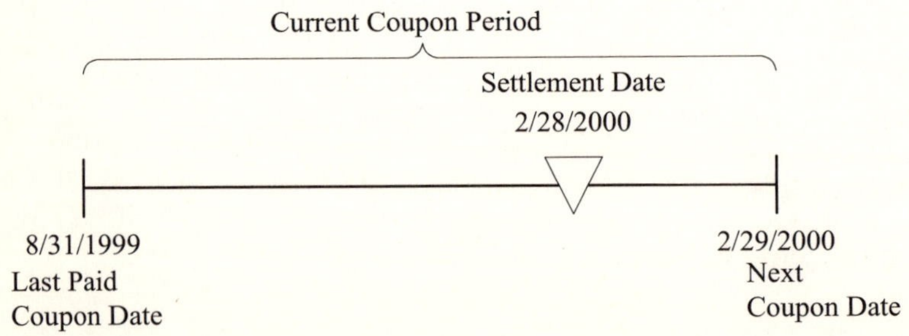

$$\text{AIF} = \frac{178}{180}$$

$$\text{FCF} = 1$$

$$\text{DF} = \frac{2}{180}$$

$$\text{LCF} = 1$$

$$\text{LDF} = 1$$

$$n = 6$$

$$\text{AI} = 0.05068055556$$

$$P = 0.9786457920$$

$$\frac{dP}{dY} = -2.806994443$$

$$\text{DUR} = 2.877007030$$

$$\text{MD} = 2.727020881$$

$$\text{CONV} = 9.830017529$$

Example 44

Normal last coupon period and settlement date coincides with a coupon date. Coupon dates are on February 28th or 29th.

Maturity Date:	8/31/2003
Settlement Date:	2/29/2000
Nominal Annual Coupon Rate:	10.25%
Nominal Annual Yield to Maturity:	11%

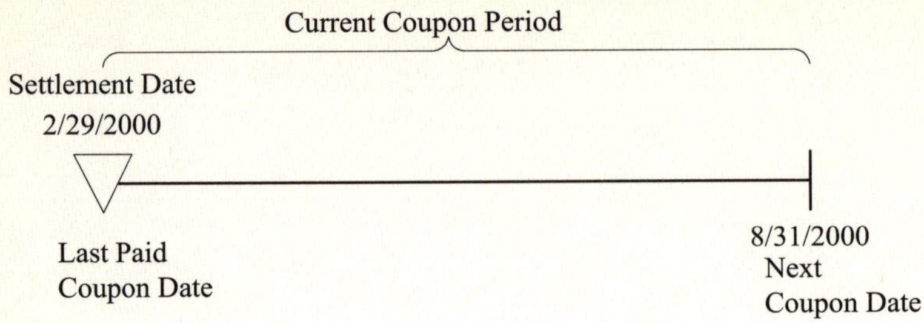

AIF = 0

FCF = 1

DF = 1

LCF = 1

LDF = 1

n = 5

AI = 0

P = 0.9786888733

$$\frac{dP}{dY} = -2.803241228$$

DUR = 3.021817839

MD = 2.864282312

CONV = 10.31195422

Example 45

Normal last coupon period and settlement date coincides with a coupon date. Coupon dates are on February 28th or 29th.

Maturity Date:	8/31/2003
Settlement Date:	2/28/2001
Nominal Annual Coupon Rate:	10.25%
Nominal Annual Yield to Maturity:	11%

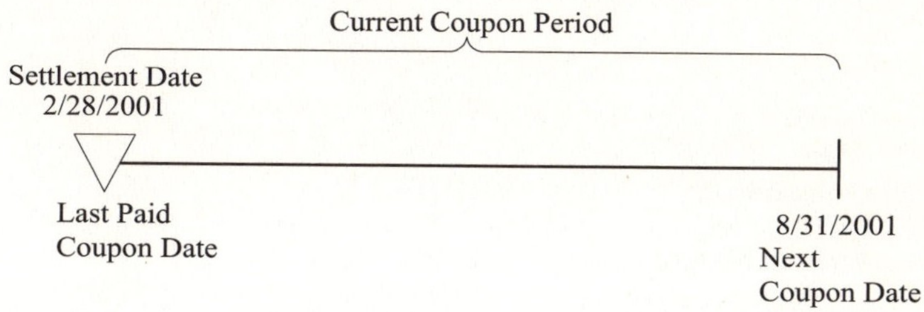

$$AIF = 0$$

$$FCF = 1$$

$$DF = 1$$

$$LCF = 1$$

$$LDF = 1$$

$$n = 3$$

$$AI = 0$$

$$P = 0.9839864332$$

$$\frac{dP}{dY} = -2.113185807$$

$$DUR = 2.265692850$$

MD = 2.147576161

CONV = 5.901880789

Example 46

Normal last coupon period and settlement date is in neither the first nor the last coupon period. Coupon dates are on February 28th or 29th.

Maturity Date:	8/31/2003
Settlement Date:	3/1/2001
Nominal Annual Coupon Rate:	10.25%
Nominal Annual Yield to Maturity:	11%

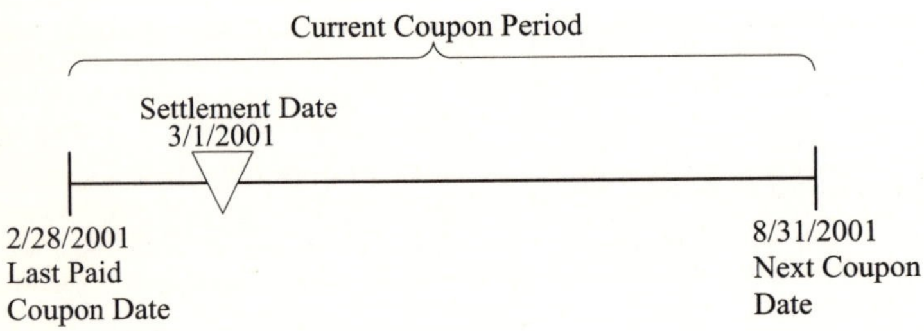

$$AIF = \frac{1}{180}$$

$$FCF = 1$$

$$DF = \frac{179}{180}$$

LCF = 1

LDF = 1

n = 3

AI = 0.0002847222222

P = 0.9839944400

$$\frac{dP}{dY} = -2.111222892$$

DUR = 2.262915072

MD = 2.144943196

CONV = 5.889330886

Treasury Investment Growth Receipts (TIGRs)

Everything is the same as for U.S. government bonds, with coupon equal to zero.

Example 1

The settlement date is in the last coupon period.

Maturity Date: 11/15/2002

Settlement Date: 10/16/2002

Nominal Annual Yield to Maturity: 5%

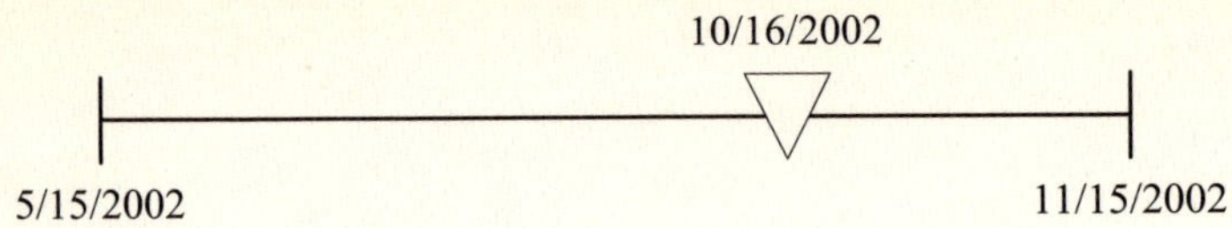

$$DF = \frac{30}{184}$$

$$P = \frac{1}{1 + \frac{0.05}{2} \cdot \frac{30}{184}} = 0.99594046$$

Chapter 11

Foreign Government Bonds

EMU (European Monetary Union) Countries

There are 12 countries in the EMU as of 1/1/2001:

- Austria
- Belgium
- Finland
- France
- Germany
- Greece
- Ireland
- Italy
- Luxembourg
- The Netherlands
- Portugal
- Spain

Conventions

- Quoted in prices
- The day count method is Actual/Actual (in period) for everything.

- Coupon payments are annual.
- End-of-Month rule is in effect.
- No ex-dividend trading
- The settlement date is three business days after the trade date.
- Simple interest is in the last coupon period for Belgium, Finland, Germany, Greece, Italy, Luxembourg, and the Netherlands. Compound interest is in the last coupon period for Austria, France, Ireland, Portugal, and Spain.

Exceptions

Only one Portuguese bond (10.625%, 6/23/2003), has semiannual coupon payments. All Italian bonds have semiannual coupon payments. Irish bonds issued before 1/1/1999 may have a different day count method, frequency of payments per year, End-of-Month rule, and ex-dividend trading. Greek bonds issued before 1/1/2001 have a 30E/360 day count method (see the sections on these countries later in this chapter).

Example 1: Portugal

Maturity Date:	10/14/2005
Settlement Date:	1/9/2001
Coupon Rate:	5.25%
Effective Yield:	3%

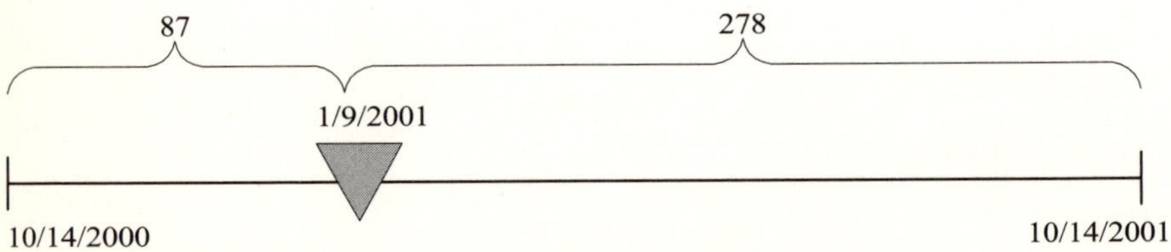

$$\text{AIF} = \frac{87}{365}$$

$$\text{FCF} = 1$$

$$\text{DF} = \frac{278}{365}$$

$$\text{LCF} = 1$$

$$\text{LDF} = 1$$

$$n = 3$$

$$\text{AI (per day)} = \frac{0.0525}{365} = 0.0001438356164 \approx 0.00014383562$$

$$\text{AI} = 0.00014383562 \cdot 87 = 0.0125136989$$

$$P = 1.098328672$$

$$P_{\text{FULL}} = 1.11084237$$

$$\frac{dP}{dY} = -4.651317994$$

$$\text{DUR} = 4.312814905$$

$$\text{MD} = 4.187198937$$

$$\text{CONV} = 22.68957903$$

$$\text{PV01Y} = 0.046513180$$

$$\text{YV01P} = 0.002149928$$

Example 2: Germany

Maturity Date:	2/16/2006
Settlement Date:	6/15/2001
Coupon Rate:	6%
Effective Yield:	5%

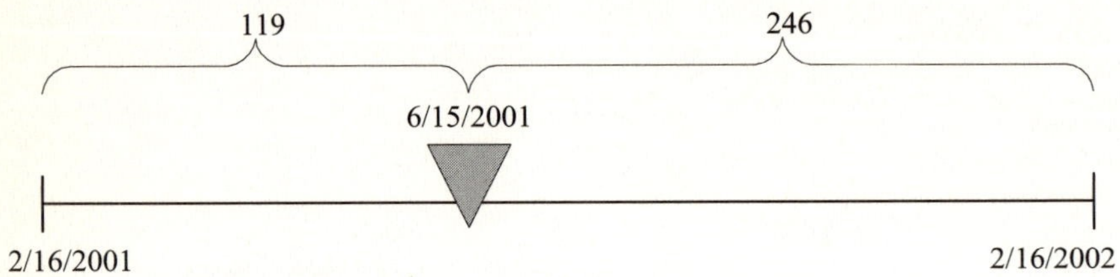

$$\text{AIF} = \frac{119}{365}$$

$$\text{FCF} = 1$$

$$\text{DF} = \frac{246}{365}$$

$$\text{LCF} = 1$$

$$\text{LDF} = 1$$

$$n = 3$$

$$\text{AI} = 0.06 \cdot \frac{119}{365} = 0.019561644$$

$$P = 1.040461435$$

$$P_{\text{FULL}} = 1.060023079$$

$$\frac{dP}{dY} = -4.191355328$$

$$\text{DUR} = 4.151723846$$

$$MD = 3.95402271$$

$$CONV = 20.5964963$$

$$PV01Y = 0.041913553$$

$$YV01P = 0.002385863$$

Example 3: Austria

The settlement date is in the last coupon period.

Maturity Date:	10/21/2001
Settlement Date:	1/31/2001
Coupon Rate:	7.25%
Effective Yield:	8%

Compound interest in the last coupon period.

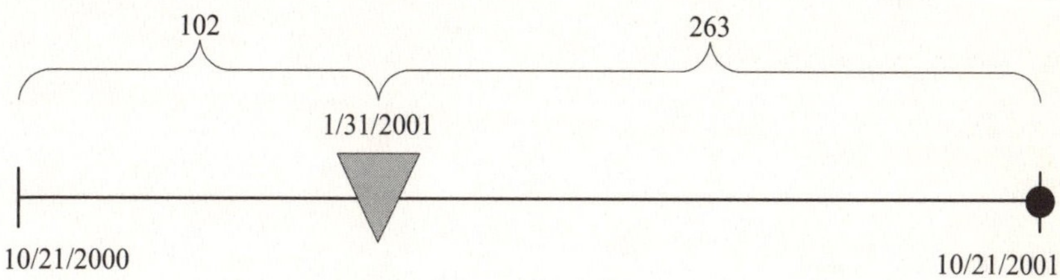

$$AIF = \frac{102}{365}$$

$$DF = \frac{263}{365}$$

$$LCF = 1$$

$$AI = 0.0725 \cdot \frac{102}{365} = 0.020260274$$

$$P = \frac{1+0.0725}{(1+0.08)^{\frac{263}{365}}} - 0.020260274 = 0.994384172$$

$$P_{full} = 1.014644446$$

$$\frac{dP}{dY} = -0.676944417$$

$$DUR = 0.720547945$$

$$MD = 0.667174023$$

$$CONV = 1.062874903$$

$$PV01Y = 0.006769444$$

$$YV01P = 0.014772262$$

Example 4: Ireland

Maturity Date:	4/18/2010
Settlement Date:	3/21/2001
Issue Date:	5/14/1999
Coupon Rate:	4%
Effective Yield:	5%

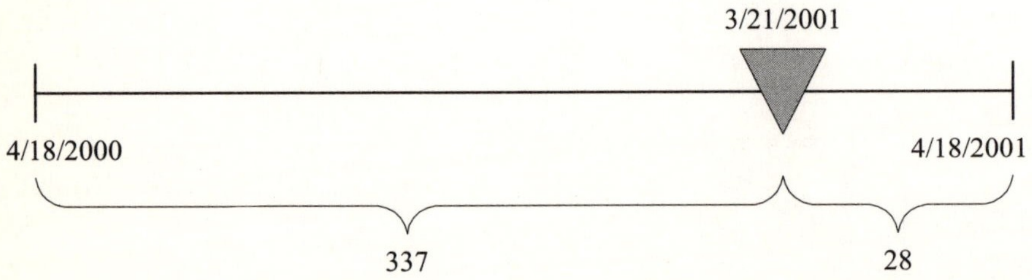

$$AIF = \frac{337}{365}$$

$$FCF = 1$$

$$DF = \frac{28}{365}$$

$$LCF = 1$$

$$LDF = 1$$

$$n = 8$$

$$AI = 0.036931507$$

$$P = 0.928370567$$

$$P_{full} = 0.965302074$$

$$\frac{dP}{dY} = -6.836454528$$

$$DUR = 7.436301493$$

$$MD = 7.082191898$$

$$CONV = 64.22853818$$

$$PV01Y = 0.068364545$$

$$YV01P = 0.001462747$$

Example 5: Spain

Maturity Date:	2/28/2005
Settlement Date:	2/14/2001
Coupon Rate:	10%
Effective Yield:	5%

The EOM rule is not in effect (this is the exception for bonds issued before 1/1/1999).

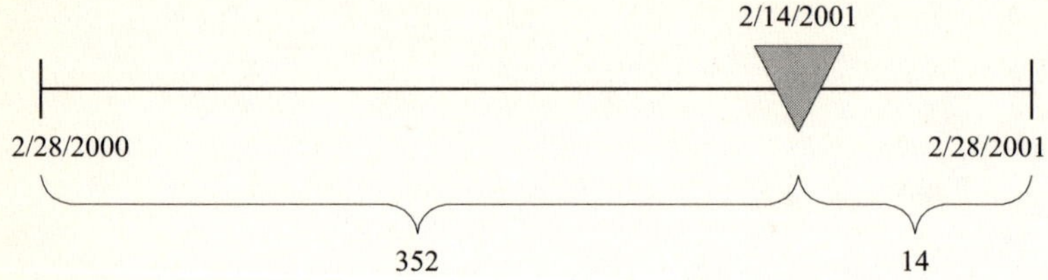

$$AIF = \frac{352}{366}$$

$$FCF = 1$$

$$DF = \frac{14}{366}$$

$$LCF = 1$$

$$LDF = 1$$

$$n = 3$$

$$AI = 0.096174863$$

$$P = 1.178741077$$

$$P_{full} = 1.27491594$$

$$\frac{dP}{dY} = -3.996861858$$

$$DUR = 3.291750318$$

$$MD = 3.135000303$$

$$CONV = 14.37232433$$

$$\text{PV01Y} = 0.039968619$$

$$\text{YV01P} = 0.002501963$$

Example 6: Luxembourg

The settlement date is in the last coupon period.

Maturity Date:	4/21/2005
Settlement Date:	5/25/2004
Coupon Rate:	8%
Effective Yield:	4%

Simple Interest in last coupon period

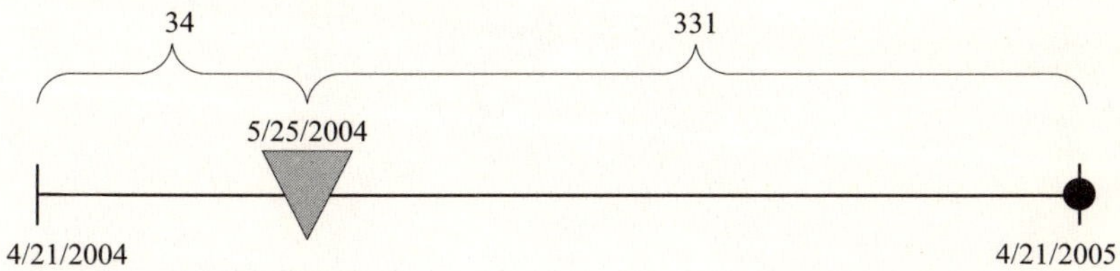

$$\text{AIF} = \frac{34}{365}$$

$$\text{DF} = \frac{331}{365}$$

$$\text{LCF} = 1$$

$$\text{AI} = 0.08 \cdot \frac{34}{365} = 0.007452054$$

$$\text{P} = \frac{1+0.08}{1+0.04 \cdot \frac{331}{365}} - 0.007452054 = 1.034743377$$

$$\text{P}_{\text{full}} = 1.042195431$$

$$\frac{dP}{dY} = -0.912031217$$

$$DUR = 0.906849315$$

$$MD = 0.875105753$$

$$CONV = 1.531620158$$

$$PV01Y = 0.009120312$$

$$YV01P = 0.010964537$$

Example 7: French Government Bond (OAT Obligations Assimilabtes du Tresor)

Maturity Date:	10/25/2016
Settlement Date:	8/9/2001
Coupon Rate:	5%
Effective Yield:	7%

Simple Interest in last coupon period

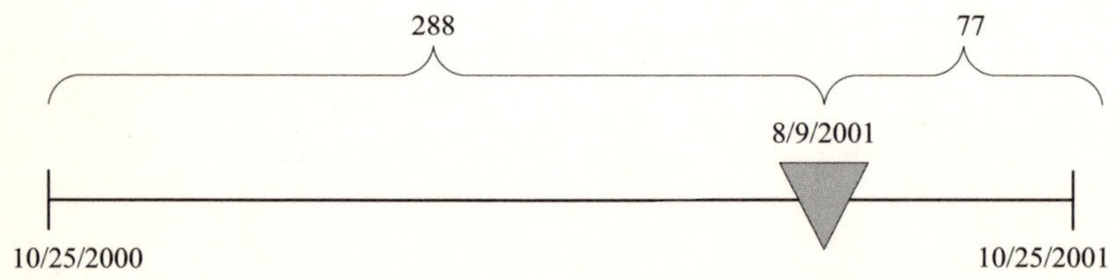

$$AIF = \frac{288}{365}$$

$$FCF = 1$$

$$DF = \frac{77}{365}$$

LCF = 1

LDF = 1

n = 14

AI = $0.05 \cdot \frac{288}{365} = 0.039452055 \approx 0.03945$

(Accrued interest is rounded to five decimal places per one Franc of face value, for OATs only).

P = $0.816092827377 \approx 0.81609$

(Price is rounded to five decimal places per one Franc of face value, for OATs only).

P_{full} = 0.85554

$\frac{dP}{dY}$ = -8.01327914

DUR = 10.02195145

MD = 9.36630977

CONV = 123.5488528

PV01Y = 0.08013279

YV01P = 0.00124793

Australia

Conventions

- Quoted in yields
- Price (capital price) and full price (gross price) are rounded to five decimal places per one Australian dollar of face value (except when the settlement date is in the last coupon period, where they are rounded to nine decimal places).
- Coupon payments are semiannual.
- The maturity date is always on the 15th of the month.
- The day count method is Actual/365 for discount factor when the settlement date is in the last coupon period. Actual/Actual (in period) for everything else.
- The settlement date is three business days after the trade date.
- There is no odd last coupon period.
- There is no callable feature.
- The ex-dividend date is the seventh calendar day before the coupon date.
- Accrued interest is rounded to five decimal places per one Australian dollar of face value.
- Simple interest is used when the settlement date is in the last coupon period.

Example 1

The settlement date is in neither the first nor the last coupon period.

Maturity Date:	7/15/2005
Settlement Date:	3/10/2000
Nominal Annual Coupon Rate:	7%
Nominal Annual Yield to Maturity:	7.5%

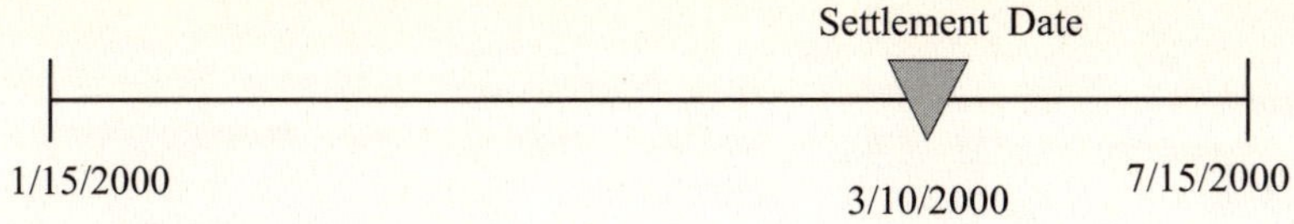

Ex-dividend date: 7/8/2000

This is cum-dividend trading.

$$AIF = \frac{55}{182}$$

$$FCF = 1$$

$$DF = \frac{127}{182}$$

$$LCF = 1$$

$$LDF = 1$$

$$n = 9$$

$$AI = 0.010576923 \approx 0.01058$$

$$P = 0.978162455 \approx 0.97816$$

$$P_{full} = 0.988739378 \approx 0.98874$$

$$\frac{dP}{dY} = -4.284632315$$

$$DUR = 4.495933029$$

$$MD = 4.333429426$$

$$CONV = 23.04976975$$

$$PV01Y = 0.042846323$$

$$YV01P = 0.002333923$$

Example 2

Maturity Date:	5/15/2004
Settlement Date:	5/11/2000
Nominal Annual Coupon Rate:	5.4%
Nominal Annual Yield to Maturity:	6.5%

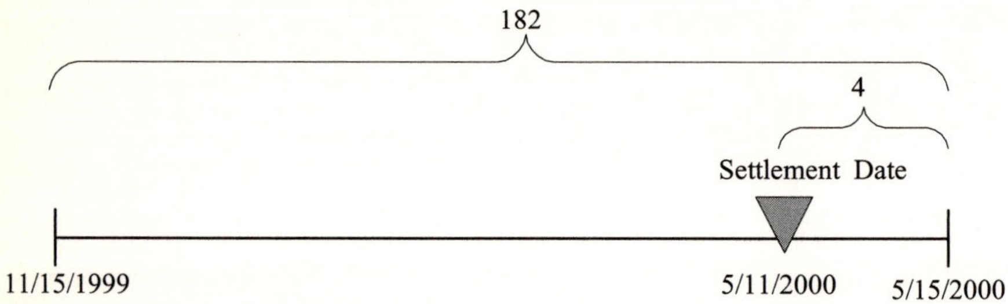

Ex-dividend date: 5/8/2000

This is ex-dividend trading.

$$AIF = -\frac{4}{182}$$

$$FCF = 0$$

$$DF = \frac{4}{182}$$

$$LCF = 1$$

$$LDF = 1$$

$$n = 7$$

$$AI = -0.000593407 \approx -0.00059$$

$$P = 0.961713217 \approx 0.96171$$

$$P_{full} = 0.96111981 \approx 0.96112$$

$$\frac{dP}{dY} = -3.400817616$$

$$DUR = 3.653388632$$

$$MD = 3.538390927$$

$$CONV = 14.96819851$$

$$PV01Y = 0.034008176$$

$$YV01P = 0.002940469$$

Example 3

The settlement date is within the ex-dividend period before the last coupon date.

Maturity Date:	2/15/2001
Settlement Date:	8/9/2000
Nominal Annual Coupon Rate:	7%
Nominal Annual Yield to Maturity:	7.6%

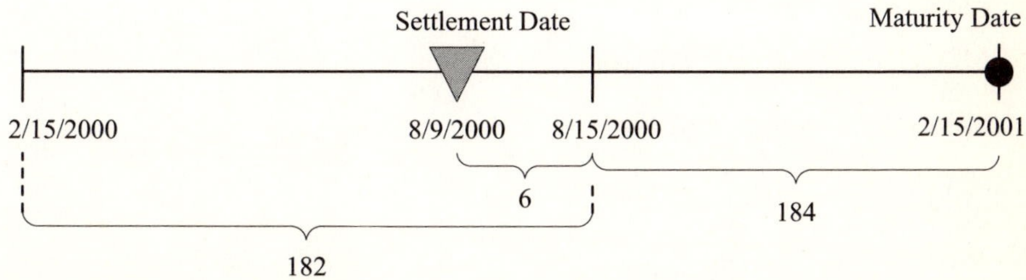

Ex-dividend date: 8/8/2000

This is ex-dividend trading.

$$AIF = -\frac{6}{182}$$

$$FCF = 0$$

$$DF = \frac{6}{182}$$

$$LCF = 1$$

$$LDF = 1$$

$$n = 0$$

$$AI = -0.001153846 \approx -0.00115$$

$$P = \frac{1 + \frac{0.07}{2}}{\left(1 + \frac{0.076}{2}\right)^{1+\frac{6}{182}}} + 0.001153846 = 0.997038448$$

$$P_{full} = 0.99588$$

$$\frac{dP}{dY} = -0.49552792$$

$$DUR = 0.516483516$$

$$MD = 0.497575642$$

$$CONV = 0.487261501$$

$$PV01Y = 0.00495528$$

$$YV01P = 0.020180498$$

Example 4

The settlement date is in the last coupon period.

Maturity Date:	7/15/2001
Settlement Date:	4/13/2001

Nominal Annual Coupon Rate: 5.25%

Nominal Annual Yield to Maturity: 7%

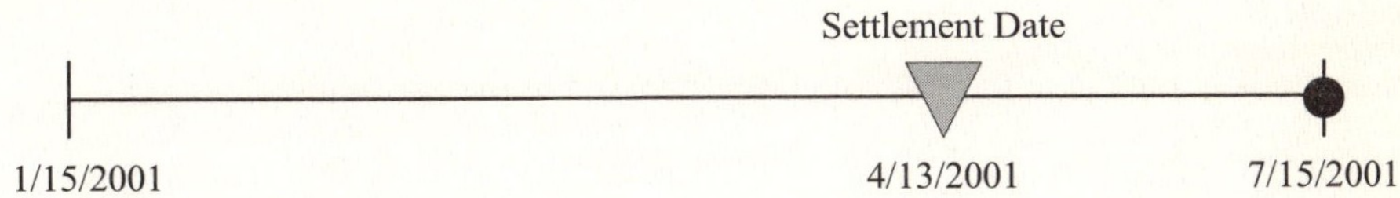

Ex-dividend date: 7/8/2001

This is cum-dividend trading.

$$AIF = \frac{88}{181}$$

$$LCF = 1$$

$$DF = \frac{93}{182.5}$$

$$AI = 0.01276$$

$$P = \frac{1+\frac{0.0525}{2}}{1+\frac{0.07}{2}\cdot\frac{93}{182.5}} - 0.01276$$

$$P = 0.995506938$$

$$P_{full} = 1.008266938$$

$$\frac{dP}{dY} = -0.252399196$$

$$DUR = 0.254794521$$

$$MD = 0.250329735$$

$$CONV = 0.125329953$$

$$\text{PV01Y} = 0.002523992$$

$$\text{YV01P} = 0.039619778$$

Example 5

The settlement date is in the last coupon period and in the ex-dividend period.

Maturity Date:	7/15/2001
Settlement Date:	7/12/2001
Nominal Annual Coupon Rate:	5.25%
Nominal Annual Yield to Maturity:	7%

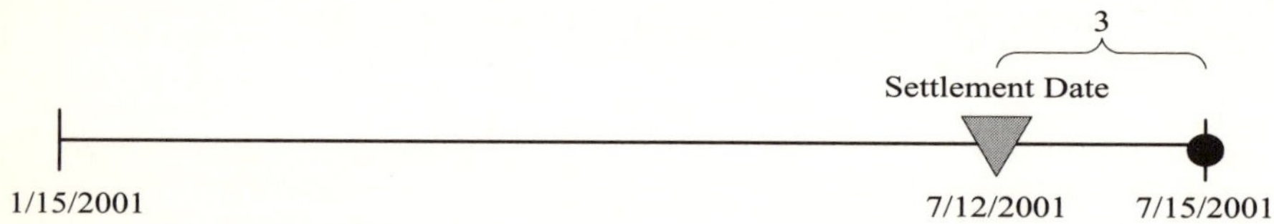

Ex-dividend date: 7/8/2001

This is ex-dividend trading.

$$\text{AIF} = -\frac{3}{181}$$

$$\text{LCF} = 0 \text{ (Because of ex-dividend trading)}$$

$$\text{DF} = \frac{3}{182.5}$$

$$\text{AI} = -0.00044$$

$$P = \frac{1}{1 + \frac{0.07}{2} \cdot \frac{3}{182.5}} + 0.00044 = 0.999864988$$

$$P_{\text{full}} = 0.999424988$$

$$\frac{dP}{dY} = -0.008209729$$

$$DUR = \frac{3}{365} = 0.008219178$$

$$MD = 0.008214452$$

$$CONV = 0.000134954$$

$$PV01Y = 0.000082097$$

$$YV01P = 1.218067069$$

Canada

Conventions

- Quoted in prices
- Coupon payments are semiannual.
- The settlement date is three business days after the trade date for bonds with more than three years remaining to maturity (from trade date) and two business days after the trade date for bonds with three years or less remaining to maturity (from trade date).
- Day count method is Actual/365 for:
    - Accrued-interest factor (AIF) for:

      Accrued interest to be paid

      Accrued interest in price/true yield calculation

      Accrued interest in price/U.S. government bond equivalent yield calculation
    - First coupon factor (FCF) and last coupon factor (LCF) (when they are fraction of a period) in forward pricing, futures analytics, and cash flow calculations.

Note that, if first (last) coupon period is short and has 183 days, then

$$FCF = \frac{181.5}{182.5}$$

$$\left(LCF = \frac{181.5}{182.5} \right)$$

- Discount factor (DF), when settlement date is in the last coupon period

- Day count method is Actual/Actual (in period) for:
  - Accrued-interest factor (AIF) in price/yield calculation
  - First coupon factor (FCF) and last coupon factor (LCF) in price/yield, first derivative and second derivative calculation
  - Discount factor everywhere else
  - Last discount factor (LDF) everywhere

- Full price

  $P_{full} = P + AI$, where AI is accrued interest to be paid.

  Note that this means that full price, calculated as the sum of present values, at the settlement date of all future cash flows, *will not* be equal to the above full price.

- For calculation of first derivative, second derivative, duration, modified duration, and convexity we use full price above.

- Simple interest is used when settlement date is in the last coupon period.

Example 1

Normal last coupon period.

The settlement date is in neither the first nor the last coupon period.

Maturity Date:	3/15/2002
Settlement Date:	7/16/2000
Nominal Annual Coupon Rate:	10.75%
Price:	107.4%

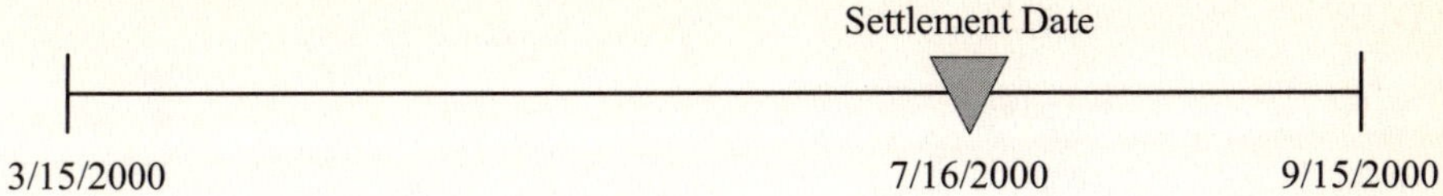

$$\text{AIF} = \frac{123}{182.5} \text{ (Actual/365)}$$

$$\text{AIF} = \frac{123}{184} \text{ [Actual/Actual (in period)]}$$

$$\text{FCF} = 1$$

$$\text{DF} = \frac{61}{184}$$

$$\text{LCF} = 1$$

$$\text{LDF} = 1$$

$$n = 2$$

$$\text{AI} = \frac{0.1075}{2} \cdot \frac{123}{182.5} = 0.036226027397$$

$$1.074 = \left(1+\frac{Y}{2}\right)^{-\frac{61}{184}} \left\{ \frac{0.1075}{2} = \frac{0.1075}{Y}\left[1-\frac{1}{\left(1+\frac{Y}{2}\right)^{2}}\right] + \left(1+\frac{0.1075}{2}\right)\left(1+\frac{Y}{2}\right)^{-2-1} \right\} - \frac{0.1075}{2} \cdot \frac{123}{184}$$

$$Y = 6.00414098\%$$

$$P_{\text{full}} = 1.074 + 0.036226027397 = 1.110226027397$$

$$\frac{dP}{dY} = -1.643007$$

$$\text{DUR} = 1.524313$$

$$\text{MD} = 1.479885$$

$$\text{CONV} = 3.046319$$

$$\text{PV01Y} = 0.016430$$

$$\text{YV01P} = 0.006086$$

U.S. Government Bond Equivalent Yield

$$\text{AIF} = \frac{123}{182.5}$$

$$\text{DF} = \frac{61}{184}$$

$$1.074 = \left(1+\frac{Y_{EQ}}{2}\right)^{-\frac{61}{184}} \left\{\frac{0.1075}{2} + \frac{0.1075}{Y_{EQ}}\left[1 - \frac{1}{\left(1+\frac{Y_{EQ}}{2}\right)^{2}}\right] + \left(1+\frac{0.1075}{2}\right)\left(1+\frac{Y_{EQ}}{2}\right)^{-2-1}\right\} - \frac{0.1075}{2}\cdot\frac{123}{182.5}$$

$$Y_{EQ} = 5.98616935\ \%$$

True Yield

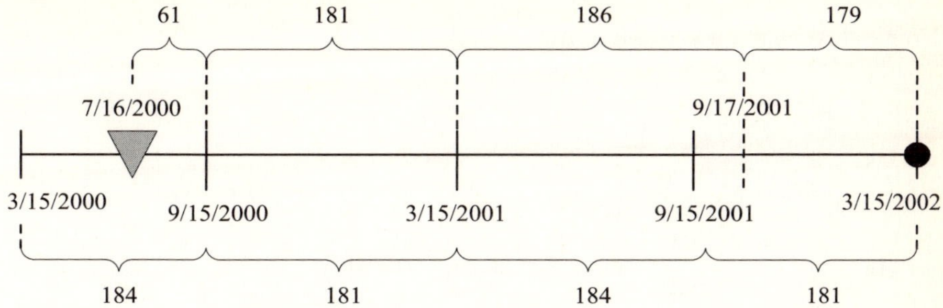

$$\text{AIF} = \frac{123}{182.5}$$

$$\text{DF} = \frac{61}{184}$$

$$1.074 = \frac{\frac{0.1075}{2}}{\left(1+\frac{Y_T}{2}\right)^{\frac{61}{184}}} + \frac{\frac{0.1075}{2}}{\left(1+\frac{Y_T}{2}\right)^{\frac{61}{184}+\frac{181}{181}}} + \frac{\frac{0.1075}{2}}{\left(1+\frac{Y_T}{2}\right)^{\frac{61}{184}+\frac{181}{181}+\frac{186}{184}}}$$

$$+ \frac{1+\frac{0.1075}{2}}{\left(1+\frac{Y_T}{2}\right)^{\frac{61}{184}+\frac{181}{181}+\frac{186}{184}+\frac{179}{181}}} - \frac{0.1075}{2}\cdot\frac{123}{182.5}$$

$$Y_T = 5.9854997\ \%$$

Example 2

Short last coupon period; the settlement date is in neither the first nor the last coupon period.

Maturity Date:	10/12/2005
Settlement Date:	8/31/2001
Last Coupon Date:	9/1/2005

Nominal Annual Coupon Rate: 4.5%

Nominal Annual Yield to Maturity: 11%

$$AIF = 1 - \frac{1}{182.5} \text{ (Actual/365)}$$

$$AIF = \frac{183}{184} \text{ [Actual/Actual (in period)]}$$

$$FCF = 1$$

$$DF = \frac{1}{184}$$

$$LCF = \frac{41}{181}$$

$$LDF = \frac{41}{181}$$

$$n = 8$$

$$AI = \frac{0.045}{2} \cdot \left(1 - \frac{1}{182.5}\right) = 0.02237671233$$

$$P = 0.7894387145$$

$$P_{full} = 0.8118154268$$

$$\frac{dP}{dY} = -2.8089514$$

$$DUR = 3.650391$$

$$MD = 3.4600863$$

$$CONV = 14.6764039$$

PV01Y = 0.0280895

YV01P = 0.00356

Example 3

Normal last coupon period.

The settlement date is in neither the first nor the last coupon period. The settlement date is in a leap year.

Maturity Date:	5/1/2010
Settlement Date:	3/10/2000
Nominal Annual Coupon Rate:	8%
Nominal Annual Yield to Maturity:	8.5%

$$\text{AIF} = \frac{130}{182.5} \text{ (Actual/365)}$$

$$\text{AIF} = \frac{130}{182} \text{ [Actual/Actual (in period)]}$$

$$\text{FCF} = 1$$

$$\text{DF} = \frac{52}{182}$$

$$\text{LCF} = 1$$

$$\text{LDF} = 1$$

$$n = 19$$

$$\text{AI} = 0.02849315068$$

$$P = 0.9662912176$$

$$P_{\text{full}} = 0.9947843683$$

$$\frac{dP}{dY} = -6.561077$$

$$DUR = 6.875784$$

$$MD = 6.595476$$

$$CONV = 58.74765$$

$$PV01Y = 0.065611$$

$$YV01P = 0.001524$$

Example 4

Short first coupon period.

Normal last coupon period.

The settlement date is in the first coupon period.

Maturity Date:	6/30/2004
Settlement Date:	10/5/2000
Dated Date:	7/6/2000
First Coupon Date:	12/31/2000
Nominal Annual Coupon Rate:	14.875%
Nominal Annual Yield to Maturity:	11%

$$AIF = \frac{91}{182.5} \text{ (Actual/365)}$$

$$AIF = \frac{91}{184} \text{ [Actual/Actual (in period)]}$$

$$FCF = \frac{178}{184}$$

$$DF = \frac{87}{184}$$

$$LCF = 1$$

$$LDF = 1$$

$$n = 6$$

$$AI = 0.0370856164$$

$$P = 1.115725191$$

$$P_{full} = 1.152810807$$

$$\frac{dP}{dY} = -3.221430$$

$$DUR = 2.948107$$

$$MD = 2.794414$$

$$CONV = 10.395528$$

$$PV01Y = 0.032214$$

$$YV01P = 0.003104$$

Example 5

Normal last coupon period.

The settlement date is in the last coupon period.

Maturity Date:	2/1/2002
Settlement Date:	12/27/2001
Nominal Annual Coupon Rate:	8.75%
Nominal Annual Yield to Maturity:	11%

$$\text{AIF} = \frac{148}{182.5} \text{ (Actual/365)}$$

$$\text{AIF} = \frac{148}{184} \text{ [Actual/Actual(in period)]}$$

$$\text{DF} = \frac{36}{182.5}$$

$$\text{LCF} = 1$$

$$\text{AI} = 0.03547945205$$

$$\text{P} = \frac{1+\dfrac{0.0875}{2}}{1+\dfrac{0.11}{2}\cdot\dfrac{36}{182.5}} - 0.03547945205 = 0.997068114$$

$$\text{P}_{\text{full}} = 1.0325475662$$

$$\frac{\text{dP}}{\text{dY}} = -0.10074727$$

$$\text{DUR} = 0.09863014$$

$$\text{MD} = 0.09757155$$

$$\text{CONV} = 0.01966013$$

$$\text{PV01Y} = 0.00100747$$

$$\text{YV01P} = 0.09925827$$

Example 6

Long first coupon period.

The settlement date is in the first coupon period after the normal issue date.

The number of accrued-interest days is greater than 182.

Maturity Date:	9/1/2006
Settlement Date:	8/31/2002
Dated Date:	1/5/2002
First Coupon Date:	9/1/2002
Nominal Annual Coupon Rate:	8.5%
Nominal Annual Yield to Maturity:	11%

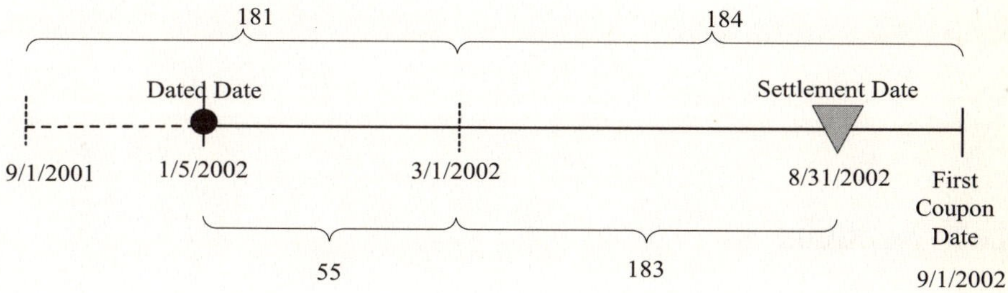

$$\text{AIF} = 1 + \frac{55}{182.5} \quad \text{(Actual/365)}$$

$$\text{AIF} = \frac{55}{181} + \frac{183}{184} = \frac{43243}{33304} \quad \text{[Actual/Actual (in period)]}$$

$$\text{FCF} = \frac{55}{181} + 1 = \frac{236}{181}$$

$$\text{DF} = \frac{1}{184}$$

$$\text{LCF} = 1$$

$$\text{LDF} = 1$$

$$n = 7$$

$$AI = 0.055308219$$

$$P = 0.9207648783$$

$$P_{full} = 0.976073097$$

$$\frac{dP}{dY} = -3.010565776$$

$$DUR = 3.254005158$$

$$MD = 3.084365079$$

$$CONV = 12.4963652$$

$$PV01Y = 0.03010566$$

$$YV01P = 0.00332163$$

Czech Republic

Conventions

- Quoted in prices
- Coupon payments are annual.
- The day count method is 30 E/360 for everything.
- The settlement date is four business days after the trade date.
- The ex-dividend date is the thirtieth calendar day before the coupon date.

Example 1

Maturity Date:	2/14/2006
Settlement Date:	2/25/2002
Coupon Rate:	10.55%
Effective Yield:	15%

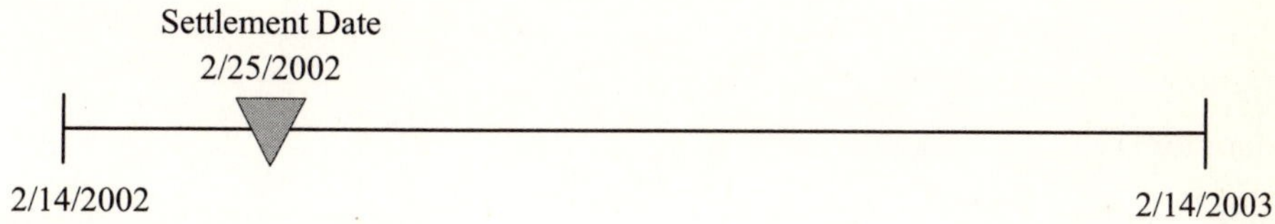

Ex-dividend date: 1/15/2003

This is cum-dividend trading.

$$AIF = \frac{11}{360}$$

$$FCF = 1$$

$$DF = \frac{349}{360}$$

$$LCF = 1$$

$$LDF = 1$$

$$n = 2$$

$$AI = 0.003223611$$

$$P = 0.873465774$$

$$P_{full} = 0.876689385$$

$$\frac{dP}{dY} = -2.585809255$$

$$DUR = 3.39194325$$

$$MD = 2.949515869$$

$$CONV = 12.063913074$$

$$PV01Y = 0.02585809$$

$$YV01P = 0.003867261$$

Example 2

Maturity Date:	8/16/2005
Settlement Date:	7/17/2002
Coupon Rate:	10.95%
Effective Yield:	14%

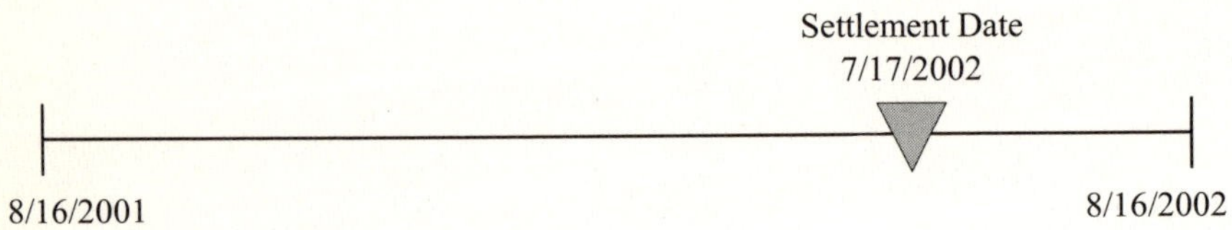

Ex-dividend date: 7/17/2002

This is ex-dividend trading.

$$AIF = -\frac{29}{360}$$

$$FCF = 0$$

$$DF = \frac{29}{360}$$

$$LCF = 1$$

$$LDF = 1$$

$$n = 2$$

$$AI = -0.008820833$$

$$P = 0.928254982$$

$$P_{full} = 0.919434148$$

$$\frac{dP}{dY} = -2.244655869$$

$$DUR = 2.783133186$$

$$MD = 2.4413449$$

$$CONV = 8.421568668$$

$$PV01Y = 0.022446559$$

$$YV01P = 0.004455026$$

Denmark

Conventions

- Quoted in prices
- Coupon payments are annual.
- The day count method is Actual/Actual (in period) for everything.
- The settlement date is three business days after the trade date.
- The ex-dividend date is one month before the coupon date. "One month before the coupon date" means the same day one month earlier (or the end of the previous month if there is no same day) or the end of previous month if the coupon date is on the end of the month.
- Compound interest is used when the settlement date is in the last coupon period.

Example 1

Maturity Date: 11/15/2007

Settlement Date: 10/22/2001

Coupon Rate: 7%

Effective Yield : 6.4%

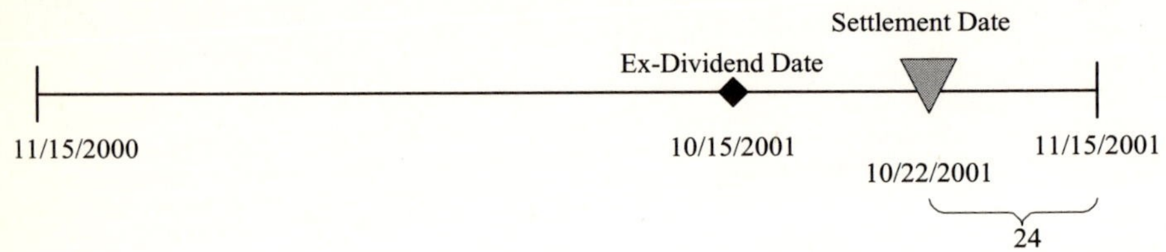

Ex-dividend date: 10/15/2001

This is ex-dividend trading.

$$AIF = -\frac{24}{365}$$

$$FCF = 0 \text{ (Because of ex-dividend trading)}$$

$$DF = \frac{24}{365}$$

$$LCF = 1$$

$$LDF = 1$$

$$n = 5$$

$$AI = 0.07 \cdot \left(-\frac{24}{365}\right) = -0.0046027397$$

$$P = \left(1+\frac{0.064}{1}\right)^{-\frac{23}{360}} \left\{0+\frac{0.07}{0.064}\left[1-\frac{1}{\left(1+\frac{0.064}{1}\right)^{2}}\right] + \left(1+\frac{0.07}{1}\right)\left(1+\frac{0.064}{1}\right)^{-5-1}\right\} + 0.0046027397$$

$$P = 1.0295501619$$

$$P_{full} = 1.0249474222$$

$$\frac{dP}{dY} = -4.99023047$$

$$DUR = 5.18036839$$

$$MD = 4.86876728$$

$$CONV = 30.5296798$$

$$PV01Y = 0.04990230$$

$$YV01P = 0.00200392$$

Example 2

The settlement date is in the last coupon period.

Maturity Date: 11/15/2002

Settlement Date: 4/10/2002

Coupon Rate: 6%

Effective Yield: 4%

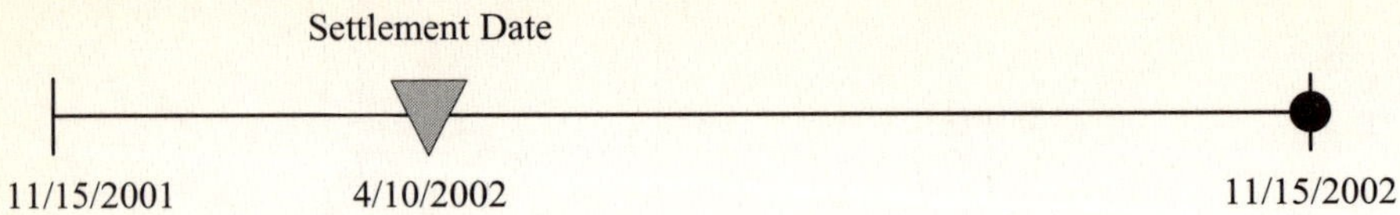

Ex-dividend date: 10/15/2002

This is cum-dividend trading.

$$\text{AIF} = \frac{146}{365}$$

$$\text{DF} = \frac{219}{365}$$

$$\text{LCF} = 1$$

$$\text{AI} = 0.06 \cdot \frac{146}{365} = 0.024$$

$$\text{P} = \frac{1+0.06}{(1+0.04)^{\frac{219}{365}}} - 0.024 = 1.011346838$$

$$\text{P}_{\text{full}} = 1.035346838$$

$$\frac{dP}{dY} = -0.59731548$$

$$\text{DUR} = 0.6$$

$$\text{MD} = 0.57692308$$

$$\text{CONV} = 0.88757396$$

$$\text{PV01Y} = 0.00597316$$

$$\text{YV01P} = 0.01674157$$

Greece

Conventions

- Quoted in prices
- Coupon payments are annual.
- The day count method is 30E/360 for everything.
- No ex-dividend trading
- The settlement date is three business days after the trade date.
- The End-of-Month rule is in effect.
- Simple interest is used when settlement date is in the last coupon period.
- Tax rates for coupon income only:

0%	for bonds issued before 1/1/97
7.5%	for bonds issued in 1997
10%	for bonds issued in 1998
0%	for bonds issued in 1999 and after

Example 1

Maturity Date:	3/21/2004
Settlement Date:	7/23/2001
Coupon Rate:	8.9%
Effective Yield:	9%
Dated Date:	3/21/97
Issue Date:	3/21/97
Tax Rate for Interest Income:	7.5%

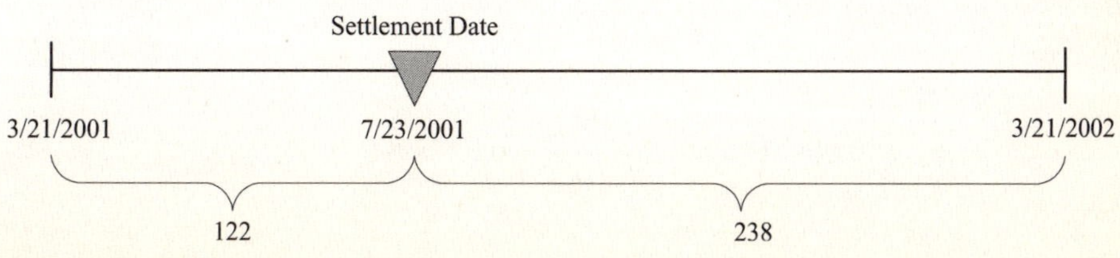

$$\text{AIF} = \frac{122}{360}$$

$$\text{FCF} = 1$$

$$\text{DF} = \frac{238}{360}$$

$$\text{LCF} = 1$$

$$\text{LDF} = 1$$

$$n = 1$$

Before Tax Calculations

$$\text{AI} = 0.03016111$$

$$P = 0.99686788$$

$$P_{full} = 1.02702899$$

$$\frac{dP}{dY} = -2.28235458$$

$$\text{DUR} = 2.42229432$$

$$\text{MD} = 2.22228837$$

$$\text{CONV} = 7.26816313$$

$$\text{PV01Y} = 0.02282355$$

$$\text{YV01P} = 0.00438144$$

After Tax Calculations

TX = 7.5%

$$\text{AI} = 0.089 \cdot (1 - 0.075) \cdot \frac{122}{360} = 0.02789903$$

$$P = (1+0.09)^{-\frac{238}{360}}\left[0.089\cdot 0.925+\frac{0.089\cdot 0.925}{1+0.09}+\frac{1+0.089\cdot 0.925}{(1+0.09)^2}\right] - 0.02789903$$

$$P = 0.98173284$$

$$P_{full} = 1.00963187$$

$$\frac{dP}{dY} = -2.25675799$$

$$DUR = 2.43639913$$

$$MD = 2.23522856$$

$$CONV = 7.32320863$$

$$PV01Y = 0.02256758$$

$$YV01P = 0.00443114$$

Hungary

Conventions

- Quoted in prices
- Coupon payments are semiannual (there are six fixed coupon rate bonds with annual coupon payments).
- The settlement date is two business days after the trade date.
- Day count method is actual (NL)/365 for:
    - Accrued interest to be paid
    - Accrued interest in price/yield formula
    - Cash flows
- The day count method is Actual/365 for all discount factors (DF, LDF, and discount factors for each coupon payment period).

- Coupon payments are calculated with the Actual (NL)/365 day count method, which means they are different for different coupon periods.
- No ex-dividend trading
- All coupon payments are rounded to four decimal places per one forint of face value.
- Price and accrued interest are rounded to six decimal places per one forint of face value.
- Input or output yield is the effective yield.
- Simple interest is used when the bond has one year or less remaining to maturity. 'One year' means the same day one year later or 2/28 of one year and 2/29 of the next year, which is a leap year, or vice versa.

Settlement Date Is More Than One Year from Maturity Date

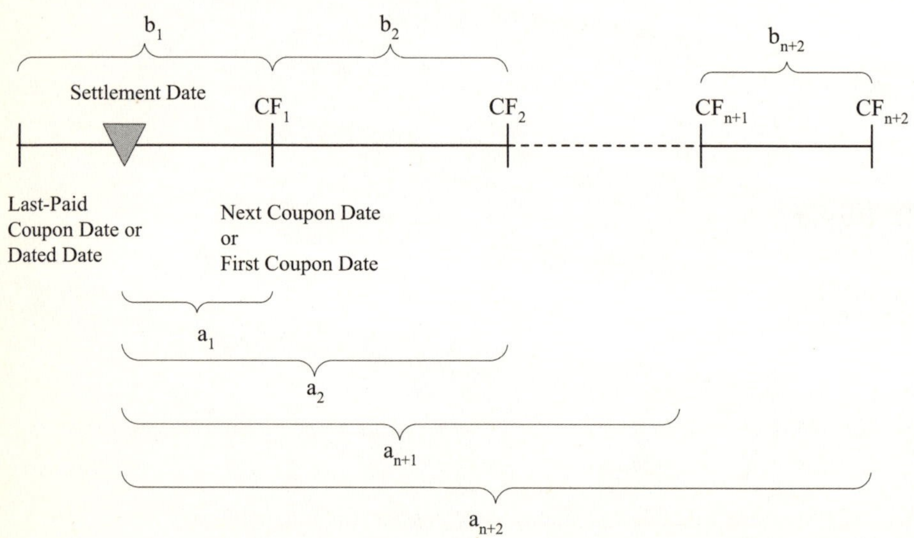

Accrued Interest

$$AI = \frac{C}{F} \cdot AIF$$

$$AIF = \frac{d}{182.5}$$

d is the actual number of days from last paid coupon date (or dated date, if settlement date is in first coupon period) to settlement date (not counting February 29th).

Cash Flows

$$CF_1 = C \cdot \frac{b_1}{365}$$

$$CF_2 = C \cdot \frac{b_2}{365}$$

$$\vdots$$

$$CF_{n+2} = 1 + C \cdot \frac{b_{n+2}}{365}$$

Conversion from effective to nominal annual yield compounded semiannually.

$$Y_s = \left[\left(1 + Y_{eff} \right)^{0.5} - 1 \right] \cdot 2$$

Y_S is the nominal annual yield compounded semiannually.

Y_{eff} is the effective yield.

Price/Yield Formula

$$P = \frac{CF_1}{\left(1 + \frac{Y_F}{F}\right)^{\frac{a_1 \cdot F}{365}}} + \frac{CF_2}{\left(1 + \frac{Y_F}{F}\right)^{\frac{a_2 \cdot F}{365}}} + \ldots + \frac{CF_{n+1}}{\left(1 + \frac{Y_F}{F}\right)^{\frac{a_{n+1} \cdot F}{365}}} + \frac{CF_{n+2}}{\left(1 + \frac{Y_F}{F}\right)^{\frac{a_{n+2} \cdot F}{365}}}$$

Y_F is the nominal annual **y**ield compounded **F** times per year.

F is the **f**requency of coupon payments per year.

Sensitivities with Respect to Effective Yield

$$\frac{dP}{dY_{eff}} = \frac{P\left(Y_{eff} + \Delta Y\right) - P\left(Y_{eff} - \Delta Y\right)}{2 \cdot \left(\Delta Y\right)} \qquad \text{(A)}$$

If F = 1 and the yield is effective yield (yield compounding frequency is 1),

increase effective yield by $\Delta Y = 1\text{bp} = 0.01\% = 0.0001$ and calculate the price $P(Y_{eff} + \Delta Y)$.

Decrease effective yield by $\Delta Y = 0.0001$ and calculate price $P\ (Y_{eff} - \Delta Y)$.

Now calculate $\frac{dP}{dY_{eff}}$ with formula (A).

If F = 2 and the yield is effective yield (yield compounding frequency is 1),

increase effective yield by $\Delta Y = 0.0001$, then convert that yield to nominal annual yield compounded semiannually, and then calculate price $P\ (Y_{eff} + \Delta Y)$ with that converted yield.

Repeat above with effective yield decreased by $\Delta Y = 0.0001$.

Now calculate $\frac{dP}{dY_{eff}}$ with formula (A).

If F = 1 and the yield is nominal annual yield compounded semiannually, convert nominal annual yield compounded semiannually to effective yield.

Increase the effective yield by $\Delta Y = 0.0001$ and calculate the price $P\ (Y_{eff} + \Delta Y)$.

Decrease the effective yield by $\Delta Y = 0.0001$ and calculate the price $P\ (Y_{eff} - \Delta Y)$.

Now calculate $\frac{dP}{dY_{eff}}$ with formula (A).

If F = 2 and the yield is nominal annual yield compounded semiannually,

convert nominal annual yield compounded semiannually to effective yield.

Increase effective yield by $\Delta Y = 0.0001$.

Convert this yield to nominal annual yield compounded semiannually.

Calculate price $P\ (Y_{eff} + \Delta Y)$ with this converted yield.

Repeat the above with the effective yield decreased by $\Delta Y = 0.0001$.

Now calculate $\frac{dP}{dY_{eff}}$ with formula (A).

$$DUR_{eff} = \frac{-\frac{dP}{dY_{eff}}}{P_{full}}\left(1 + Y_{eff}\right)$$

$$MD_{eff} = \frac{-\frac{dP}{dY_{eff}}}{P_{full}}$$

$$CONV_{eff} = \frac{P\left(Y_{eff} + \Delta Y\right) + P\left(Y_{eff} - \Delta Y\right) - 2P\left(Y_{eff}\right)}{P_{full} \cdot \left(\Delta Y\right)^2}$$

$$PV01Y_{eff} = \frac{\left|\frac{dP}{dY_{eff}}\right|}{100}$$

$$YV01P_{eff} = \frac{1}{100\left|\frac{dP}{dY_{eff}}\right|}$$

Settlement Date Is in the Last Coupon Period

Yield is always with simple interest. That means there is no need for any conversion of yields.

$$AI = \frac{C}{F} \cdot AIF$$

$$CF_1 = 1 + C \cdot \frac{b_1}{365}$$

b_1 is the actual number of days (not including February 29th) from last coupon date to maturity date

$$P = \frac{CF_1}{1+\frac{Y}{F}\cdot DF} - AI$$

$$Y = \left(\frac{CF_1}{P+AI} - 1\right)\frac{F}{DF}$$

$$\frac{dP}{dY} = -\frac{CF_1 \cdot DF}{F \cdot \left(1+\frac{Y}{F}\cdot DF\right)^2}$$

$$DUR = \frac{DF}{F}$$

$$MD = \frac{-\frac{dP}{dY}}{P_{full}}$$

$$CONV = \frac{2 \cdot CF_1 \cdot DF^2}{P_{full} \cdot F^2 \left(1+\frac{Y}{F}\cdot DF\right)^3}$$

$$PV01Y = \frac{\left|\frac{dP}{dY}\right|}{100}$$

$$YV01P = \frac{1}{100\left|\frac{dP}{dY}\right|}$$

Settlement Date Is in the Next-to-Last Coupon Period When Frequency of Payments per Year Is Semiannual

Yield is always with simple interest, and there is no need for yield conversion.

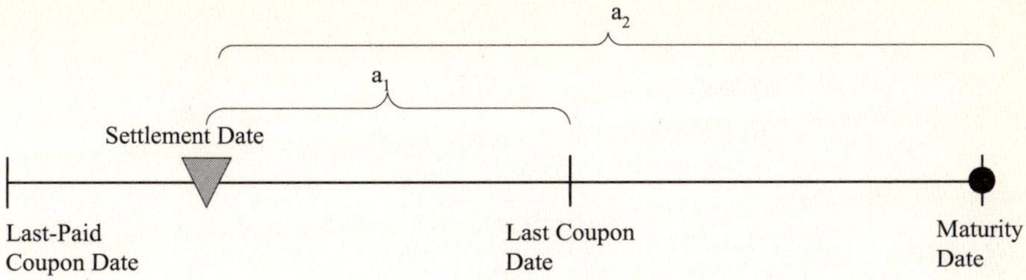

$$P = \frac{CF_1}{1+Y_{eff}\frac{a_1}{365}} + \frac{CF_2}{1+Y_{eff}\frac{a_2}{365}} - AI$$

$$\frac{dP}{dY_{eff}} = -\frac{CF_1 \cdot a_1}{365\left(1+Y_{eff}\frac{a_1}{365}\right)^2} - \frac{CF_2 \cdot a_2}{365\left(1+Y_{eff}\frac{a_2}{365}\right)^2}$$

$$DUR_{eff} = \frac{\frac{CF_1}{1+Y_{eff}\cdot\frac{a_1}{365}}\cdot\frac{a_1}{365} + \frac{CF_2}{1+Y_{eff}\cdot\frac{a_2}{365}}\cdot\frac{a_2}{365}}{P_{full}}$$

$$MD_{eff} = \frac{-\frac{dP}{dY_{eff}}}{P_{full}}$$

$$CONV_{eff} = \frac{1}{P_{full}}\left[\frac{2\cdot CF_1 \cdot a_1^{\,2}}{365^2\left(1+Y_{eff}\cdot\frac{a_1}{365}\right)^3} + \frac{2\cdot CF_2 \cdot a_2^{\,2}}{365^2\left(1+Y_{eff}\cdot\frac{a_2}{365}\right)^3}\right]$$

$$PV01Y_{eff} = \frac{\left|\frac{dP}{dY_{eff}}\right|}{100}$$

$$YV01P_{eff} = \frac{1}{100\left|\frac{dP}{dY_{eff}}\right|}$$

Example 1

Maturity Date:	11/24/2000
Settlement Date:	6/8/99
Nominal Annual Coupon Rate:	16%
Effective Yield:	14%
Coupon Payment Frequency per Year:	2

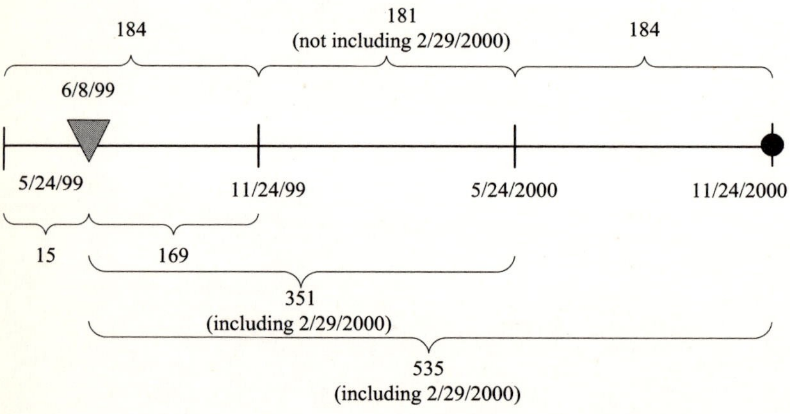

$$\text{AIF} = \frac{15}{182.5}$$

$$a_1 = 169$$
$$a_2 = 351$$
$$a_3 = 535$$

$$b_1 = 184$$
$$b_2 = 181$$
$$b_3 = 184$$

$$\text{AI} = \frac{0.16}{2} \cdot \frac{15}{182.5} = 0.006575342 \approx 0.006575$$

$$Y_s = \left(1.14^{0.5} - 1\right) \cdot 2 = 0.13541565$$

$$CF_1 = 0.16 \cdot \frac{184}{365} = 0.080657534 \approx 0.0807$$

$$CF_2 = 0.16 \cdot \frac{181}{365} = 0.079342465 \approx 0.0793$$

$$CF_3 = 1 + 0.16 \cdot \frac{184}{365} = 1.080657534 \approx 1.0807$$

$$P = \frac{0.0807}{\left(1 + \frac{0.13541565}{2}\right)^{\frac{169}{182.5}}} + \frac{0.0793}{\left(1 + \frac{0.13541565}{2}\right)^{\frac{351}{182.5}}}$$

$$+ \frac{1.0807}{\left(1 + \frac{0.13541565}{2}\right)^{\frac{535}{182.5}}} - 0.006575$$

$$= 1.031146505 \approx 1.031147$$

$$P_{full} = 1.031147 + 0.006575 = 1.037722$$

$$\frac{dP}{dY} = \frac{1.031022865 - 1.031270171}{0.0002} = -1.23653$$

$$\text{DUR} = \frac{1.23653}{1.037722} \cdot \left(1 + 0.14\right) = 1.358402539$$

$$\text{MD} = \frac{1.23653}{1.037722} = 1.191581175$$

$$\text{CONV} = \frac{1.031022865 + 1.031270171 - 2 \cdot 1.031146505}{1.037722 \cdot 0.00000001}$$

$$= 2.505487982$$

$$\text{PV01Y} = \frac{1.23653}{100} = 0.0123653$$

$$\text{YV01P} = \frac{1}{100 \cdot 1.23653} = 0.00808714709$$

Example 2

The settlement date is in the last coupon period.

Maturity Date:	10/24/2001
Settlement Date:	5/28/2001
Nominal Annual Coupon Rate:	21%
Effective Yield:	11%
Coupon Payment Frequency per Year:	2

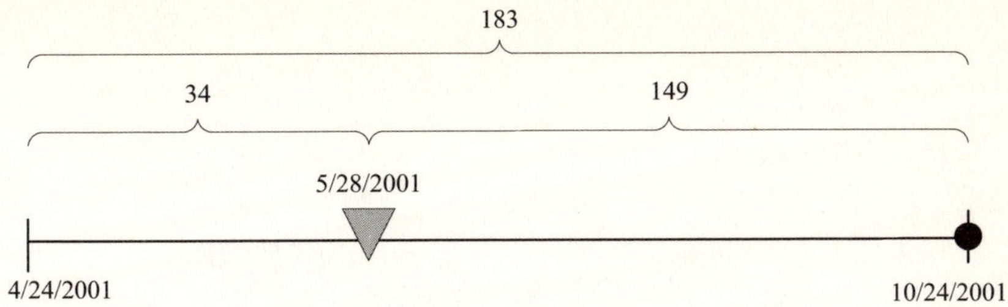

$$AIF = \frac{34}{182.5}$$

$$DF = \frac{149}{182.5}$$

$$b_1 = 183$$

$$AI = \frac{0.21}{2} \cdot \frac{34}{182.5} = 0.019561643 \approx 0.019562$$

$$CF_1 = 1 + 0.21 \cdot \frac{183}{365} = 1.105287671 \approx 1.1053$$

$$P = \frac{1.1053}{1 + \frac{0.11}{2} \cdot \frac{149}{182.5}} - 0.019562 = 1.038238414 \approx 1.038238$$

$$P_{full} = 1.0578$$

$$\frac{dP}{dY} = -\frac{1.1053 \cdot \frac{149}{182.5}}{2 \cdot \left(1 + \frac{0.11}{2} \cdot \frac{149}{182.5}\right)^2} = -0.413257457$$

$$DUR = \frac{149}{365} = 0.408219178$$

$$\text{MD} = \frac{0.413257457}{1.0578} = 0.390676363$$

$$\text{CONV} = \frac{2 \cdot 1.1053 \cdot \left(\frac{149}{182.5}\right)^2}{1.0578 \cdot 2^2 \cdot \left(1 + \frac{0.11}{2} \cdot \frac{149}{182.5}\right)^3} = 0.305255922$$

$$\text{PV01Y} = \frac{0.413257457}{100} = 0.004132575$$

$$\text{YV01P} = \frac{1}{100 \cdot 0.413257457} = 0.02419799$$

Example 3

The settlement date is in the next-to-last coupon period.

Maturity Date:	1/12/2002
Settlement Date:	3/5/2001
Nominal Annual Coupon Rate:	16%
Effective Yield:	15%
Coupon Payment Frequency per Year:	2

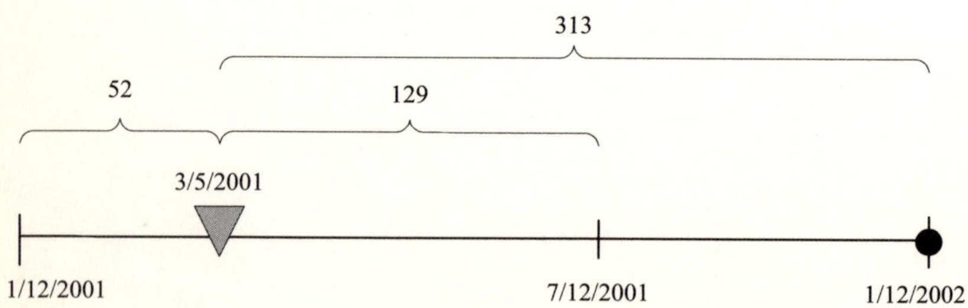

$$\text{AIF} = \frac{52}{182.5}$$

$$a_1 = 129$$
$$a_2 = 313$$

$$b_1 = 181$$
$$b_2 = 184$$

$$\text{AI} = \frac{0.16}{2} \cdot \frac{52}{182.5} = 0.02279452 \approx 0.022795$$

$$\text{CF}_1 = \frac{0.16}{2} \cdot \frac{181}{182.5} = 0.079342465 \approx 0.0793$$

$$\text{CF}_2 = 1 + \frac{0.16}{2} \cdot \frac{184}{182.5} = 1.080657534 \approx 1.0807$$

$$P = \frac{0.0793}{1 + 0.15 \cdot \frac{129}{365}} + \frac{1.0807}{1 + 0.15 \cdot \frac{313}{365}} - 0.022795$$

$$P = 1.01004513 \approx 1.010045$$

$$P_{\text{full}} = 1.03284$$

$$\frac{dP}{dY} = -\frac{0.0793 \cdot 129}{365 \cdot \left(1 + 0.15 \cdot \frac{129}{182.5}\right)^2} - \frac{1.0807 \cdot 313}{365 \cdot \left(1 + 0.15 \cdot \frac{313}{365}\right)^2}$$

$$\frac{dP}{dY} = -0.752809705$$

$$\text{DUR} = \frac{\frac{0.0793}{1 + 0.15 \cdot \frac{129}{365}} \cdot \frac{129}{365} + \frac{1.0807}{1 + 0.15 \cdot \frac{313}{365}} \cdot \frac{313}{365}}{1.03284}$$

$$DUR = 0.820778114$$

$$MD = 0.728873499$$

$$CONV = \frac{1}{1.03284}\left[\frac{2\cdot 0.0793\cdot 129^2}{365^2\cdot\left(1+0.15\cdot\dfrac{129}{365}\right)^3}+\frac{2\cdot 1.0807\cdot 313^2}{365^2\cdot\left(1+0.15\cdot\dfrac{313}{365}\right)^3}\right]$$

$$CONV = 1.08683703$$

$$PV01Y = 0.007528097$$

$$YV01P = 0.013283569$$

Example 4

Maturity Date:	10/26/2004
Settlement Date:	4/12/2000
Coupon Rate:	23%
Effective Yield:	12%
Coupon Payment Frequency per Year:	1

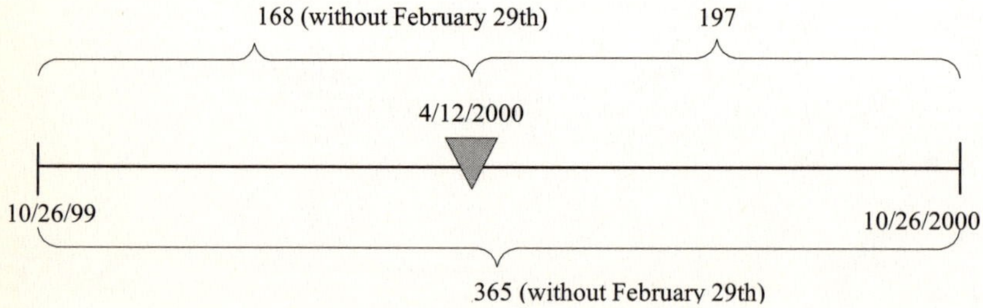

$$\text{AIF} = \frac{168}{365}$$

$$a_1 = 197$$
$$a_2 = 562$$
$$a_3 = 927$$
$$a_4 = 1292$$
$$a_5 = 1658 \text{ (including February 29th of 2004)}$$

$$b_1 = 365$$
$$b_2 = 365$$
$$b_3 = 365$$
$$b_4 = 365$$
$$b_5 = 365$$

$$\text{AI} = 0.23 \cdot \frac{168}{365} = 0.105863013 \approx 0.105863$$

$$\text{CF}_1 = \text{CF}_2 = \text{CF}_3 = \text{CF}_4 = 0.23$$

$$\text{CF}_5 = 1+0.23 = 1.23$$

$$\text{P} = \frac{0.23}{(1+0.12)^{\frac{197}{365}}} + \frac{0.23}{(1+0.12)^{\frac{562}{365}}} + \frac{0.23}{(1+0.12)^{\frac{927}{365}}} + \frac{0.23}{(1+0.12)^{\frac{1292}{365}}} + \frac{1.23}{(1+0.12)^{\frac{1658}{365}}} - 0.105863$$

$$\text{P} = 1.365213381 \approx 1.365213$$

$$\text{P}_{\text{full}} = 1.471076$$

$$\frac{dP}{dY} = -4.228945$$

$$\text{DUR} = 3.219696603$$

MD	=	2.87472911
CONV	=	12.71178376
PV01Y	=	0.04228945
YV01P	=	0.002364656

Ireland

Conventions

- Quoted in prices
- The day count convention is:
  - Act/365 for everything if the issue date is before 6/14/1993.
  - 30E/360 for everything if the issue date is on or after 6/14/1993 and before 9/1/1997.
  - Act/Act (in period) for everything if the issue date is on or after 9/1/1997.
- Coupon payment frequency per year is semiannual if the issue date is before 6/14/1993, annual if the issue date is on or after 6/14/1993.
- The End-of-Month rule is not in effect.
- The ex-dividend date is the sixth business day before coupon date.
- Compound interest is used when settlement date is in the last coupon period.
- The settlement date is one business day after the trade date.
- Input yield and calculated yield (output) should always be the effective yield.
- All sensitivity measures should be calculated with respect to effective yield. Effective yield is the annual yield compounded annually.

Sensitivity measures with respect to effective yield, when the coupon payment frequency is semiannual:

$$\left(1+\frac{Y_s}{2}\right)^2 = 1+Y_{eff}$$

$$Y_s = \left[\left(1+Y_{eff}\right)^{\frac{1}{2}} - 1\right]\cdot 2$$

$$\frac{dY_s}{dY_{eff}} = \left(1+Y_{eff}\right)^{-\frac{1}{2}}$$

$$\frac{dP}{dY_{eff}} = \frac{dP}{dY_s}\cdot\frac{dY_s}{dY_{eff}}$$

$\frac{dP}{dY_s}$ is the first derivative from General Price/Yield formula.

$$\frac{d^2Y_s}{dY_{eff}^{\,2}} = -\frac{1}{2}\left(1+Y_{eff}\right)^{-\frac{3}{2}}$$

$$\frac{d^2P}{dY_{eff}^{\,2}} = \frac{d^2P}{dY_S^{\,2}}\left(\frac{dY_S}{dY_{eff}}\right)^2 + \frac{dP}{dY_S}\cdot\frac{d^2Y_S}{dY_{eff}^{\,2}}$$

$\frac{d^2P}{dY_S^{\,2}}$ is the second derivative from General Price/Yield formula.

$$DUR = \frac{-\frac{dP}{dY_{eff}}}{P_{full}}\left(1+Y_{eff}\right)$$

$$MD = \frac{-\frac{dP}{dY_{eff}}}{P_{full}}$$

$$\text{CONV} = \frac{\dfrac{d^2P}{dY_{eff}^{\ 2}}}{P_{full}}$$

$$\text{PV01Y} = \frac{\left|\dfrac{dP}{dY_{eff}}\right|}{100}$$

$$\text{YV01P} = \frac{1}{100\left|\dfrac{dP}{dY_{eff}}\right|}$$

Example 1

Maturity Date:	12/15/2005
Settlement Date:	5/17/99
Issue Date:	12/15/84
Nominal Annual Coupon Rate:	12.5%
Effective Yield:	4%
Frequency of Coupon Payments per Year:	2
Day Count Method:	Act / 365

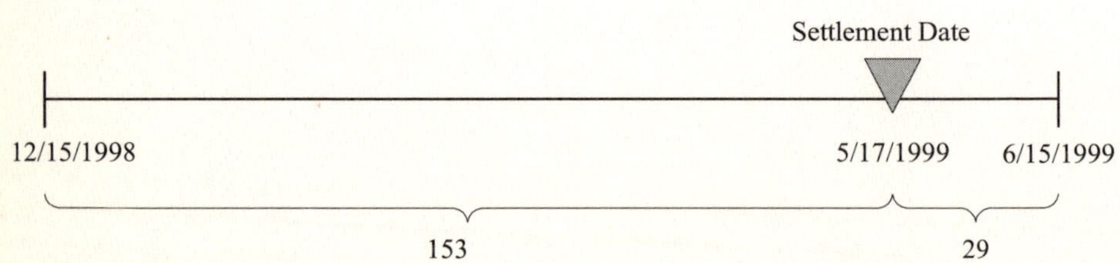

Ex-dividend date: 6/4/1999

This is cum-dividend trading.

$$\text{AIF} = \frac{153}{182.5}$$

$$\text{FCF} = 1$$

$$\text{DF} = \frac{29}{182.5}$$

$$\text{LCF} = 1$$

$$\text{LDF} = 1$$

$$n = 12$$

Nominal annual yield compounded semiannually:

$$Y_s = \left[(1 + 0.04)^{\frac{1}{2}} - 1\right] \cdot 2 = 0.039607805$$

$$\text{AI} = \frac{0.125}{2} \cdot \frac{153}{182.5} = 0.05239726$$

$$P = 1 + \frac{Y_s}{2}^{-\frac{29}{182.5}} \left\{ \frac{0.125}{2} + \frac{0.125}{Y_s}\left[1 - \frac{1}{\left(1 + \frac{Y_s}{2}\right)^{12}}\right] + \left(1 + \frac{0.125}{2}\right)\left(1 + \frac{Y_s}{2}\right)^{-12-1} \right\} - 0.05239726$$

$$P = 1.490445618$$

$$P_{\text{full}} = 1.542842878$$

$$\frac{dP}{dY_s} = -7.37891865$$

$$\frac{d^2P}{dY_s^2} = 46.21674249$$

$$\frac{dY_s}{dY_{eff}} = (1+0.04)^{-\frac{1}{2}} = 0.980580675$$

$$\frac{d^2Y_s}{dY_{eff}^2} = -\frac{1}{2}(1+0.04)^{-\frac{3}{2}} = -0.471433017$$

$$\frac{dP}{dY_{eff}} = -7.37891865 \cdot 0.980580675 = -7.235625031$$

$$DUR = \frac{7.235625031}{1.542842878}(1+0.04) = 4.877392338$$

$$MD = \frac{7.235625031}{1.542842878} = 4.689800325$$

$$\frac{d^2P}{dY_{eff}^2} = 46.21674249 \cdot (0.980580675)^2 + (-7.37891865) \cdot (-0.471433017) = 47.91784129$$

$$CONV = \frac{47.91784129}{1.542842878} = 31.05814725$$

$$PV01Y = \frac{7.235625031}{100} = 0.072356250$$

$$YV01P = \frac{1}{100 \cdot 7.235625031} = 0.0013820506$$

Example 2

Maturity Date:	10/18/2004
Settlement Date:	5/14/1999
Issue Date:	10/18/1993
Coupon Rate:	6.25%
Effective Yield:	3%
Frequency of Coupon Payments per Year:	1
Day Count Method:	30E / 360

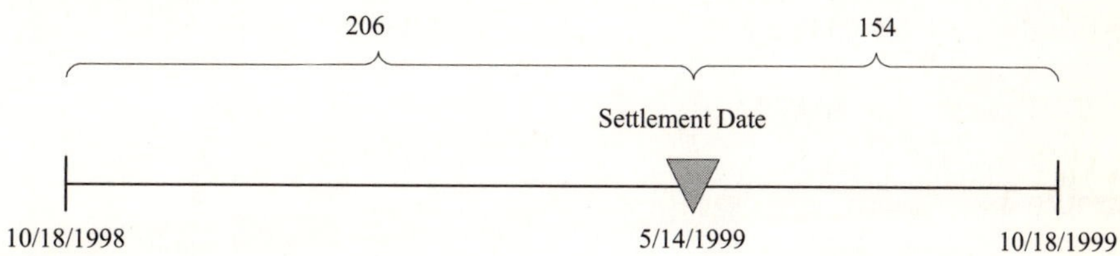

Ex-dividend date: 10/8/1999.

This is cum-dividend trading.

$$\text{AIF} = \frac{206}{360}$$

$$\text{FCF} = 1$$

$$\text{DF} = \frac{154}{360}$$

$$\text{LCF} = 1$$

$$\text{LDF} = 1$$

$$n = 4$$

$$\text{AI} = 0.035763889$$

$$P = 1.160356112$$

$$P_{full} = 1.196120001$$

$$\frac{dP}{dY} = -5.438570218$$

$$DUR = 4.683248606$$

$$MD = 4.546843306$$

$$CONV = 27.17083604$$

$$PV01Y = 0.05438561$$

$$YV01P = 0.001838719$$

Example 3

Maturity Date:	8/18/2006
Settlement Date:	8/11/1999
Issue Date:	5/16/1995
Coupon Rate:	8%
Effective Yield:	3%
Frequency of Coupon Payments per Year:	1
Day Count Method:	30E / 360

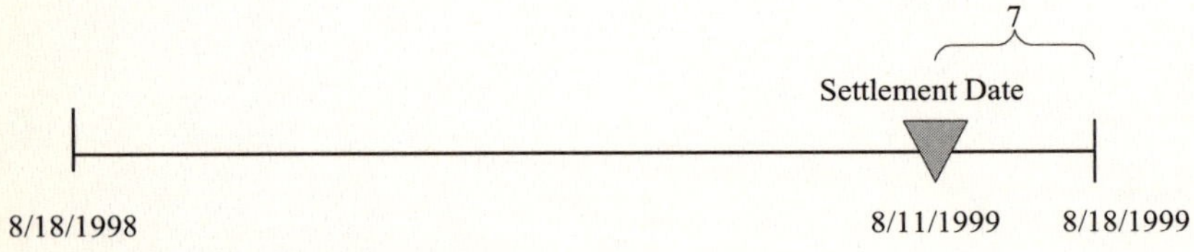

Ex-dividend date: 8/10/1999.

This is ex-dividend trading.

$$\text{AIF} = -\frac{7}{360}$$

$$\text{FCF} = 0$$

$$\text{DF} = \frac{7}{360}$$

$$\text{LCF} = 1$$

$$\text{LDF} = 1$$

$$n = 6$$

$$\text{AI} = 0.08\left(-\frac{7}{360}\right) = -0.001555556$$

$$P = 1.312316121$$

$$P_{\text{full}} = 1.31076057$$

$$\frac{dP}{dY} = -7.424803711$$

$$\text{DUR} = 5.834435383$$

$$\text{MD} = 5.664500372$$

$$\text{CONV} = 41.17512444$$

$$\text{PV01Y} = 0.074248037$$

$$\text{YV01P} = 0.001346837$$

Example 4

The settlement date is in the last coupon period.

Maturity Date:	7/15/1999
Settlement Date:	7/9/1999

Issue Date:	11/4/1986
Nominal Annual Coupon Rate:	7.5%
Effective Yield:	3%
Frequency of Coupon Payments per Year:	2
Day Count Method:	Act / 365

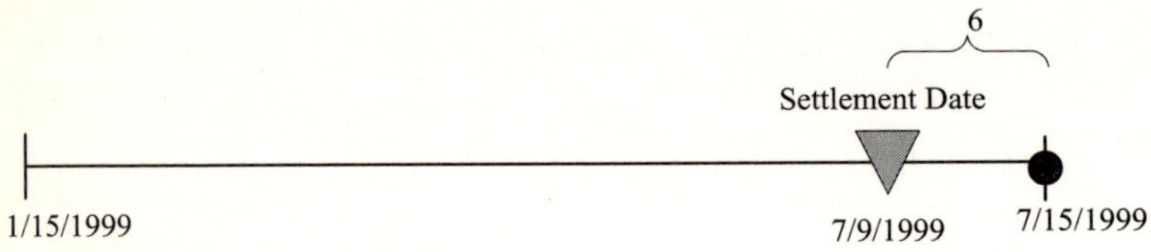

Ex-dividend date: 7/7/1999.

This is ex-dividend trading.

$$Y_s = \left[(1+0.03)^{\frac{1}{2}} - 1\right] \cdot 2$$

$$Y_s = 0.029778313$$

$$\text{AIF} = -\frac{6}{182.5}$$

$$\text{DF} = \frac{6}{182.5}$$

$$\text{LCF} = 0$$

$$\text{AI} = \frac{0.075}{2}\left(-\frac{6}{182.5}\right) = -0.001232876$$

$$\text{P} = \frac{1}{\left(1+\frac{0.029778313}{2}\right)^{\frac{6}{182.5}}} + 0.001232876 = 1.000747096$$

$$\text{P}_{\text{full}} = 0.999514219$$

$$\frac{dP}{dY_s} = -0.016189325$$

$$\frac{dY_s}{dY_{eff}} = 0.985329278$$

$$\frac{d^2P}{dY_s^{\ 2}} = 0.008238129$$

$$\frac{d^2Y_s}{dY_{eff}^{\ 2}} = -0.478315183$$

$$\frac{dP}{dY_{eff}} = -0.015951815$$

DUR = 0.016438356

MD = 0.015959569

CONV = 0.015749434

PV01Y = 0.000159518

YV01P = 0.6268878728

Example 5

The settlement date is in the last coupon period.

Maturity Date:	7/15/2001
Settlement Date:	3/8/2001
Issue Date:	5/22/1991
Nominal Annual Coupon Rate:	9%
Effective Yield:	3%
Frequency of Coupon Payments per Year:	2
Day Count Method:	Act / 365

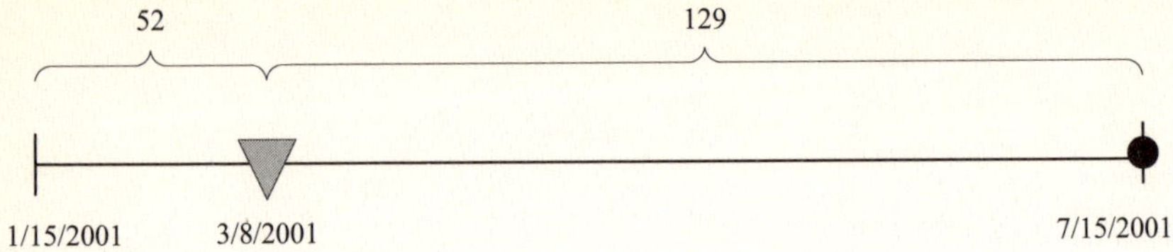

Ex-dividend date: 7/6/2001.

This is cum-dividend trading.

$$Y_s = \left[(1+0.03)^{\frac{1}{2}} - 1 \right] \cdot 2$$

$$Y_s = 0.029778313$$

$$\text{AIF} = \frac{52}{182.5}$$

$$\text{DF} = \frac{129}{182.5}$$

$$\text{LCF} = 1$$

$$\text{AI} = \frac{0.09}{2}\left(\frac{52}{182.5}\right) = 0.012821918$$

$$P = \frac{1+\frac{0.09}{2}}{\left(1+\frac{0.029778313}{2}\right)^{\frac{129}{182.5}}} - 0.012821918 = 1.021317991$$

$$P_{\text{full}} = 1.034139909$$

$$\frac{dP}{dY_s} = -0.360128533$$

$$\frac{dY_s}{dY_{eff}} = 0.985329278$$

$$\frac{d^2P}{dY_s^2} = 0.302833633$$

$$\frac{d^2Y_s}{dY_{eff}^2} = -0.478315183$$

$$\frac{dP}{dY_{eff}} = -0.354845187$$

DUR = 0.353424657

MD = 0.343130735

CONV = 0.450875337

PV01Y = 0.003548452

YV01P = 0.028181303

Italy

Conventions

- Quoted in prices
- Coupon payments are semiannual (for BPTs—Buoni Poliennali del Tesoro).
- The day count method is actual/actual (in period) for everything.
- No ex-dividend trading
- The settlement date is three business days after a trade date.

- The interest income and the spread between redemption value and base price for taxes [price at issue (fiscal price in this case)] are taxable. If the price at issue is greater than 100, then 100 should be used as the base price for taxes.
- The reform date is the first coupon date in 1997.
- The tax rate is 12.50%.
- Price/yield formula is the general price/yield formula for periodic payment fixed income securities with some adjustments for taxes depending on when the bond is issued and gross or net yield (see examples).
- In price/yield calculations with net (or true net) yield, there is a term, at the settlement date, that is subtracted from the full price. It represents the portion of original issue discount after tax [TXG(1–fiscal price)], which depends on issue date of a bond (see examples).
- Simple yield is used when settlement date is in the last coupon period.

True yield is calculated as follows: all coupon dates and maturity date that are on nonbusiness days are moved to the next business day.

> In order to do this, we need to know the holidays in each year up to the maturity date of security. If we don't know this, we will count only Saturdays and Sundays.

The day count method (for discounting of cash flows) is actual/actual (in period).

- Input yield and calculated yield (output) should always be the effective yield. Effective yield is the annual yield compounded annually. In the price yield formula, the annual yield compounded semiannually is used. That means the effective yield must be converted to annual yield compounded semiannually.

  The conversion formula is as follows:

$$Y_S = \left[(1 + Y_{eff})^{\frac{1}{2}} - 1\right] \cdot 2$$

- All sensitivity measures should be calculated with respect to effective true (gross or net) yield. First derivative (risk) should be calculated by moving effective true yield up and down (see Chapter 3).

Example 1

Issued on or after 1/1/1999.

Maturity Date:	9/1/2002
Issue Date:	9/1/1999
Settlement Date:	9/8/2000
Nominal Annual Coupon Rate:	3.75%
Base Price for Taxes:	99.24%
Day Count Method:	Actual/actual (in period)

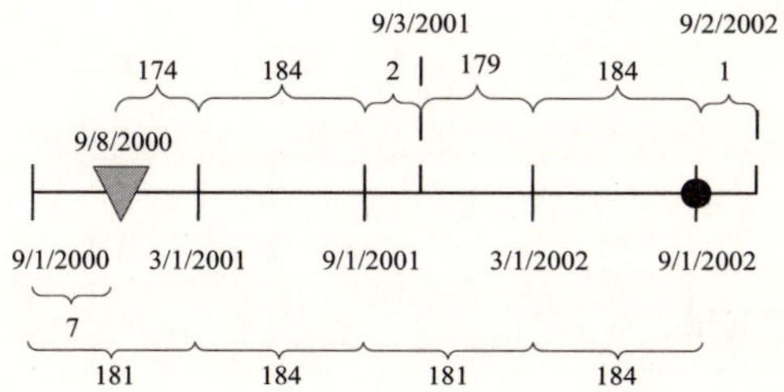

$$AIF = \frac{7}{181}$$

$$FCF = 1$$

$$DF = \frac{174}{181}$$

$$LCF = 1$$

$$LDF = 1$$

$$n = 2$$

$$TX = TXG = 12.5\%$$

Gross Accrued Interest

$$AI_G = \frac{0.0375}{2}\cdot\frac{7}{181} = 0.000725138 \approx 0.0007251$$

Net Accrued Interest

$$AI_N = \frac{0.0375}{2}\cdot\frac{7}{181}\cdot(1-0.125) = 0.000634496 \approx 0.0006345$$

Gross Effective True Yield 5%

$$Y_S = \left(1.05^{\frac{1}{2}} - 1\right)\cdot 2 = 0.049390153$$

$$P = \left(1+\frac{Y_S}{2}\right)^{\frac{174}{181}}\left[0.01875 + \frac{0.01875}{\left(1+\frac{Y_S}{2}\right)^{1+\frac{2}{181}}} + \frac{0.01875}{\left(1+\frac{Y_S}{2}\right)^{1+\frac{2}{181}+\frac{179}{181}}} + \frac{1+0.01875}{\left(1+\frac{Y_S}{2}\right)^{1+\frac{2}{181}+\frac{179}{181}+1+\frac{1}{181}}}\right] - 0.0007251$$

$$P = 0.977686545$$

Net Effective True Yield 5%

$$Y_S = 0.049390153$$

$$P = \left(1+\frac{Y_S}{2}\right)^{-\frac{174}{181}}\left[0.01875 \cdot 0.875 + \frac{0.01875 \cdot 0.875}{\left(1+\frac{Y_S}{2}\right)^{1+\frac{2}{181}}}\right.$$

$$\left. + \frac{0.01875 \cdot 0.875}{\left(1+\frac{Y_S}{2}\right)^{1+\frac{2}{181}+\frac{179}{181}}} + \frac{1-0.125\,(1-0.9924) + 0.01875 \cdot 0.875}{\left(1+\frac{Y_S}{2}\right)^{1+\frac{2}{181}+\frac{179}{181}+1+\frac{1}{181}}}\right]$$

$$-\ 0.0006345$$

$$P = 0.968083723$$

Gross Effective Yield 5%

$Y_S = 0.049390153$

$$P = \left(1+\frac{Y_s}{2}\right)^{-\frac{174}{181}}\left[0.01875 + \frac{0.01875}{1+\frac{Y_s}{2}} + \frac{0.01875}{\left(1+\frac{Y_s}{2}\right)^2} + \frac{1+0.01875}{\left(1+\frac{Y_s}{2}\right)^3}\right] - 0.0007251$$

$P = 0.977816013$

Net Effective Yield 5%

$Y_S = 0.049390153$

$$P = \left(1+\frac{Y_s}{2}\right)^{-\frac{174}{181}}\left[0.01875\cdot 0.875 + \frac{0.01875\cdot 0.875}{1+\frac{Y_s}{2}} + \frac{0.01875\cdot 0.875}{\left(1+\frac{Y_s}{2}\right)^2}\right.$$

$$\left. + \frac{1-0.125(1-0.9924)+0.01875\cdot 0.875}{\left(1+\frac{Y_s}{2}\right)^3}\right] - 0.0006345$$

$P = 0.968212185$

Example 2

Issued after 1/1/1997 and before 1/1/1999

Maturity Date:	3/1/2002
Issue Date:	3/1/1997
Settlement Date:	9/20/2000
Nominal Annual Coupon Rate:	6.25%
Base Price for Taxes:	98.15%

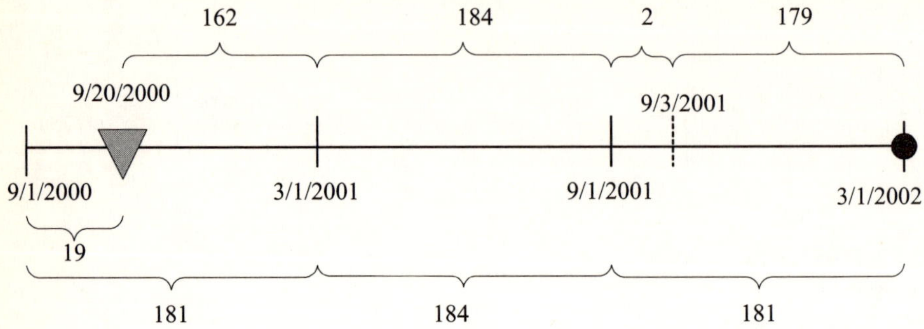

$$\text{AIF} = \frac{19}{181}$$

$$\text{FCF} = 1$$

$$\text{DF} = \frac{162}{181}$$

$$\text{LCF} = 1$$

$$\text{LDF} = 1$$

$$n = 1$$

$$\left.\begin{array}{l}\text{Dated date to maturity date: } 3/1/1997 \text{ to } 3/1/2002 = 1826 \\ \text{Dated date to settlement date: } 3/1/1997 \text{ to } 9/20/2000 = 1299\end{array}\right\} \text{Actual number of days}$$

Gross Accrued Interest

$$AI_G = \frac{0.0625}{2} \cdot \frac{19}{181} = 0.003280387 \approx 0.0032804$$

Net Accrued Interest

$$AI_N = \frac{0.0625}{2} \cdot \frac{19}{181} \cdot 0.875 = 0.002870338 \approx 0.0028703$$

Gross Effective True Yield 5%

$Y_S = 0.049390153$

$$P = \left(1+\frac{Y_s}{2}\right)^{-\frac{162}{181}} \left[0.03125 + \frac{0.03125}{\left(1+\frac{Y_s}{2}\right)^{1+\frac{2}{181}}} + \frac{1+0.03125}{\left(1+\frac{Y_s}{2}\right)^{1+\frac{2}{181}+\frac{179}{181}}} \right] - 0.0032804$$

$P = 1.018055748$

Net Effective True Yield 5%

$Y_S = 0.049390153$

$$P = \left(1+\frac{Y_s}{2}\right)^{-\frac{162}{181}} \left[0.03125 \cdot 0.875 + \frac{0.03125 \cdot 0.875}{\left(1+\frac{Y_s}{2}\right)^{1+\frac{2}{181}}} \right.$$

$$\left. + \frac{1-0.0125(1-0.9815)+0.03125 \cdot 0.875}{\left(1+\frac{Y_s}{2}\right)^{1+\frac{2}{181}+\frac{179}{181}}} \right]$$

$$-0.0028703 + 0.125(1-0.9815)\frac{1299}{1826}$$

$P = 1.006765577$

Gross Effective Yield 5%

$Y_S = 0.049390153$

$$P = \left(1+\frac{Y_S}{2}\right)^{-\frac{162}{181}} \left[0.03125 + \frac{0.03125}{1+\frac{Y_S}{2}} + \frac{1+0.03125}{\left(1+\frac{Y_S}{2}\right)^2}\right] - 0.0032804$$

P = 1.01806379

Net Efffective Yield 5%

$Y_s = 0.049390153$

$$P = \left(1+\frac{Y_S}{2}\right)^{-\frac{162}{181}} \left[0.03125\cdot 0.875 + \frac{0.03125\cdot 0.875}{1+\frac{Y_S}{2}} + \frac{1-0.125(1-0.9815)+0.3125\cdot 0.875}{\left(1+\frac{Y_S}{2}\right)^2}\right] - 0.0028703 + 0.125(1-0.9815)\frac{1299}{1826}$$

P = 1.006772614

Example 3

Issued before 1/1/1997

Maturity Date:	1/1/2002
Issue Date:	1/1/1992
Settlement Date:	9/13/2000
Nominal Annual Coupon Rate:	12%
Base Price for Taxes:	93.85%

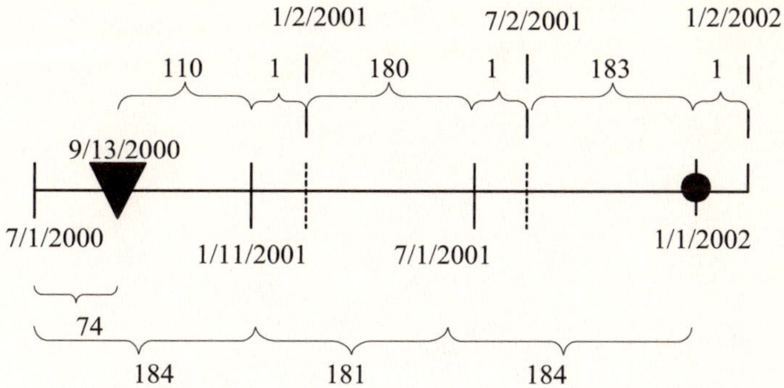

$$\text{AIF} = \frac{74}{184}$$

$$\text{FCF} = 1$$

$$\text{DF} = \frac{110}{184}$$

$$\text{LCF} = 1$$

$$\text{LDF} = 1$$

$$n = 1$$

$$\left.\begin{array}{l}\text{Dated date to maturity date: } 1/1/1992 \text{ to } 1/1/2002 = 3653 \\ \text{Dated date to reform date: } 1/1/1992 \text{ to } 1/1/1997 = 1827 \\ \text{Reform date to settlement date: } 1/1/1997 \text{ to } 9/13/2000 = 1351\end{array}\right\} \text{Actual number of days}$$

Gross Accrued Interest

$$AI_G = \frac{0.12}{2} \cdot \frac{74}{184} = 0.024130435 \approx 0.0241304$$

Net Accrued Interest

$$AI_N = \frac{0.12}{2} \cdot \frac{74}{184} \cdot 0.875 = 0.021114130 \approx 0.0211141$$

Gross Effective True Yield 5%

$Y_s = 0.049390153b$

$$P = \left(1 + \frac{Y_s}{2}\right)^{-\frac{110}{181} - \frac{1}{181}} \left[0.06 + \frac{0.06}{\left(1 + \frac{Y_s}{2}\right)^{\frac{180}{181} + \frac{1}{184}}} \right.$$

$$\left. + \frac{1 - 0.125(1 - 0.9385) \cdot \frac{1827}{3653} + 0.06}{\left(1 + \frac{Y_s}{2}\right)^{\frac{180}{181} + \frac{1}{184} + \frac{183}{184} + \frac{1}{181}}} \right] - 0.0241304$$

$P = 1.083856976$

Net Effective True Yield 5%

$Y_S = 0.049390153$

$$P = \left(1 + \frac{Y_s}{2}\right)^{-\frac{110}{184} - \frac{1}{181}} \left[0.06 \cdot 0.875 + \frac{0.06 \cdot 0.875}{\left(1 + \frac{Y_s}{2}\right)^{\frac{180}{181} + \frac{1}{184}}} \right.$$

$$\left. + \frac{1 - 0.125(1 - 0.9385) + 0.06 \cdot 0.875}{\left(1 + \frac{Y_s}{2}\right)^{\frac{180}{181} + \frac{1}{184} + \frac{183}{184} + \frac{1}{181}}} \right] - 0.0211141 + 0.125(1 - 0.9385)\frac{1351}{3653}$$

$P = 1.064468892$

Gross Effective Yield 5%

$Y_S = 0.049390153$

$$P = \left(1 + \frac{Y_S}{2}\right)^{-\frac{110}{184}} \left[0.06 + \frac{0.06}{\left(1 + \frac{Y_S}{2}\right)} + \frac{1 - 0.125(1 - 0.9385)\frac{1827}{3653} + 0.06}{\left(1 + \frac{Y_S}{2}\right)^2} \right] - 0.0241304$$

$P = 1.084006194$

Net Effective Yield 5%

$Y_S = 0.049390153$

$$P = \left(1 + \frac{Y_S}{2}\right)^{-\frac{110}{184}} \left[0.06 \cdot 0.875 + \frac{0.06 \cdot 0.875}{1 + \frac{Y_S}{2}} + \frac{1 - 0.125(1 - 0.9385) + 0.06 \cdot 0.875}{\left(1 + \frac{Y_S}{2}\right)^2} \right] - 0.0211141 + 0.125(1 - 0.9385)\frac{1351}{3653}$$

$P = 1.064614722$

Japan

Conventions

- Quoted in prices
- Coupon payments are semiannual.
- The day count is Actual/365 (see descriptions of t_{sm} and t_{ps} in formulas below).
- The settlement date is three business days after the trade date, but there is a lockout period of seven business days before the coupon date.
- The maturity date is never on a nonbusiness day.
- If the settlement date (T + 3) falls in the lockout period, then the settlement date should be moved to the next coupon date or the next business day after the next coupon date if the next coupon date is not a business day.
- If the settlement date is in the first coupon period, then both the dated date and the settlement date should be included in the number of accrued-interest days.

  Note that if the settlement date is on the dated date, then the number of Accrued-Interest Days is 0 (the above rule does not apply). If the settlement date is one day after the dated date, the number of Accrued-Interest Days is 2 (the above rule applies).

  For bonds issued on or after 3/1/2001, only one date should be included.
- If the number of accrued-interest days is 183 (or 184 if the settlement date is in the normal first coupon period), then the accrued interest is equal to full coupon payment, that is, AI = C/2.
- Coupon dates are always on the 20th of the month, except the maturity date, which is on the first business day after the 20th, if the 20th is a nonbusiness day.
- Dated date may not be on the 20th of the month, but on the first business day after the 20th, if the 20th is a nonbusiness day.
- The first coupon period may be normal, short, or long.
- If the first coupon period is normal, then the first coupon payment is:

$$\frac{C}{2}\left(1+\frac{1}{182.5}\right)$$ for bonds issued before 3/1/2001.

- If the first coupon period is long, then the first coupon payment is:

$$\frac{C}{2}\left(1+\frac{d_{dn}}{182.5}\right)$$

d_{dn} is the actual number of days from the dated date to the normal issue date.

- If the first coupon period is short, then the first coupon payment is:

$$\frac{C}{2}\cdot\frac{d_{df}}{182.5}$$

d_{df} is the actual number of days from the dated date to the first coupon date.

- The last coupon period can be normal or long.
- Price is truncated to five decimal places per 1 yen of face value.

1. Accrued interest

$$AI = C\cdot\frac{t_{ps}}{365}$$

AI is the accrued interest per 1 yen of face value.
t_{ps} is the actual number of days from the last-paid coupon date (dated date, if settlement date is in the first coupon period) to the settlement date. In a leap year, February 29th is always counted.

2. Price/Yield

Settlement date in any coupon period

$$P=\frac{RV+C\cdot\frac{t_{sm}}{365}}{1+Y\cdot\frac{t_{sm}}{365}}$$

$$Y=\frac{C+(RV-P)\cdot\frac{365}{t_{sm}}}{P}$$

Note that this is simple interest.

P is the price per 1 yen of face value.

C is the nominal annual coupon rate, expressed as a decimal.

Y is the simple yield, expressed as a decimal.

RV is the redemption value per 1 yen of face value.

t_{sm} is the actual number of days from the settlement date to the maturity date. In a leap year, February 29th is not counted, except when the settlement date is 1 year or less before the maturity date (in which case February 29th is counted).

LEAP YEAR EXPLANATION

Notation:

T_{ps} = actual number of days between the previous coupon date (dated date if the settlement date is in the first coupon period) and the settlement date (number of accrued days).

T_{sm} = actual number of days between the settlement date and the maturity date.

Rules:

If T_{sm} is less than or equal to one year, February 29th should be included in T_{sm}.

If T_{sm} is greater than one year, February 29th should not be included in T_{sm}.

The way of not including February 29th is this: always count February 29th and then subtract one.

February 29th should always be included in T_{ps}.

One year means the period from one date to the same date a year later or earlier. This should include the period from 2/28 of one year to 2/29 of the next year or from 2/29 of one year to 2/28 of the next year.

Example 1

Maturity Date: 1/20/2001

Settlement Date: 2/29/2000

T_{sm} = 2/29/2000 to 1/20/2001 < one year

T_{sm} = 326 (February 29th is included)

T_{ps} = 1/20/2000 to 2/29/2000 = 40
(February 29th is included)

Example 2

Maturity Date:	2/28/2001
Settlement Date:	2/29/2000
T_{sm} =	2/29/2000 to 2/28/2001 = one year
T_{sm} =	365 (February 29th is included)
T_{ps} =	2/29/2000 to 2/29/2000 = 0 (February 29th is included)

Example 3

Maturity Date:	4/20/2001
Settlement Date:	2/29/2000
T_{sm} =	2/29/2000 to 4/20/2001 > one year
T_{sm} =	415 (February 29th is not included)
T_{ps} =	10/20/99 to 2/29/2000 = 132 (February 29th is included)

Example 4

Maturity Date:	6/20/2000
Settlement Date:	2/5/2000
T_{sm} =	2/5/2000 to 6/20/2000 < one year
T_{sm} =	136 (February 29th is included)
T_{ps} =	12/20/99 to 2/5/2000 = 47

Example 5

Maturity Date:	1/20/2001
Settlement Date:	1/20/2000

T_{sm} =	1/20/2000 to 1/20/2001 = one year
T_{sm} =	366 (February 29th is included)
T_{sm} =	1/20/2000 to 1/20/2000 = 0

Example 6

Maturity Date:	3/20/2002
Settlement Date:	2/15/2000
T_{sm} =	2/15/2000 to 3/20/2002 > one year
T_{sm} =	763 (February 29th is not included)
T_{sm} =	9/20/99 to 2/15/2000 = 148

Notes:

The numerator in formula for price can be rewritten like this:

$$RV + C\frac{t_{sm}}{365} = RV + \frac{C}{2} \cdot \frac{t_{sm}}{182.5}$$

$\frac{C}{2}$ is the full coupon payment.

$\frac{t_{sm}}{182.5}$ is the number of half-a-year coupon periods from the settlement date to the maturity date, which includes the fraction of a current coupon period (from the settlement date to the next coupon date). The denominator has time from the settlement date to the maturity date, which means that price is calculated as if all the coupon payments are made on the maturity date (in reality it is not true, because payments are made every half-year on coupon dates).

Price is without accrued interest, because the next coupon payment (according to note 1 above) is only the fraction (from the settlement date to the next coupon date) of the full coupon payment. It does not include the accrued-interest portion of the current coupon period.

3. Full price

$$P_{full} = P + AI$$

4. First derivative of price with respect to yield:

$$\frac{dP}{dY} = -\frac{RV + C\dfrac{t_{sm}}{365}}{\left(1 + Y\dfrac{t_{sm}}{365}\right)^2} \cdot \frac{t_{sm}}{365}$$

5. Duration

$$DUR = \frac{\left|\dfrac{dP}{dY}\right|}{P_{full}}\left(1 + \frac{Y}{2}\right)$$

In last coupon period,

$$DUR = \frac{t_{sm}}{365}$$

6. Modified Duration

$$MD = \frac{\left|\dfrac{dP}{dY}\right|}{P_{full}}$$

7. Convexity

$$CONV = \frac{\dfrac{d^2P}{dY^2}}{P_{full}}$$

$$\frac{d^2P}{dY^2} = \frac{2\left(RV + C\dfrac{t_{sm}}{365}\right)\left(\dfrac{t_{sm}}{365}\right)^2}{\left(1 + Y\dfrac{t_{sm}}{365}\right)^3}$$

8. Price value of 0.01

$$PV01Y = \frac{\left|\dfrac{dP}{dY}\right|}{100}$$

9. Yield value of 0.01

$$\text{YV01P} = \frac{1}{100\left|\frac{dP}{dY}\right|}$$

Example 1

Normal last coupon period.
The settlement date is in neither the first nor the last coupon period.

Maturity Date:	3/20/2009
Settlement Date:	11/10/99
Nominal Annual Coupon Rate:	2%
Simple Yield:	3%

$t_{sm} = 3415$ (February 29th is not included), $t_{ps} = 51$

$$\text{AI} = 0.002794520$$

$$P = 0.926944058 \approx 0.92694$$

$$P_{full} = 0.92973452$$

$$\frac{dP}{dY} = -6.771877118$$

$$\text{DUR} = 7.392922525$$

$$\text{MD} = 7.283667507$$

$$\text{CONV} = 106.4230379$$

$$\text{PV01Y} = 0.067718771$$

$$\text{YV01P} = 0.001476695$$

Example 2

Normal last coupon period

The settlement date is in neither the first nor the last coupon period.

Maturity Date:	6/20/2005
Settlement Date:	4/2/2000
Nominal Annual Coupon Rate:	4%
Simple Yield:	7%

$t_{sm} = 1904$, $t_{ps} = 104$ (February 29th is included)

$$AI = 0.04 \cdot \frac{104}{365} = 0.011397260$$

$$P = \frac{1 + 0.04 \cdot \frac{1904}{365}}{1 + 0.07 \cdot \frac{1904}{365}} = 0.885365658 \approx 0.88536$$

$$P_{full} = 0.89675726$$

$$\frac{dP}{dY} = -3.383110325$$

$$DUR = 3.904645483$$

$$MD = 3.772604332$$

$$CONV = 28.83133438$$

$$PV01Y = 0.033831103$$

$$YV01P = 0.00295586$$

Example 3

Normal last coupon period

The settlement date is on February 29th.

The settlement date is less than one year from the maturity date.

Maturity Date:	3/20/2000
Settlement Date:	2/29/2000
Nominal Annual Coupon Rate:	2.6%
Simple Yield:	0.5%

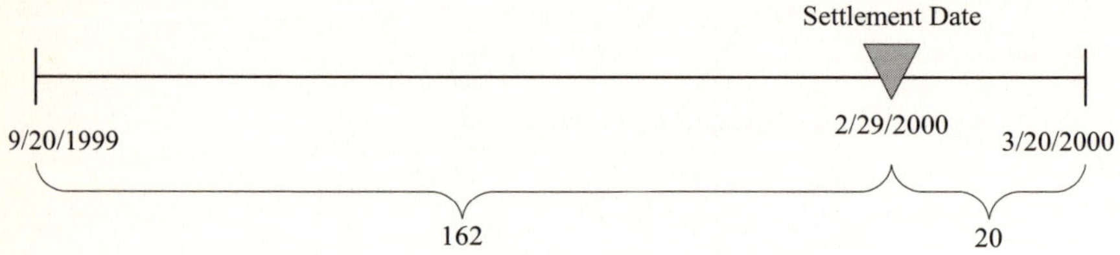

t_{ps} = 9/20/1999 to 2/29/2000 = 162 (February 29th is included)

t_{sm} = 2/29/2000 to 3/20/2000 = 20 (February 29th is included)

$$AI = 0.026 \cdot \frac{162}{365} = 0.011539726$$

$$P = \frac{1 + 0.026 \cdot \frac{20}{365}}{1 + 0.005 \cdot \frac{20}{365}} = 1.00115$$

$$P_{full} = 1.012689726$$

$$\frac{dP}{dY} = -0.05484253$$

$$DUR = 0.05429070$$

$$MD = 0.05415531$$

$$CONV = 0.00593320$$

$$\text{PV01Y} = 0.00054843$$

$$\text{YV01P} = 0.18234024$$

Example 4

Short first coupon period

Long last coupon period

The settlement date is in the first coupon period.

Maturity Date:	12/21/2010
Settlement Date:	11/18/2000
Dated Date:	10/20/2000
First Coupon Date:	12/20/2000
Last Coupon Date:	6/20/2010
Nominal Annual Coupon Rate:	8%
Simple Yield:	9.4%

$t_{sm} = 3683$, $t_{ps} = 30$

$$\text{AI} = 0.08 \cdot \frac{30}{365} = 0.006575342$$

$$\text{P} = \frac{1 + 0.08 \cdot \frac{3683}{365}}{1 + 0.094 \cdot \frac{3683}{365}} = 0.9275002039 \approx 0.92750$$

$$\text{P}_{\text{full}} = 0.934075342$$

$$\frac{dP}{dY} = -4.803112549$$

$$\text{DUR} = 5.383782881$$

$$\text{MD} = 5.142103994$$

$$\text{CONV} = 53.25735588$$

$$\text{PV01Y} = 0.048031125$$

$$\text{YV01P} = 0.002081983$$

Example 5

Long last coupon period

The settlement date is in neither the first nor the last coupon period.

Maturity Date:	3/21/2011
Settlement Date:	2/14/2001
Last Coupon Date:	9/20/2010
Nominal Annual Coupon Rate:	6.7%
Simple Yield:	10%

$t_{sm} = 3685$, $t_{ps} = 147$

$$\text{AI} = 0.067 \cdot \frac{147}{365} = 0.026983561$$

$$\text{P} = \frac{1 + 0.067 \cdot \dfrac{3685}{365}}{1 + 0.10 \cdot \dfrac{3685}{365}} - 0.026983561 \approx 0.83421$$

$$P_{full} = 0.861193561$$

$$\frac{dP}{dY} = -4.190966219$$

$$\text{DUR} = 5.109785682$$

$$\text{MD} = 4.866462554$$

$$\text{CONV} = 48.89683575$$

$$\text{PV01Y} = 0.041909662$$

$$\text{YV01P} = 0.002386085$$

Example 6

Normal last coupon period

The settlement date coincides with the coupon date.

Maturity Date: 6/20/2005

Settlement Date: 6/20/2001

Nominal Annual Coupon Rate: 1.1%

Simple Yield: 1%

$t_{sm} = 1460, \ t_{ps} = 0$

$$\text{AI} = 0$$

$$P = \frac{1 + 0.011 \cdot \dfrac{1460}{365}}{1 + 0.01 \cdot \dfrac{1460}{365}} = 1.00384$$

$$P_{full} = 1.00384$$

$$\frac{dP}{dY} = -3.860946746$$

$$\text{DUR} = 3.865408311$$

$$\text{MD} = 3.846177424$$

$$\text{CONV} = 29.58598019$$

$$\text{PV01Y} = 0.038609467$$

$$\text{YV01P} = 0.002590038$$

Example 7

Issue date is after 3/1/2001.

Maturity Date:	3/20/2007
Settlement Date:	4/18/2001
Nominal Annual Coupon Rate:	0.7%
Simple Yield:	0.6%
Issue Date:	3/20/2001

$t_{sm} = 2161$, $t_{ps} = 3/20/2001$ to $4/18/2001 = 29$ (including only one date, because the issue date is after 3/1/2001).

$$AI = \frac{0.007}{2} \cdot \frac{29}{182.5} = 0.000556164$$

$$P = \frac{1 + 0.007 \cdot \dfrac{2161}{365}}{1 + 0.006 \cdot \dfrac{2161}{365}} = 1.0057174 \approx 1.00571$$

$$P_{full} = 1.006266164$$

$$\frac{dP}{dY} = -5.75013467$$

$$DUR = 5.73147073$$

$$MD = 5.71432775$$

$$CONV = 65.34271479$$

$$PV01Y = 0.05750135$$

$$YV01P = 0.00173909$$

New Zealand

Conventions

- Quoted in yields
- Coupon payments are semiannual.
- The maturity date is always on the 15th of the month.
- Day count method is actual/365 for discount factor when the settlement date is in the last coupon period and is Actual/Actual (in period) for everything else.
- The settlement date is three business days after the trade date.
- There is no odd last coupon period.
- There is no callable feature.
- The ex-dividend date is the ninth calendar day before the coupon date. Bond is trading ex-dividend, if the settlement date is on or after the ex-dividend date and before the coupon date immediately after that ex-dividend date.
- Simple interest is used when the settlement date is in the last coupon period.

Example 1

The settlement date is in the last coupon period.

Maturity Date:	3/15/2002
Settlement Date:	3/6/2002
Nominal Annual Coupon Rate:	10%
Nominal Annual Yield to Maturity:	11%

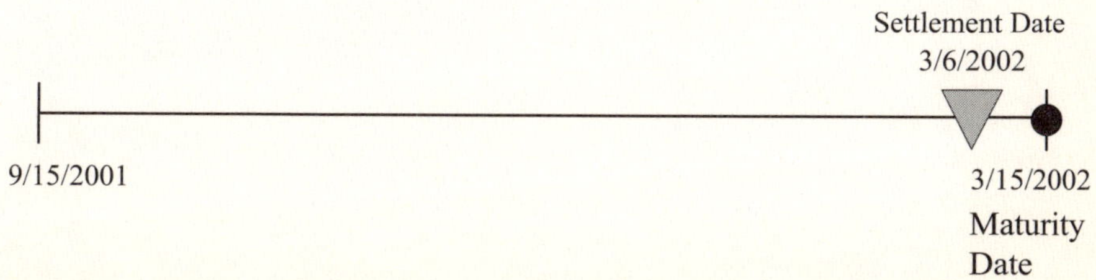

Ex-dividend date: 3/6/2002

This is ex-dividend trading.

$$AIF = -\frac{9}{181}$$

$$DF = \frac{9}{182.5}$$

$$LCF = 0$$

$$AI = -0.002486188$$

$$P = \frac{1}{1+\frac{0.11}{2}\cdot\frac{9}{182.5}} + 0.002486188$$

$$P = 0.999781196$$

$$P_{full} = 0.997295008$$

$$\frac{dP}{dY} = -0.024524318$$

$$DUR = 0.024657534$$

$$MD = 0.024590836$$

$$CONV = 0.001209418$$

$$PV01Y = 0.00245243$$

$$YV01P = 0.407758539$$

Norway

Conventions

- Quoted in prices.
- Coupon payments are annual. Old bonds with issue dates up to and including 1986 have semiannual coupon payments.
- The day count method is Actual/365 for everything, but for fractional periods only. (Cash flows for normal coupon periods are full coupon payments, that is, C/F.)
- The settlement date is three business days after the trade date.
- The ex-dividend date is the fourteenth calendar day before the coupon date.
- Non-End-of-Month rule is in effect.
- The price is rounded to five decimal places per one Kroner of face value.
- Compound interest is used when the settlement date is in the last coupon period.
- Input yield and calculated yield (output) should always be effective yield (see Italy).

Example 1

Maturity Date:	1/15/2007
Settlement Date:	7/5/2001
Coupon Rate:	6.75%
Effective Yield to Maturity:	7%

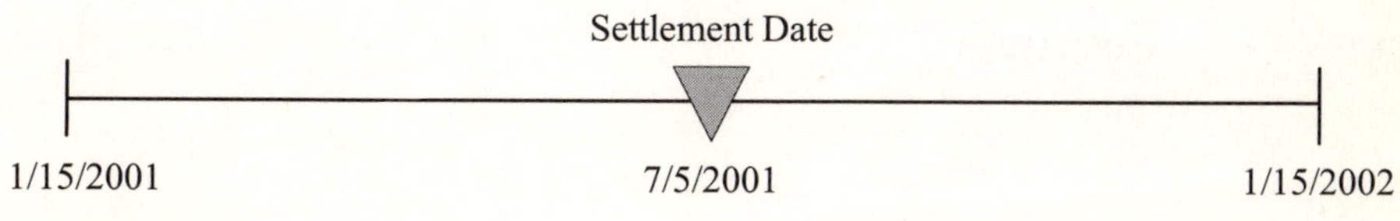

Ex-dividend date: 1/1/2002

This is cum-dividend trading.

$$AIF = \frac{171}{365}$$

$$FCF = 1$$

$$DF = \frac{194}{365}$$

$$LCF = 1$$

$$LDF = 1$$

$$n = 4$$

$$AI = 0.0316232877$$

$$P = 0.98828$$

$$P_{full} = 1.019903287$$

$$\frac{dP}{dY} = -4.435516282$$

$$DUR = 4.653384769$$

$$MD = 4.348957728$$

$$CONV = 25.19529393$$

$$PV01 = 0.04435516$$

$$YV01 = 0.00225453$$

Example 2

Maturity Date:	11/30/2004
Settlement Date:	11/19/2001
Coupon Rate:	5.75%
Effective Yield to Maturity:	6%

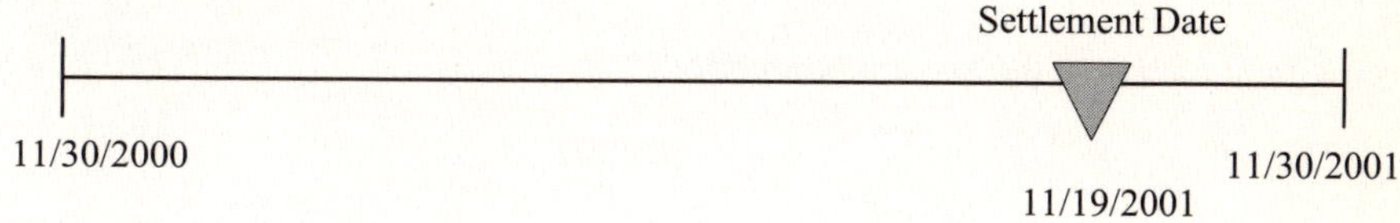

Ex-dividend date: 11/16/2001

This is ex-dividend trading.

$$AIF = -\frac{11}{365}$$

$$DF = \frac{11}{365}$$

$$FCF = 0$$

$$LCF = 1$$

$$LDF = 1$$

$$n = 2$$

$$AI = -0.001732877$$

$$P = 0.993307563 \approx 0.99331$$

$$P_{full} = 0.991577123$$

$$\frac{dP}{dY} = -2.684171608$$

$$DUR = 2.869390427$$

$$MD = 2.706972101$$

$$CONV = 10.09873108$$

$$PV01 = 0.026841716$$

$$YV01 = 0.003725544$$

Example 3

The settlement date is in the last coupon period.

Maturity Date:	5/31/2001
Settlement Date	7/2/2000
Coupon Rate:	7%
Effective Yield to Maturity:	3%

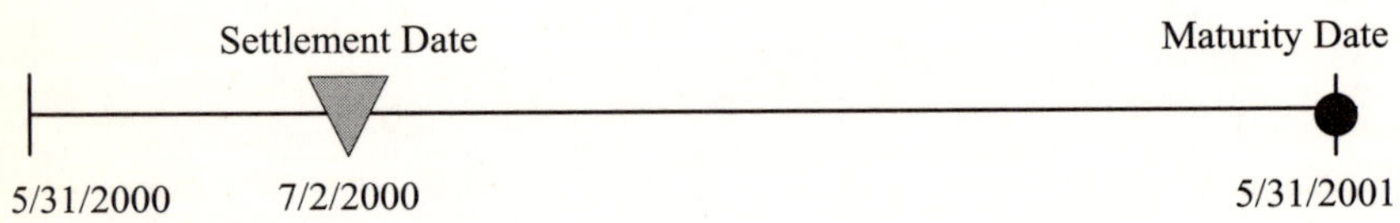

Ex-dividend date: 5/17/2001

This is cum-dividend trading.

$$AIF = \frac{32}{365}$$

$$DF = \frac{333}{365}$$

$$LCF = 1$$

$$AI = \frac{0.07}{1} \cdot \frac{32}{365} = 0.006136986$$

$$P = \frac{1+0.07}{(1+0.03)^{\frac{333}{365}}} - 0.006136986$$

$$P = 1.03539355 \approx 1.03539$$

$$P_{\text{full}} = 1.041526986$$

$$\frac{dP}{dY} = -0.92254201$$

$$DUR = 0.91233187$$

$$MD = 0.88575910$$

$$CONV = 1.64452121$$

$$PV01 = 0.00922542$$

$$YV01 = 0.01083961$$

Example 4

Short first coupon period

Maturity Date:	2/15/2005
Settlement Date	4/11/2001
Dated Date:	3/1/2001
First Coupon Date:	2/15/2002
Coupon Rate:	8%
Effective Yield to Maturity:	6%
Frequency of Coupon Payments per Year:	1

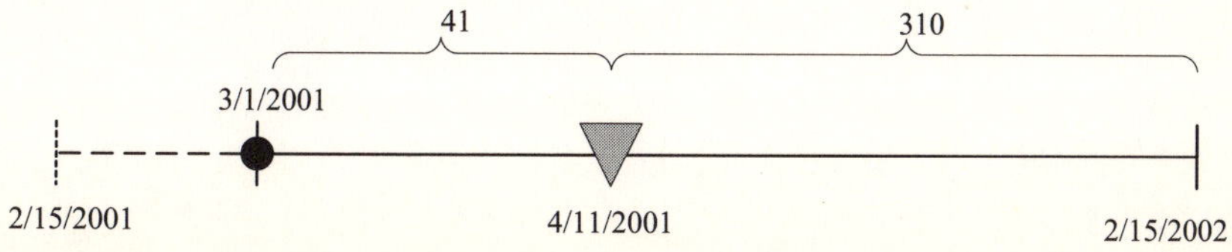

$$AIF = \frac{41}{365}$$

$$FCF = \frac{351}{365}$$

$$DF = \frac{310}{365}$$

$$LCF = 1$$

$$LDF = 1$$

$$n = 2$$

$$AI = 0.08 \cdot \frac{41}{365} = 0.008986301$$

$$P = 1.0668255517 \approx 1.06683$$

$$P_{full} = 1.075816301$$

$$\frac{dP}{dY} = -3.5000668$$

$$DUR = 3.44860996$$

$$MD = 3.25340562$$

$$CONV = 14.34992923$$

$$PV01Y = 0.03500067$$

$$YV01P = 0.00285709$$

Poland

Conventions

- Quoted in prices (when there is ex-dividend trading, the quoted price is full price).
- Coupon payments are annual.
- The settlement date is two business days after the trade date.
- The day count method is the Actual/Actual (in period) for everything
- The ex-dividend date is the tenth business day before the coupon date.
- Accrued interest is rounded to five decimal places per one Zloty of face value.
- Simple interest is used when settlement date is in the last coupon period.

Example 1

Maturity Date:	5/12/2006
Settlement Date:	6/16/2002
Coupon Rate:	8.5%
Effective Yield to Maturity:	10%

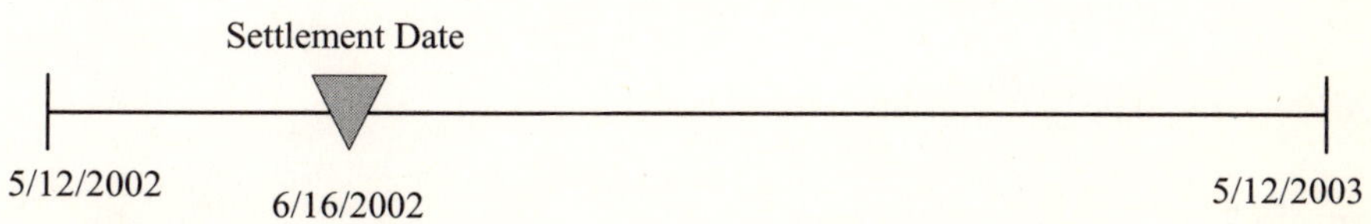

Ex-dividend date: 4/28/2003

This is cum-dividend trading.

$$AIF = \frac{35}{365}$$

$$FCF = 1$$

$$DF = \frac{330}{365}$$

$$LCF = 1$$

$$LDF = 1$$

$$n = 2$$

$$AI = 0.00815$$

$$P = 0.953046693$$

$$P_{full} = 0.961196693$$

$$\frac{dP}{dY} = -3.011306174$$

$$DUR = 3.446159163$$

$$MD = 3.132871966$$

$$CONV = 13.3923103$$

$$PV01Y = 0.030113062$$

$$YV01P = 0.003320818$$

Example 2

Maturity Date: 7/22/2004

Settlement Date: 7/17/2002

Coupon Rate: 8.5%

Effective Yield to Maturity: 10%

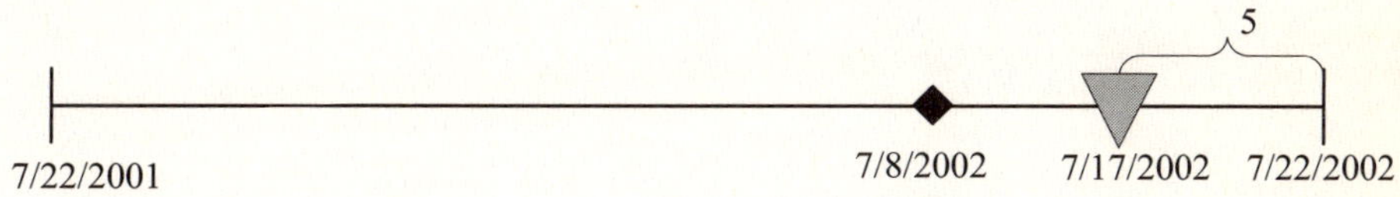

Ex-dividend date: 7/8/2002

This is ex-dividend trading.

$$AIF = -\frac{5}{365}$$

$$FCF = 0$$

$$DF = \frac{5}{365}$$

$$LCF = 1$$

$$LDF = 1$$

$$n = 1$$

$$AI = -0.085\frac{5}{365} \approx -0.00116$$

$$P = 0.973860526$$

$$P_{full} = 0.972696142$$

$$\frac{dP}{dY} = -1.71049544$$

$$DUR = 1.93436049$$

MD	=	1.75850954
CONV	=	4.75136743
PV01Y	=	0.01710495
YV01P	=	0.00584626

Portugal

Conventions

- Quoted in prices
- Coupon payments are annual (only one fixed coupon bond has semiannual coupon payments).
- The settlement date is three business days after the trade date.
- The maturity date of almost all bonds is on the 23rd of the month.
- There is no ex-dividend trading.
- The day count method is Actual/Actual (in period) for everything.
- Accrued interest is calculated in three steps: 1) Find accrued interest per one day and one Escudo of face value, 2) round that number to 11 decimal places, and 3) multiply the amount in step 2 by the number of accrued interest days.
- Compound interest is used when the settlement date is in the last coupon period.

Example 1

Maturity Date:	6/23/2003
Settlement Date:	5/5/2001
Issue Date:	6/23/93
Nominal Annual Coupon Rate:	10.625%

Nominal Annual Yield to Maturity: 3%

Frequency of Coupon Payments per Year: 2

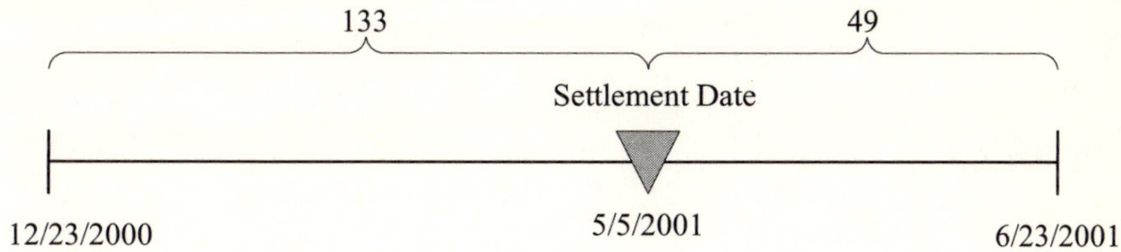

$$\text{AIF} = \frac{133}{182}$$

$$\text{FCF} = 1$$

$$\text{DF} = \frac{49}{182}$$

$$\text{LCF} = 1$$

$$\text{LDF} = 1$$

$$n = 3$$

$$\text{AI (per one day)} = \frac{0.10625}{2} \cdot \frac{1}{182} = 0.000291895604 \approx 0.00029189560$$

$$\text{AI} = 0.00029189560 \cdot 133 = 0.0388221148$$

$$P = 1.1564504669$$

$$P_{\text{full}} = 1.1952725817$$

$$\frac{dP}{dY} = -2.256912163$$

$$\text{DUR} = 1.916521704$$

$$\text{MD} = 1.888198723$$

CONV = 4.768383818

PV01Y = 0.022569122

YV01P = 0.004430833

South Africa

Conventions

- Quoted in yields
- Coupon payments are semiannual.
- The day count method is Actual/365 for accrued interest to be paid, accrued interest in price/yield formula, and discount factor (when the settlement date is in the last coupon period) and Actual/Actual (in period) for everything else.
- The End-of-Month rule is in effect.

  Exceptions: for bonds 11.5%, 11/30/2000 End-of-Month rule is not in effect. For bonds 12%, 2/28/2005, and 13%, 8/31/2010, the coupon payment dates are 2/28 (in leap year, too) and 8/31.
- The settlement date is three business days after the trade date.
- The ex-dividend date is one month before the coupon date. "One month before the coupon date" means the same day one month earlier (or the end of the previous month if there is no same day) or the end of previous month if the coupon date is on the end of the month.

  February 29th in a leap year is never an ex-dividend date. It is always February 28th.
- Price and accrued interest are rounded to seven decimal places per one Rand of face value.
- Simple interest is used when the settlement date is in the last coupon period.

Example 1

Maturity Date:	10/15/2006
Settlement Date:	11/6/2001
Nominal Annual Coupon Rate:	14.5%
Nominal Annual Yield to Maturity:	14%

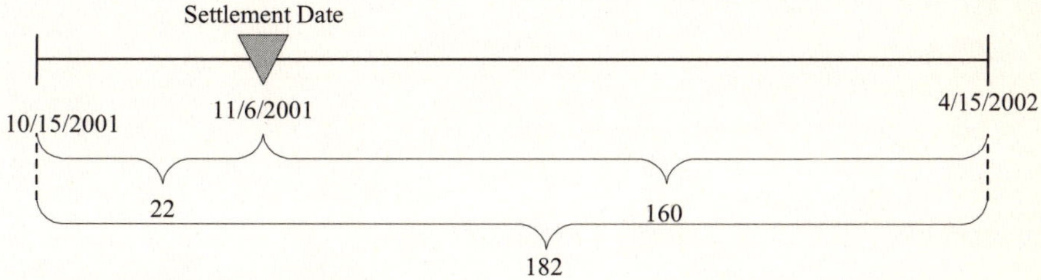

Ex-dividend date: 3/15/2002

This is cum-dividend trading.

$$AIF = \frac{22}{182.5}$$

$$FCF = 1$$

$$DF = \frac{160}{182}$$

$$LCF = 1$$

$$LDF = 1$$

$$n = 8$$

$$AI = \frac{0.145}{2} \cdot \frac{22}{182.5} = 0.0087397$$

$$P = 1.0171755$$

$$P_{full} = 1.0259152$$

$$\frac{dP}{dY} = -3.523596748$$

$$DUR = 3.675009896$$

$$MD = 3.43458868$$

$$CONV = 15.676207$$

$$PV01Y = 0.035235967$$

$$YV01P = 0.002838009$$

Example 2

Maturity Date:	9/15/2006
Settlement Date:	8/16/2001
Nominal Annual Coupon Rate:	9.25%
Nominal Annual Yield to Maturity:	14%

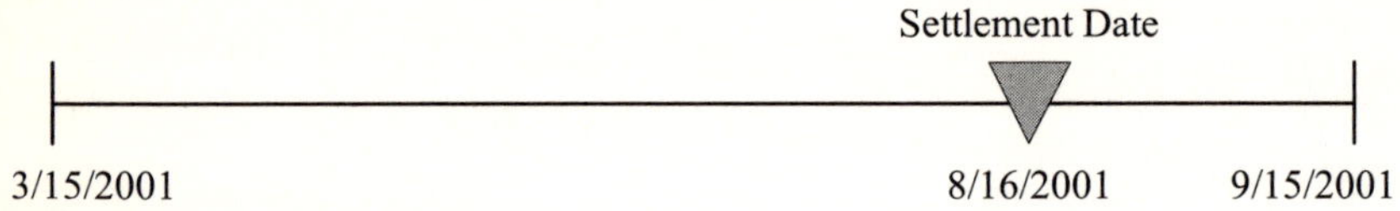

Ex-dividend date: 8/15/2001

This is ex-dividend trading.

$$AIF = -\frac{30}{182.5}$$

$$FCF = 0$$

$$DF = \frac{30}{184}$$

$$\text{LCF} = 1$$

$$\text{LDF} = 1$$

$$n = 8$$

$$\text{AI} = \frac{0.0925}{2} \cdot \left(-\frac{30}{182.5}\right) = -0.0076027$$

$$P = 0.8316520$$

$$P_{\text{full}} = 0.8240493$$

$$\frac{dP}{dY} = -3.154737$$

$$\text{DUR} = 4.096319$$

$$\text{MD} = 3.828336$$

$$\text{CONV} = 18.458207$$

$$\text{PV01Y} = 0.031547$$

$$\text{YV01P} = 0.003170$$

Example 3

The settlement date is in the last coupon period.

Maturity Date:	10/1/2001
Settlement Date:	5/22/2001
Nominal Annual Coupon Rate:	10.35%
Nominal Annual Yield to Maturity:	16%
Ex-dividend Date:	9/1/2001

This is cum-dividend trading.

$$\text{AIF} = \frac{51}{182.5}$$

$$\text{DF} = \frac{132}{182.5}$$

$$\text{LCF} = 1$$

$$\text{AI} = \frac{0.1035}{2} \cdot \frac{51}{182.5} = 0.0144616$$

$$P = \frac{1+\dfrac{0.1035}{2}}{1+\dfrac{0.16}{2}\cdot\dfrac{132}{182.5}} - 0.0144616$$

$$P = 0.9797597$$

$$P_{\text{full}} = 0.9942213$$

$$\frac{dP}{dY} = -0.339887$$

$$\text{DUR} = 0.361644$$

$$\text{MD} = 0.341863$$

$$\text{CONV} = 0.233740$$

$$\text{PV01Y} = 0.003399$$

$$\text{YV01P} = 0.029422$$

Example 4

The settlement date is in the last coupon period.

Maturity Date:	7/15/2001
Settlement Date:	7/6/2001
Nominal Annual Coupon Rate:	8.75%
Nominal Annual Yield to Maturity:	8%

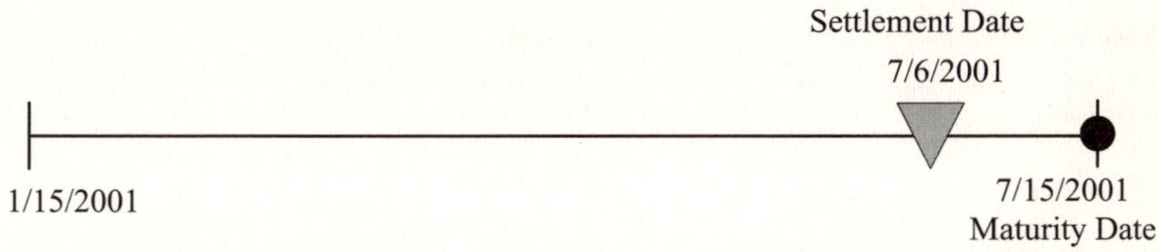

Ex-dividend date: 6/15/2001

This is ex-dividend trading.

$$AIF = -\frac{9}{182.5}$$

$$LCF = 0$$

$$DF = \frac{9}{182.5}$$

$$AI = \frac{0.0875}{2} \cdot \left(-\frac{9}{182.5} \right) = -0.0021575$$

$$P = \frac{1}{1 + \frac{0.08}{2} \cdot \frac{9}{182.5}} + 0.0021575 = 1.0001888$$

$$P_{full} = 0.9980313$$

$$\frac{dP}{dY} = -0.024561$$

$$DUR = 0.024658$$

$$MD = 0.024609$$

$$CON = 0.001211$$

$$PV01Y = 0.000246$$

$$YV01P = 0.407157$$

Example 5

Maturity Date:	2/28/2005
Settlement Date:	3/26/2000
Nominal Annual Coupon Rate:	12%
Nominal Annual Yield to Maturity:	15%

The EOM is in effect, but excluding February 29 [this means that the coupon payment dates are 2/28 (in leap year, too) and 8/31].

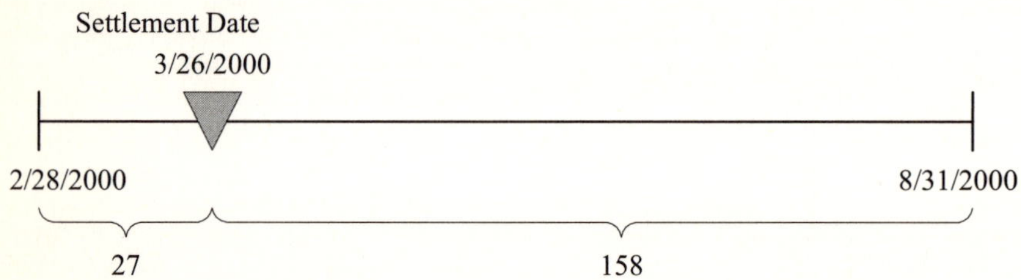

Ex-dividend date: 7/31/2000

This is cum-dividend trading.

$$AIF = \frac{27}{182.5}$$

$$FCF = 1$$

$$DF = \frac{158}{185}$$

$$\text{LCF} = 1$$

$$\text{LDF} = 1$$

$$n = 8$$

$$\text{AI} = \frac{0.12}{2} \cdot \left(\frac{27}{182.5} \right) = 0.0088767$$

$$P = 0.8976804$$

$$P_{full} = 0.9065571$$

$$\frac{dP}{dY} = -3.169359$$

$$\text{DUR} = 3.758242$$

$$\text{MD} = 3.496039$$

$$\text{CONV} = 16.039185$$

$$\text{PV01Y} = 0.031694$$

$$\text{YV01P} = 0.003155$$

Spain

Conventions

- Quoted in prices
- Coupon payments are annual.
- The day count method is Actual/Actual (in period) for everything.
- The End-of-Month rule is not in effect.
- The settlement date is three business days after the trade date.

- Dated date can be after the issue date, because the bonds are usually issued in three or four tranches and accrued interest starts to accrue after the last tranche is issued.
- There is no ex-dividend trading.
- The maturity date is always moved from a nonbusiness day to the next business day, but the coupon payment does not change.
- Compound interest is used when the settlement date is in the last coupon period.

  Note that when the settlement date is before dated date, then AIF = 0, FCF = 0, and DF is the portion from the settlement date to the dated date, and the dated date should be counted in determining n.

Example 1

Maturity Date:	4/30/2006 (Sunday)
Settlement Date:	3/9/2001
Coupon Rate:	8.8%
Effective Yield to Maturity:	4%

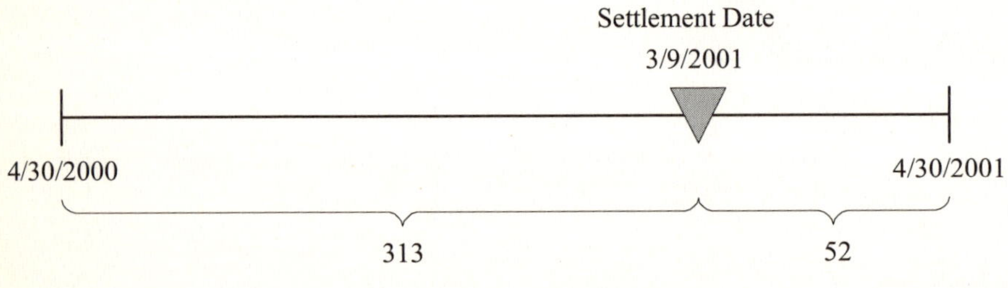

The maturity date is moved to 5/2/2006.

$$AIF = \frac{313}{365}$$

$$FCF = 1$$

$$DF = \frac{52}{365}$$

$$LCF = 1$$

$$LDF = \frac{367}{365}$$

$$n = 4$$

$$AI = 0.07546301$$

$$P = 1.21878033$$

$$P_{full} = 1.29424334$$

$$\frac{dP}{dY} = -5.20503063$$

$$DUR = 4.18254564$$

$$MD = 4.02167850$$

$$CONV = 22.50947588$$

$$PV01Y = 0.05205031$$

$$YV01P = 0.00192122$$

Example 2

The dated date is after the issue date. The settlement date is before the dated date.

Maturity Date:	7/30/2011 (Saturday)
Settlement Date:	3/14/2001
Coupon Rate:	5.4%
Issue Date:	9/19/2000

Dated Date:	7/30/2001
First Coupon Date:	7/30/2002
Effective Yield to Maturity:	5%

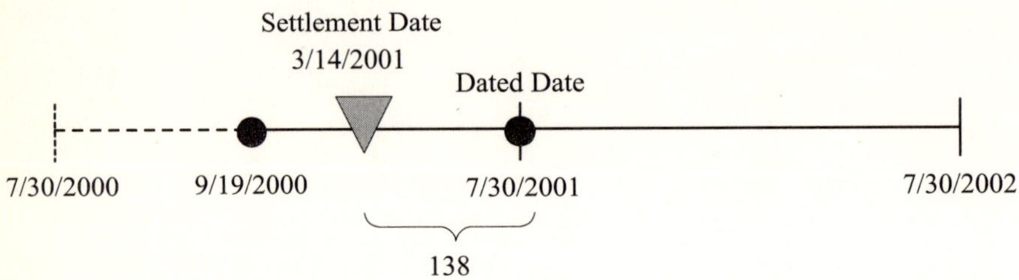

The maturity date is moved to 8/1/2011.

$$AIF = 0$$

$$FCF = 0$$

$$DF = \frac{138}{365}$$

$$LCF = 1$$

$$LDF = \frac{367}{365}$$

$$n = 9$$

$$AI = 0$$

$$P = 1.0118750035$$

$$P_{full} = 1.0118750035$$

$$\frac{dP}{dY} = -8.09390515$$

$$DUR = 8.39886387$$

$$\text{MD} = 7.99891798$$

$$\text{CONV} = 79.85224965$$

$$\text{PV01Y} = 0.08093905$$

$$\text{YV01P} = 0.00123550$$

Example 3

The settlement date is in the last coupon period.

Maturity Date:	2/28/2002
Settlement Date:	3/21/2001
Coupon Rate:	7.9%
Effective Yield to Maturity:	3%

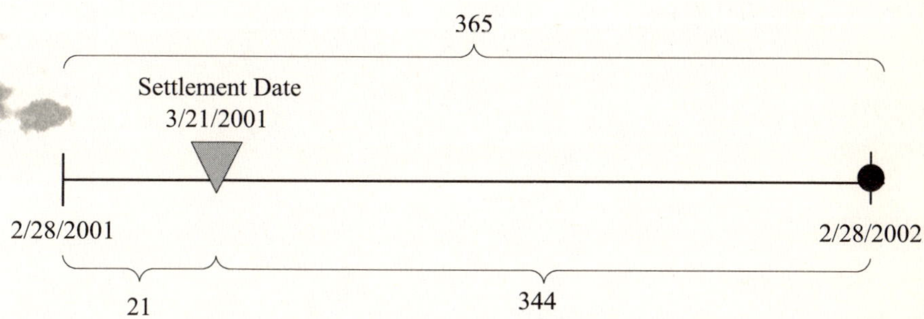

$$\text{AIF} = \frac{21}{365}$$

$$\text{DF} = \frac{344}{365}$$

$$\text{LCF} = 1$$

$$\text{AI} = 0.079 \cdot \frac{21}{365} = 0.0045452055$$

$$P = \frac{1+0.079}{(1+0.03)^{\frac{344}{365}}} - 0.0045452055$$

$$P = 1.044810674$$

$$P_{full} = 1.049355879$$

$$\frac{dP}{dY} = -0.96017668$$

$$DUR = 0.94246575$$

$$MD = 0.91501530$$

$$CONV = 1.72561735$$

$$PV01Y = 0.00960177$$

$$YV01P = 0.01041475$$

Sweden

Conventions

- Quoted in yields
- Coupon payments are annual.
- The day count method is 30E/360 for everything.
- The settlement date is three business days after the Trade date.
- The ex-dividend date is the fourth business day before the coupon date.
- Simple interest should be used when the settlement date is in the last coupon period.

Example 1

Maturity Date: 10/25/2006

Settlement Date: 10/20/2001

Coupon Rate: 6.5%

Effective Yield to Maturity: 5%

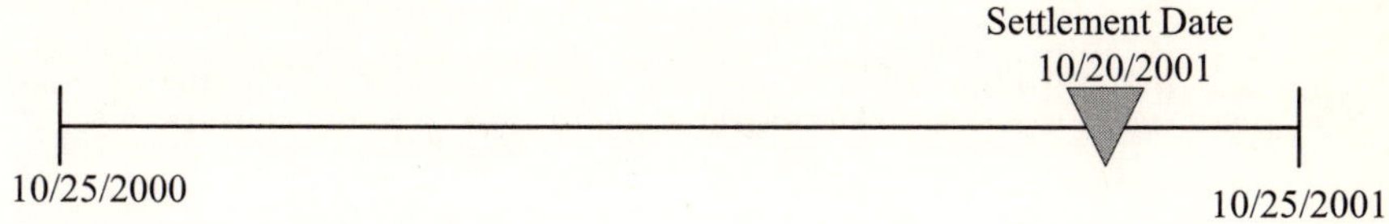

Ex-dividend date: 10/19/2001

This is ex-dividend trading.

$$\text{AIF} = -\frac{5}{360}$$

$$\text{FCF} = 0$$

$$\text{DF} = \frac{5}{360}$$

$$\text{LCF} = 1$$

$$\text{LDF} = 1$$

$$n = 4$$

$$\text{AI} = \frac{0.065}{2} \cdot \left(-\frac{5}{360}\right) = -0.000902778$$

$$P = 1.06512352$$

$$P_{\text{full}} = 1.064220746$$

$$\frac{dP}{dY} = -4.52001912$$

$$DUR = 4.45961996$$

$$MD = 4.24725711$$

$$CONV = 23.33792448$$

$$PV01Y = 0.04520019$$

$$YV01P = 0.00221238$$

Switzerland

Conventions

- Quoted in prices
- Coupon payments are annual.
- The settlement date is three business days after the trade date.
- The day count method is 30E/360 for everything.
- No ex-dividend trading
- Compound interest is used when the settlement date is in the last coupon period.

Example 1

Maturity Date:	4/8/2006
Settlement Date:	3/9/2001
Coupon Rate:	4.5%
Effective Yield to Maturity:	3%

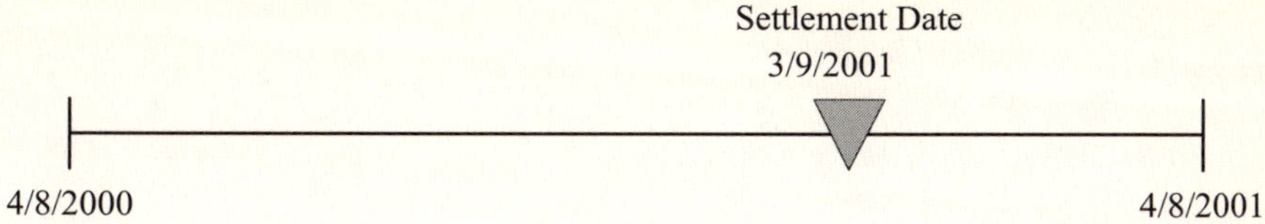

$$AIF = \frac{331}{360}$$

$$FCF = 1$$

$$DF = \frac{29}{360}$$

$$LCF = 1$$

$$LDF = 1$$

$$n = 4$$

$$AI = 0.041375$$

$$P = 1.0696719132$$

$$P_{full} = 1.1110469132$$

$$\frac{dP}{dY} = -4.85138594$$

$$DUR = 4.49749463$$

$$MD = 4.36649964$$

$$CONV = 25.02535308$$

$$PV01Y = 0.04851386$$

$$YV01P = 0.00206127$$

Example 2

The settlement date is in the last coupon period.

Maturity Date:	2/5/2002
Settlement Date:	12/7/2001
Coupon Rate:	6.5%
Effective Yield to Maturity:	3%

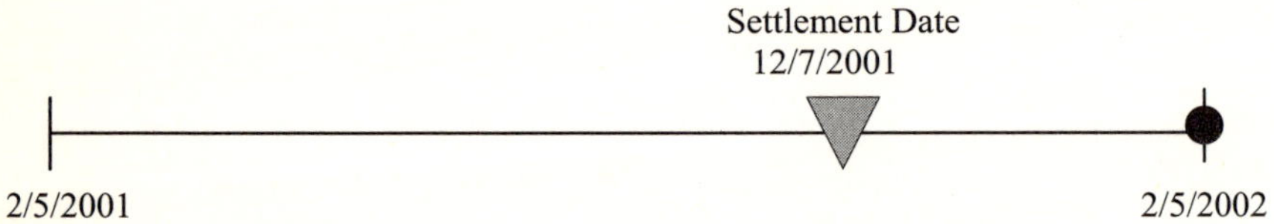

$$\text{AIF} = \frac{302}{360}$$

$$\text{DF} = \frac{58}{360}$$

$$\text{LCF} = 1$$

$$\text{AI} = 0.054527778$$

$$P = \frac{1+0.065}{(1+0.03)^{\frac{58}{360}}} - 0.054527778 = 1.005412482$$

$$P_{\text{full}} = 1.05994026$$

$$\frac{dP}{dY} = -0.16579432$$

$$\text{DUR} = 0.16111111$$

$$\text{MD} = 0.15641855$$

CONV = 0.17632944

PV01Y = 0.00165794

YV01P = 0.06031570

United Kingdom Gilts

Conventions

- Quoted in prices
- Coupon payments are semiannual.
- The day count method is Actual/Actual (in period) for everything.
- The settlement date is one business day after the trade (bargain) date.
- The End-of-Month rule is not in effect.
- The ex-dividend date is the sixth business day before the coupon date. The exception is for 3.5% war loans, where the ex-dividend date is the ninth business day before the coupon date.
- Compound interest is used when settlement date is in the last coupon period.

Stocks can be issued in a partly paid form. This means that the bid price is paid in installments during a number of months after the issue date. There can be a maximum of three installments. The first installment is always on the issue date. The second and third installment dates are known as "second call" and "third call." This does not refer to early redemption of stocks, but rather those dates after the issue date at which the issuer "calls" for additional payments toward the full bid price. The sum of all installments must be 1 (per £1 of face value). The last issued partly paid Gilt was on 1/27/1994.

Stocks cannot be ex-dividend before any call date.

The price/yield formula is the same as general price/yield formula for periodic payment fixed income securities in Chapter 1, with subtraction of the following two terms (if there are three installments) or one term (if there are two installments) from the right side of equation (1):

$$\frac{A_2}{\left(1+\frac{Y}{F}\right)^{\frac{m_2}{d}}} \quad \text{and} \quad \frac{A_3}{\left(1+\frac{Y}{F}\right)^{\frac{m_3}{d}}}$$

A_2 is the partly paid **A**mount on second call per £1of face value.

m_2 is the actual number of days between the settlement date and second call.

A_3 is the partly paid **A**mount on third call per £1 of face value.

m_3 is the actual number of days between the settlement date and third call.

The amounts of A_2 and A_3 are treated as negative cash flows.

d is the actual number of **d**ays in the normal first coupon period.

If first coupon period is long, then fractions m_2/d and m_3/d should be calculated in accordance with the discount factor (DF) calculation in Chapter 1. This is valid only for cum-dividend trading and when the settlement date is before the last call date. When the settlement date is on or after the call date, the corresponding term should be removed.

The first coupon factor is calculated this way:

$$FCF = \frac{1}{d}\sum_{i=1}^{m}\left[A_i\left(d_{CF}\right)_i\right]$$

d is the actual number of **d**ays in a normal first coupon period.

A_i is the ***i*th** partial **A**mount, expressed as a decimal

$(d_{CF})i$ is the actual number of **d**ays between ***i*th** partial (**c**all) payment date (including issue date) and the **f**irst coupon date.

m is the number of partial call dates.

If the first coupon period is long, then two normal coupon periods, before the first coupon date, should be taken into account.

Example 1

Maturity Date:	8/25/2017
Settlement Date:	2/21/2001
Nominal Annual Coupon Rate:	8.75%
Nominal Annual Yield to Maturity:	5%

Ex-dividend date: 2/16/2001

This is ex-dividend trading.

$$AIF = -\frac{4}{184}$$

$$FCF = 0$$

$$DF = \frac{4}{184}$$

$$LCF = 1$$

$$LDF = 1$$

$$n = 32$$

$$AI = -0.000951087$$

$$P = 1.4181628967$$

$$P_{full} = 1.4172118098$$

$$\frac{dP}{dY} = -14.16799666$$

$$DUR = 10.24701917$$

$$MD = 9.99709187$$

$$CONV = 136.128882$$

$$PV01Y = 0.14167997$$

$$YV01P = 0.00070582$$

Example 2

The settlement date is in the last coupon period.

Maturity Date:	7/12/2001
Settlement Date:	3/20/2001
Nominal Annual Coupon Rate:	9.5%
Nominal Annual Yield to Maturity:	5%

Ex-dividend date: 7/4/2001

This is cum-dividend trading.

$$\text{AIF} = \frac{67}{181}$$

$$\text{DF} = \frac{114}{181}$$

$$\text{LCF} = 1$$

$$\text{AI} = 0.0175828729$$

$$\text{P} = 1.013752168$$

$$\text{P}_{\text{full}} = 1.031335041$$

$$\frac{dP}{dY} = -0.31686348$$

$$\text{DUR} = 0.31491713$$

$$\text{MD} = 0.30723622$$

$$\text{CONV} = 0.24426542$$

$$\text{PV01Y} = 0.00316863$$

$$\text{YV01P} = 0.03155933$$

Example 3

Partly paid stock

Maturity Date:	8/1/2002
Settlement Date:	4/12/2001
Nominal Annual Coupon Rate:	6%
Nominal Annual Yield to Maturity:	7%
Issue Date:	2/1/2001
Amount at Issue:	10%
Second Call Date:	3/1/2001

Second Call Amount:	30%
Third Call Date:	4/1/2001
Third Call Amount:	60%

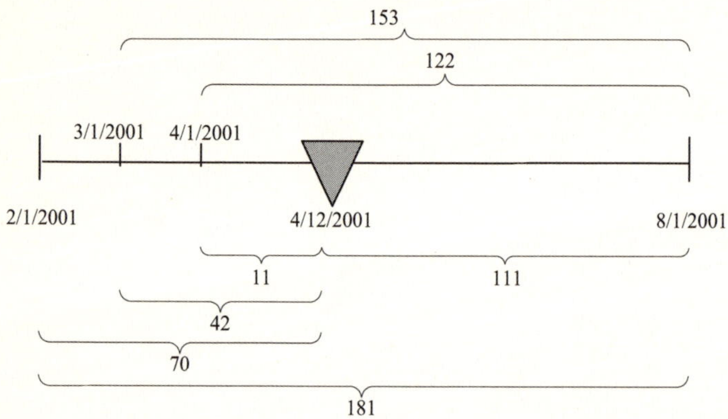

$$\text{AIF} = \frac{0.10 \cdot 70 + 0.30 \cdot 42 + 0.60 \cdot 11}{181} = 0.144751381$$

$$\text{DF} = \frac{111}{181}$$

$$\text{FCF} = \frac{0.10 \cdot 181 + 0.30 \cdot 153 + 0.60 \cdot 122}{181} = 0.758011049$$

$$\text{LCF} = 1$$

$$\text{LDF} = 1$$

$$\text{n} = 1$$

$$\text{AI} = \frac{0.06}{2} \cdot 0.144751381 = 0.0043425414$$

$$P = \left(1+\frac{0.07}{2}\right)^{-\frac{111}{181}} \left[\frac{0.06}{2}\cdot 0.758011049 + \frac{0.06}{0.07}\left(1-\frac{1}{1+\frac{0.07}{2}}\right) + \left(1+\frac{0.06}{2}\right)\cdot\left(1+\frac{0.07}{2}\right)^{-2}\right] - 0.0043425414$$

$$P = 0.9877468588$$

$$P_{full} = 0.9920894003$$

$$\frac{dP}{dY} = -1.21723459$$

$$DUR = 1.26988334$$

$$MD = 1.22694043$$

$$CONV = 2.12447421$$

$$PV01Y = 0.01217235$$

$$YV01P = 0.00821534$$

United Kingdom Index-Linked Gilts

Conventions

Everything is the same as for U.K. Gilts, plus the following:

- Quoted price is with inflation.
- The coupon payments and redemption value are dependent on the retail price index (RPI), which is the measure of inflation.
- RPI is published for every month in the middle of the next month.
- The RPI is periodically rebased to a value of 100.
- The new RPI for January 1987 was set to 100.
- The old RPI for January 1987 was 394.5.

- Before January of 1987, RPIs are "old."
- After January 1987, RPIs are "new."
- The relationship between "old" and "new" RPIs is as follows:

  $$\text{NewRPI} = \frac{100}{394.5} \cdot \text{OldRPI, or } \frac{\text{Old}}{394.5} = \frac{\text{New}}{100}$$

- New RPI should be rounded to four decimal places.
- Beside the regular input data, we need the following additional input data for index-linked GILTS: 1) Inflation rate, 2) Base RPI (RPI eight months before the issue date), and 3) At least eight most recent RPIs with corresponding month and year.

- Inflation rate can be calculated (if it is not given) as the ratio of current RPI (latest published RPI) and the RPI twelve months before the current RPI: $R_{infl} = \frac{RPI_c - RPI_{c-12}}{RPI_{c-12}} \cdot 100[\%]$, where RPI_c is the current RPI (Latest published RPI), and RPI_{c-12} is the RPI twelve months before Current RPI.

- The future RPIs are projected by current RPI and inflation rate, as follows: $RPI_k = RPI_c (1 + R_{infl})^{\frac{m_k}{12}}$, where, RPI_k ($k = 1, 2, 3, \ldots, n + 2$) are future RPIs, R_{infl} is the inflation rate, expressed as a decimal, and m_k ($k = 1, 2, \ldots, n + 2$) is the number of months between current RPI month and the month for which we want to calculate future RPI.

- Projected RPIs should not be rounded or truncated.
- In the price/yield formula, we use Money Yield. The Money Yield (Y), Real Yield (R), and Inflation Rate (R_{infl}), are related with the following formula:

  $$\left(1 + \frac{Y}{2}\right)^2 = \left(1 + \frac{R}{2}\right)^2 \cdot (1 + R_{infl})$$

Partly paid index-linked Gilts will not be considered here, because the last issued one was on 12/31/1986.

Calculation of Cash Flows

The Settlement Date is Not in the Last Coupon Period.

- Next cash flow:

$$CF_1 = \frac{C(1-TX)}{F} \cdot FCF \cdot \frac{RPI_1}{RPI_b}$$

RPI_1 is the RPI eight months before the next coupon date.

RPI_b is the Base RPI, which is eight months before the issue date.

When it is ex-dividend trading, $CF_1 = 0$.

- Other cash flows (except the last one) are:

$$CF_k = \frac{C(1-TX)}{F} \cdot \frac{RPI_k}{RPI_b}, k = 2, 3, \ldots, n+1$$

- Last cash flow (payment at maturity date) is:

$$CF_{n+2} = [RV - TXG(RV_1 - P0)] \cdot \frac{RPI_{n+2}}{RPI_b} + \frac{C(1-TX)}{F} LCF \cdot \frac{RPI_{n+2}}{RPI_b}$$

RPI_k $k = 1, 2, \ldots, n+2$ is the Retail Price Index eight months before the corresponding coupon payment dates.

All cash flows (except principal) should be truncated to four decimal places per £1 of face value for these two Index-Linked Gilts:

- 2%—7/19/2006
- 2.5%—8/23/2011

For all other Index-Linked Gilts, all cash flows (except principal) should be truncated to six decimal places per £1 of face value. Cash flow on the next coupon date should always be calculated with the corresponding RPI, which is always known. The second cash flow (cash flow on the second coupon date after the settlement date) should always be calculated with RPI eight months before the second cash flow date if that RPI is published. Otherwise, it should be projected.

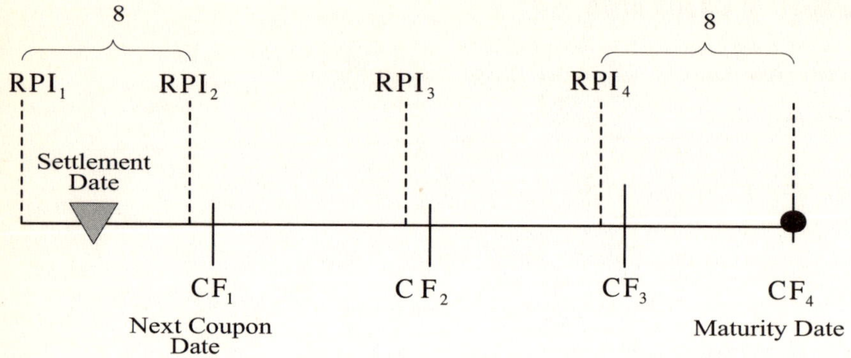

Note that CF_3 is calculated with RPI_3, which is eight months before the CF_3.

Accrued interest:

- Cum-dividend trading: $AI = CF_1 \cdot AIF$
- Ex-dividend trading: $AI = -CF_1 \cdot DF$

Price/yield formula:

- Cum-dividend or ex-dividend trading

$$P = \left(1+\frac{Y}{F}\right)^{-DF} \cdot \sum_{k=1}^{n+1}\left[\frac{CF_k}{\left(1+\frac{Y}{F}\right)^{k-1}}\right] + \frac{CF_{n+2}}{\left(1+\frac{Y}{F}\right)^{n+LDF}} - AI$$

Settlement Date in the Last Coupon Period

- Cash flow:

$$CF_1 = RV - TXG(RVI - P0) \cdot \frac{RPI_1}{RPI_b} + \frac{C(1 - TX)}{F} \cdot \frac{RPI_1}{RPI_b}$$

  The second term is zero for ex-dividend trading. RPI_1 is the RPI eight months before the maturity date.

- Price/yield Formula:

  Cum-dividend or ex-dividend trading:

$$P = \frac{CF_1}{1 + \frac{Y}{F} \cdot DF} - AI$$

Example 1

Maturity Date:	5/20/2003
Settlement Date:	10/27/2000
Nominal Annual Coupon Rate:	2.5%
Annual Inflation Rate:	3%
Base RPI:	78.75792
Current RPI:	171.7 for 9/2000
RPI_1:	168.4 for 3/2000 (eight months before the next coupon date of 11/20/2000)
RPI_2:	171.7 for 9/2000 (eight months before the second coupon date after settlement date)
Money Yield:	7%

Ex-dividend date: 11/10/2000

This is cum-dividend trading.

$$\text{AIF} = \frac{160}{184}$$

$$\text{FCF} = 1$$

$$\text{DF} = \frac{24}{184}$$

$$\text{LCF} = 1$$

$$\text{LDF} = 1$$

$$n = 4$$

Projected RPIs

$$\text{RPI}_3 \text{ (for 3/2001)} = 171.7(1+0.03)^{\frac{1}{2}} = 174.2564682$$

$$\text{RPI}_4 \text{ (for 9/2001)} = 171.7(1+0.03)^{1} = 176.851$$

$$\text{RPI}_5 \text{ (for 3/2002)} = 171.7(1+0.03)^{\frac{3}{2}} = 179.4841622$$

$$\text{RPI}_6 \text{ (for 9/2002)} = 171.7(1+0.03)^{2} = 182.15653$$

Known Cash Flows

$$CF_1 = \frac{0.025}{2} \cdot \frac{168.4}{78.75792} = 0.026727$$

$$CF_2 = \frac{0.025}{2} \cdot \frac{171.7}{78.75792} = 0.027251$$

Projected Cash Flows

$$CF_3 = \frac{0.025}{2} \cdot \frac{174.2564682}{78.75792} = 0.027656$$

$$CF_4 = \frac{0.025}{2} \cdot \frac{176.851}{78.75792} = 0.028068$$

$$CF_5 = \frac{0.025}{2} \cdot \frac{179.4841622}{78.75792} = 0.028486$$

$$CF_6 = \frac{182.15653}{78.75792} + \frac{0.025}{2} \cdot \frac{182.15653}{78.75792}$$

$$= 2.31286619 + 0.028910$$

$$= 2.34177619$$

$$AI = 0.026727 \cdot \frac{160}{184} = 0.02324086957$$

$$P = \left(1 + \frac{0.07}{2}\right)^{-\frac{24}{184}} \left[0.026727 + \frac{0.027251}{\left(1 + \frac{0.07}{2}\right)} + \frac{0.027656}{\left(1 + \frac{0.07}{2}\right)^2} + \frac{0.028068}{\left(1 + \frac{0.07}{2}\right)^3} + \frac{0.028486}{\left(1 + \frac{0.07}{2}\right)^4} + \frac{2.34177619}{\left(1 + \frac{0.07}{2}\right)^5} \right] - 0.0232408696$$

$$P = 2.0680799728$$

$$P_{full} = 2.0913208424$$

$$\frac{dP}{dY} = -4.99482126$$

$$DUR = 2.47194974$$

$$MD = 2.38835723$$

Real Yield

$$R = \left(\frac{1 + \frac{Y}{2}}{\sqrt{1 + R_{infl}}} - 1 \right) 2 = \left(\frac{1 + \frac{0.07}{2}}{\sqrt{1 + 0.03}} - 1 \right) 2$$

$$= 0.039631606 \approx 3.963\%$$

Change in Price per Change in Inflation Rate

$$\frac{dP}{dR_{infl}} = 3.8815646$$

Example 2

Maturity Date:	8/23/2011
Settlement Date:	2/20/2001
Nominal Annual Coupon Rate:	2.5%
Annual Inflation Rate:	3%
Base RPI:	74.55
Current RPI:	171.1 for 1/2001
RPI_1:	171.1 for 6/2000 (eight months before next coupon date of 2/23/2001)
RPI_2:	172.2 for 12/2000 (eight months before second coupon date after settlement date)
Money Yield:	5%

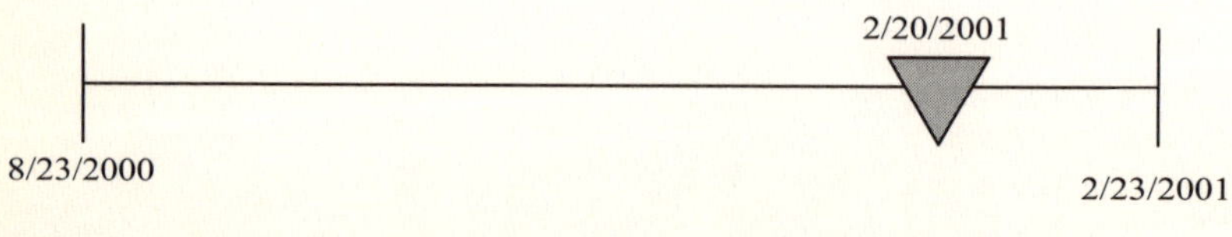

Ex-dividend date: 2/15/2001

This is ex-dividend trading.

$$\text{AIF} = -\frac{3}{184}$$

$$\text{FCF} = 0$$

$$\text{DF} = \frac{3}{184}$$

$$\text{LCF} = 1$$

$$\text{LDF} = 1$$

$$n = 20$$

$$\text{AI} = -0.00046630435$$

$$P = 2.362670171288$$

$$P_{full} = 2.362203866938$$

$$\frac{dP}{dY} = -21.5312365$$

$$\text{DUR} = 9.34276575$$

$$\text{MD} = 9.11489341$$

$$R = 0.01992502 \approx 1.993\%$$

$$\frac{dP}{dR_{infl}} = 20.0818084$$

Example 3

The settlement date is in the last coupon period.

Maturity Date: 9/24/2001

Settlement Date: 6/18/2001

Inflation Rate: 3%

Base RPI: 78.2763

RPI_1: 171.1 for 1/2001 (eight months before maturity date)

Coupon Rate: 2.5%

Money Yield: 5%

Ex-dividend date: 9/14/2001

This is cum-dividend trading.

$$AIF = \frac{86}{184}$$

$$DF = \frac{98}{184}$$

$$CF_1 = \frac{171.1}{78.2763} + \frac{0.025}{2} \cdot \frac{171.1}{78.2763}$$

$$= 2.185846802 + 0.027323 = 2.213169802$$

$$AI = 0.027323 \cdot \frac{86}{184} = 0.012770533$$

$$P = \frac{2.213169802}{1 + \frac{0.05}{2} \cdot \frac{98}{184}} - 0.012770533 = 2.17131766$$

$$P_{Full} = 2.184088193$$

$$\frac{dP}{dY} = -0.57398939$$

$$DUR = \frac{98}{368} = 0.26630435$$

$$MD = 0.26280504$$

$$R = 1.993\%$$

$$\frac{dP}{dR_{infl}} = 0$$

Index

Accrued interest
- cum-dividend trading, 39–40
- ex-dividend trading, 40
- interest factor, 25–26, 40, 85
- periodic payment fixed income securities, 86

Australian government bonds, 41–42
- conventions, 250
- examples, 250–257

Bonds, 1. *See also* Foreign Government Bonds

Breakeven repo rate calculations, given forward price, 112–113

Canadian government bonds, 42–45, 131
- conventions, 257–258
- examples, 258–268

Cash flow calculations, 98

Compound interest, 78–79
- cum-dividend trading, 17
- ex-dividend trading, 17–20
- settlement date in last coupon period, 78–79

Conversion factors
- definition of, 130–131
- Canadian 5- and 10-year government bonds,131
- conventions, 131–134
- E-bond 30-year bond, 131–132
- Euro 2-, 5-, and 10-year bonds, 131
- German 2-, 5-, 10-, and 30-year government bonds, 132
- Italian 10-year government bond, 132
- Japanese 5-, 10-, and 20-year government bonds. 132–133
- Spanish 10-year government bond, 133
- Swiss 10-year government bond, 133
- U.K. Long gilt (10-year), 134

Conversion factors *(Cont.)*
- U.S. indexed-linked note, 134
- U.S. Treasury bond (20-year), 134
- U.S. Treasury note, 134

Convexity, 75, 77, 79

Corporate bonds and notes, 175–237
- combinations of settlement date, first and last coupon periods, and other conventions, 175
- examples of, 178–237
- matrices, 175, 176

Corporate securities. *See* Corporate bonds and notes

Coupon dates, 2
- current coupon date, 3
- dated date, 2
- first coupon date, 2, 27–28
- issue date, 2
- last coupon date, 2, 28
- last-paid coupon date, 2
- next coupon date, 2
- normal issue date, 2
- normal maturity date, 3
- pseudo issue date, 3
- pseudo maturity date, 3
- settlement date, 2
- trade date, 2

Coupon periods, 94–95, 96, 97
- first coupon period, 2
- first/last coupon dates both given, 97
- last coupon period, 2
- long last period, 5, 96
- normal coupon period, 2, 94–95
- normal last period, 4–5
- short first period, 4, 95–96
- short last period, 5, 96

Current coupon date, 3

Current yield, 72

Czech Republic government bonds, 45–46
conventions, 268
examples, 269–271

Danish government bonds, 46–47
conventions, 271
examples, 272–274
Dated date, 2
Day count methods
ACT/365 method, 23
clarifications of, 23–24
30E/360 method, 22
30/360 method, 22
30/365 method, 22
Discount factor, 40, 85
Duration, 75, 77, 78

European Monetary Union (EMU) countries
government bonds, 47–50, 239
countries, 239
conventions, 239–240
examples, 240–249
End-of-Month (EOM) rule in effect, 94–95
End-of-Month (EOM) rule not in effect, 95
EURO government bonds, 51

First coupon date, 2, 27–28
First coupon factor, 85
First coupon period, 2
First derivative of price with respect to yield, 72–73, 77, 78,
by approximation, 87–88
for periodic payment fixed income securities 87–88
by summation, 88
risk factors, 87
using General Price/Yield Formula, 87
First/last coupon dates both given, 97
Fixed income periodic payment securities. *See* Periodic payment fixed income securities
Foreign government bonds, 239–373
Australian bonds, 41–42, 250–257
Canadian bonds, 42–45, 257–268
Czech Republic bonds, 45–46, 268–271
Danish bonds, 46–47, 271–274
EMU countries bonds, 47–50, 239–249

Foreign government bonds *(Cont.)*
EURO bonds, 51
German bonds, 48
Greek bonds, 50, 275–277
Hungarian bonds, 52, 277–292
Italian bonds, 49, 132, 303–313
Irish bonds, 49–50, 292–303
Japanese bonds, 52–55, 314–326
New Zealand bonds, 55–56, 327–328
Norwegian bonds, 57–58, 329–334
Polish bonds, 58–59, 335–338
Portuguese bonds, 48–49, 338–340
South African bonds, 60–61, 340–347
Spanish bonds, 50, 347–352
Swedish bonds, 61–62, 352–354
Swiss bonds, 62–63, 354–357
U.K. gilts, 63–66, 357–373
Forward price formulas
CAR formula, 106
CD method, 109–110
continuous compounding method, 111
drop calculation, 111
forward yield, 112
invoice payment, 111
net profit/loss calculation, 111
proceeds method, 104–109
scientific method, 110–111
for Treasury bills, 113
variables for, 105
Full price. *See* Price, full
Futures calculations
for $n \geq 2$, 146
for $n = 1$, 148
for $n = 0$, 148–149
variables for, 147–148

German government bonds, 48
Greek government bonds, 50
conventions, 275
examples, 275–277

Hungarian government bonds, 52
conventions, 277–284
examples, 284–292

Implied repo rate calculation by iteration
cost of carry, 152

Implied repo rate calculation by iteration *(Cont.)*
- cost of financing, 151
- coupon income, 151
- gross basis, 151–152
- gross basis in 32nds, 152
- net basis, 152
- net basis in 32nds, 152
- Newton-Raphson method, 149–151

Issue date, 2
Italian government bonds, 49
- conventions, 303–304
- examples, 305–313

Irish government bonds, 49–50
- conventions, 292–294
- examples, 294–303

Japanese government bonds, 52–55
- conventions, 314–320
- examples, 320–326

Last coupon date, 2, 28
Last coupon factor, 85
Last coupon period, 2
Last-paid coupon date, 2
Long first period, 4, 95–96
Long last period, 5, 96

Maturity-anniversary, 27
Modified duration, 75, 77, 79

Next coupon date, 2
New Zealand government bonds, 55–56
- conventions, 327
- examples, 327–328

Newton-Raphson method, 149–151
Normal coupon period, 2, 94–95
Normal first period, 3
Normal issue date, 2
Normal last period, 4–5
Normal maturity date, 3
Norwegian government bonds, 57–58
- conventions, 329
- examples, 329–334

Percent change in full price per ΔY
- actual, 92

Percent change in full price per ΔY *(Cont.)*
- not predicted by modified duration and convexity, 93
- predicted by modified duration and convexity, 92

Periodic fixed income instruments. *See* bonds
Periodic payment fixed income securities
- accrued interest, 86
- accrued-interest factor, 85
- convexity, 92
- discount factor, 85
- duration, 89
- first coupon factor, 85
- first derivative of price with respect to yield, 87–88
- full price, 86
- last coupon factor, 85
- modified duration, 89
- percentage change in full price per ΔY, 92
- price, 86
- price value of 0.01 (basis point value), 89
- second derivative of price with respect to yield, 89–91
- yield value of 0.01, 93

Polish government bonds, 58–59
- conventions, 335
- examples, 335–338

Portuguese government bonds, 48–49
- conventions, 338
- examples, 338–340

Price
- first derivative with respect to yield, 72–73, 77, 78, 87–88
- full price, 86, 92
- for periodic payment fixed income securities 86
- price/yield (P/Y) formula. *See* Price/yield formula
- second derivative of price with respect to yield, 73–74, 77, 78, 89–91
- value of 0.01 (basis point value), 75, 78, 79
- value of ΔY change in yield, 75

Price value of 0.01 (basis point value), 75, 78, 79
Price value of ΔY change in yield, 75
Price/yield (P/Y) formula
  accrued-interest factor, 25–26
  applicable markets and conventions, 29–30
  compound interest, 17–20
  for cum-dividend trading, 6
  date assumptions and conventions, 31–32
  day count methods, 21–24
  for ex-dividend trading, 6–12
  first coupon date, 27–28
  formula analysis, 13–14
  full price, 20
  iterative yield calculation, 15–16
  last coupon date, 28
  maturity-anniversary, 27
  simple interest, 17
  variables for, 7–8
Pseudo issue date, 3
Pseudo maturity date, 3

Risk factor, 87

Second derivative of price with respect to yield, 73–74, 77, 78
  by approximation, 90
  by summation, 91
  for periodic payment fixed income securities 89–91
  using General Price/Yield Formula, 89–90
Settlement date, 2
Settlement date in last coupon period,
  compound interest, 78–79
  convexity, 77, 79
  duration, 77, 78
  first derivative of price with respect to yield, 77, 78
  modified duration, 77, 79
  price value of 0.01 (basis point value), 78, 79
  second derivative of price with respect to yield, 77, 78
  simple interest, 77–78
  yield value, 78, 79
Settlement date not in last coupon period
  convexity, 75
  duration, 75
  first derivative of price with respect to yield, 72–73
  modified duration, 75
  price value of ΔY change in yield, 75
  price value of 0.01 (basis point value), 75
  second derivative of price with respect to yield, 73–74
  Taylor series of price as a function of yield, 76
  yield value of 0.01, 76
  yield value of 1/32, 76
Short first period, 4, 95–96
Short last period, 5, 96
Simple interest, 77–78
  cum-dividend trading, 16
  ex-dividend trading, 16
  settlement date in last coupon period, 77–78
South African government bonds, 60–61
  conventions, 340
  examples, 341–347
Separately Traded Registered Interest and Principal Securities (STRIPS), 174
Spanish government bonds, 50
  conventions, 347–348
  examples, 348–352
Swedish government bonds, 61–62
  conventions, 352
  examples, 353–354
Swiss government bonds, 62–63
  conventions, 354
  examples, 354–357

Taylor series of price as a function of yield, 76
Time in years to each cash flow
  settlement date in last coupon period, 99
  settlement date not in last coupon period, 99
Trade date, 2
Treasury bills,
  discount, 161–162
  discount rate, 162
  examples of conventions, 158–161
  forward price for, 113

Treasury bills *(Cont.)*
price, 162
yields, 162–173
Treasury Investment Growth Receipts (TIGRs), 237–238

U.K. gilts, 63–66
conventions, 357–359
examples, 359–363
index-linked gilts, 66–68, 363–373
U.S. corporate bonds, 70
U.S. government bonds, 68–70.
See also U. S. Treasury securities
U.S. Treasury securities
bills, forward price for, 113,
bonds, 134, 158–161
notes, 134, 158–161

Yield value, 76, 78, 79

Merrill Lynch

A global leader in
Financial Management and Advisory

Investment Banking & Capital Markets

Private Wealth Management

Investment Management

ml.com

Ask Merrill Lynch